Jackson Hole
UNCOVERED

Sierra Adare

Seaside Press

Library of Congress Cataloging-in-Publication Data

Adare, Sierra.
    Jackson Hole uncovered / Sierra Adare.
      p. cm.
    Includes bibliographical references and index.
    ISBN 1-55622-484-2 (pbk.)
    1. Jackson Hole (Wyo.)—Guidebooks.   2. Jackson Hole (Wyo.)—
    History.   I. Title.
    F767.T28A33   1996
    917.87'55--dc20   96-446
                                                        CIP

ISBN 1-55622-484-2
10 9 8 7 6 5 4 3 2 1
9610

All inquiries for volume purchases of this book should be addressed to
Wordware Publishing, Inc., at 1506 Capital Avenue, Plano, Texas 75074.
Telephone inquiries may be made by calling:

(214) 423-0090

Contents

Section One
The Settling of Jackson's Hole   1

   Snake Indians, River, and Mountains • Gros
   Ventres, a People and a Mountain Range • Chief
   Tog-we-tee and the Pass • River of the Wind •
   The Three Breasts • Wilson • Kelly • Moran
   Junction • Hoback Junction

   John Colter's Hell • John Hoback and the
   Astorians • Legends of the Rocky Mountain Fur
   Company • David Edward Jackson • Beaver Dick
   Leigh

   Bachelors and Other Early Homesteaders • Jack
   Davis, a Real "Grizzly Adams" • Mary White,
   Postmistress of Marysvale • Pony Express Rider
   Nick Wilson's Covered Wagon • Morman Row •
   Jackson, More Than a Name Change

Contents

Contents

Contents

Dedication

To Candy Moulton for sharing her love of Jackson Hole's history with me, answering countless questions, fun research trips—and, especially, for including me in the family gatherings at the Moulton Barn.

For Everyone who loves history and its relationship to the present and future. And for lovers of nature who walk on the wild side of life.

For Carolyn, Gwen, and C.W.

Acknowledgements

Several people went well out of their way to help gather information for *Jackson Hole Uncovered* and deserve more thanks than I can possibly say. Among them are Renee Leitz and Larry Kammer of the Teton County Historical Society; Jeannie Cook and Lynn Houze of the Park County Historical Society Archives; Kimberly Valentine of the National Wildlife Art Museum; Ann Nelson, Jean Brainard, and Lavaughn Breshnahan of the Wyoming State Museum; Robert Schiller, Chief Division of Science and Natural Resource Management, and Melody Webb, Assistant Superintendent, at Grand Teton National Park; James M. Griffin, Assistant Refuge Manager of Education and Visitor Services, National Elk Refuge; Jesse O'Connor, Sara Flitner and Karen A. Connelly of the Jackson Hole Chamber of Commerce, and Virginia Wakefield. A BIG THANK YOU to Sheila Bricker-Wade and her staff at the Wyoming State Historical Preservation Office.

Very special thanks to Candy Moulton for the wealth of Jackson Hole information (and all the rest) she supplied for me, Andy Breffeilh, Chris and Denny Becker, Carolyn Lampman, and to everyone who responded to my letters, phone calls, and endless questions!

Western Writers of America, the greatest writing organization in the world, deserves a big thanks, too. Also, Mike and Kathy Gear, Mike Blakely, Tom Knowles, Gwen Petersen, Bob Wiseman, Sharon Niederman, Norm Zollinger, and Dusty Richards for the laughter, great conversations, good food and music (especially the *B5* CD and Mike Blakely's *Ride the River*).

Lastly, thank you Mel Gibson for making *Braveheart*, but that's a whole other story!

Introduction

Jackson Hole: The Microcosm of the West and Its Hollywood Image

Unfortunately, language lacks the words to sufficiently describe the intensity of the Tetons—the very symbol of Jackson Hole. The valley rests in the bosom (pun intended) of the mountains. Maybe the name "Tetons" comes from more than just some female-companion-starved French trappers viewing the range and being reminded of women's breasts (which is where the Tetons obtained the name that stuck). Perhaps that cherished feeling struck the trappers as much as it does most people who come to Jackson Hole—every time they come. Something brings the estimated 2.5 million visitors annually. Of course, being on the doorstep of two diverse national parks, Yellowstone and Grand Teton, has something to do with it. But the communities on the edge of these natural wonders radiate their own brand of magic.

Of late, the media has latched onto phrases about the "Aspenization" of Jackson Hole. Ask longtime residents, recent emigrants, and visitors who have returned to the area over a period of years (like migrating birds) and you'll receive responses along the lines of "maybe it appears that way, but not really."

Granted, Jackson is a tourist town. No doubt about it. Practically since the end of the fur-trading era, the valley has relied heavily on tourism. Up until recently, businesses wooed it with the single-mindedness of a bull elk during the rut. (If you get the chance to take advantage of visiting during autumn and are lucky enough to witness the elk mating season in all its splendor of bugling and courtship, you'll realize this comparison is by no means a slam.) Nowadays, the focus leans towards extending the summer and winters heights of visitation into the slower periods of October-November and March-May.

Downtown Jackson

Photo Credit: Sierra Adare

Tourists wandering around the town square only pick up Jackson Hole's surface impression. Comments range from "quaintsy touristy" to "tourist trap extraordinaire" to "it looks more like a Hollywood set than a real place." But these people seldom experience the reality of Jackson Hole. Strip away all the tourist trappings and you'll find an authentic western town, going about the exact same businesses it has for more than the past century.

The idea of packing in the "dudes" to see the sights, wander the wilderness, taste chuckwagon cooking, and bringing money to the area hatched in Jackson Hole back in the late 1800s. Cowpokes punched cattle from the valley's earliest homesteading days, and some of their descendants still do. Long before skiing became THE winter sport, the town boasted Wyoming's first ski resort. So, the "tourist traps" have been around since the days when visitors arrived on horseback or via the mail stage. This suggests that the "fake" image is anything but! Judge for yourself.

Jackson or Jackson Hole. What's the Difference?

Over in the northwest section of the state of Wyoming, just south of Yellowstone, the country's first national park, rests a valley approximately eighty miles long by fifteen miles wide—a small hollow encompassed by mountains. Back in the early 1800s, fur trappers referred to such high mountain valleys as "holes," hence the name Jackson Hole. Technically, this name applies to the entire area; however, Jacksonites (as well as all Wyomingites) tend to call the town Jackson Hole, too. Teton County as a whole also gets included in this reference.

How Much Do You Really Know About Jackson Hole?

Test Your Knowledge

1. What did Grace Miller have to do with the town of Jackson?
   A. She platted the actual townsite.
   B. She located the town for Jackson.
   C. She became Jackson's first woman mayor.
   D. All of the above.

2. What does the term *Du'kurkant* refer to?
   A. A herd of bighorn sheep that only live at high altitude.
   B. A fur trader's expression for beaver trapping in the Mad River.
   C. An early name for Jackson Hole.
   D. A tribe of Indians known for the type of meat they ate.

3. What should you never forget to wear in Jackson Hole?
   A. Longjohns
   B. Sun block
   C. A cowboy hat
   D. A wildlife T-shirt

4. How did Mrs. O'Leary's cow change William Henry Jackson's photography career?
   A. The Chicago Fire destroyed all of the negatives of the first photos taken in Yellowstone shot by Jackson's competitor.
   B. Jackson's photos of the Chicago Fire brought him the national recognition that resulted in him being hired as the photographer on the first official government expedition into Yellowstone.

    C. Jackson lived in Chicago and the fire burned his studio, forcing him to take a photography position out West.

    D. The cow had nothing to do with Jackson's career.

5. What did John Colter find in 1807?
    A. Jackson Hole
    B. The Snake River
    C. Colter's Hell
    D. The Tetons

6. Which Jackson was Jackson Hole named after?
    A. William Henry Jackson
    B. Andrew Jackson
    C. Alexander Young Jackson
    D. David E. Jackson

7. Why did Lieutenant Gustavus Cheney Doane tackle the Mad River during the winter of 1876?
    A. He was seeking glory.
    B. His was lost and thought it was the Green River.
    C. He was fleeing from an Indian attack.
    D. He had to rescue his shipwrecked troops.

8. Who coined the term "boatercade" to describe President Clinton's trip on the Snake River?
    A. The river guide
    B. The Associated Press reporter
    C. The President himself
    D. The President's daughter

9. What takes place at the annual Jackson Hole Quick Draw Contest?
    A. Actors dramatize a fake shootout in the Town Square.
    B. The town hosts a fast draw and shoot target contest.
    C. Jackson citizens reenact a famous duel fought in the town's early days.
    D. High-caliber artists produce a piece of artwork in an hour.

10. Why did Paula Jeffries name the town's first live theatre the "Pink Garter?"
   A. The theatre had a pink curtain.
   B. The theatre building was painted pink.
   C. Her friends thought calling the theatre the "Red Garter" was too risque.
   D. Jeffries always wore pink garters.

11. How much did the skis weigh on the first winter expedition into Yellowstone during 1887?
   A. Nine pounds
   B. Five pounds
   C. Twenty pounds
   D. Thirteen pounds

12. What is a wapiti?
   A. North American elk
   B. Native American tribe
   C. A summer hail storm
   D. A fish that lives in the Snake River

ANSWERS

1. D. pp. xix, 105
2. D. p. 2
3. B. p. 43
4. A. p. 239
5. C. p. 13
6. D. p. 20
7. A. p. 117
8. B. p. 119
9. D. p. 216
10. C. p. 174
11. D. p. 123
12. A. p. 225

Jackson Hole Trivia:
Twenty Facts About the Hole

Did you know that...

...1) The town's first newspaper, the *Jackson Hole Courier*, started up on January 28, 1909. At the time, it listed the population of the town at two hundred people. Fifteen hundred, more or less, resided in the whole valley. Mail packed in from St. Anthony, Idaho reached Jackson an incredible six days a week (give or take winter storms which buried a few mail shipments until the spring thaw!). Letters and packages arrived via stage, snowshoes, backpack, or skis and sleds to nine community post offices—Brooks, Cheney, Elk, Grovont, Jackson, Moran, Teton, Wilson, and Zenith.

...2) When Grace Miller laid out the town at the turn of the century, Jackson was made up of "rocks, sagebrush, jackrabbits, mosquitoes and a few hunters in fall."

...3) When officially incorporated during 1901 as plain old "Jackson," town life consisted of Foster's saloon on the corner of present-day Cache and Deloney, "Pap" Deloney's store across the street on Cache, the Simpson building (which may have been Anderson's Hotel, depending on the source), and a place called the Clubhouse, a dance hall of sorts originally given the name Gun Club, built around 1897. On occasion, it also served as a part-time courtroom. By 1907 the number of businesses had increased to twenty-six, including Dr. Palmer's "Insanitorium."

...4) Dr. Charles William Huff came to Jackson in 1913 at the age of twenty-four, around $5,000 in debt and with sixteen cents to his name. Mrs. Reed, the owner of Ma Reed's Hotel, took him in because the town needed a doctor. She even assured him he could operate at the hotel whenever the need arose—which it did, at least once. The ironing board served as an operating table.

...5) A display in the Jackson Hole Museum claims the mountains of the West were "unknown and unexplored before 1800." In addition they were "a land of guesswork, mystery, and misconception."

...6) Jackson Hole has fewer than sixty (or thirty, depending on the source and where you stand in the Hole) frost-free days each year, making for a very short growing season.

...7) Throughout Jackson Hole's history, the United States government has established eighteen "official" post offices in the valley. Only six remain today.

...8) The town of Kelly, population eighty in 1927, rivaled Jackson for the county seat. Folks around Jackson claim it was a "landslide victory" for the town as Kelly lost its bid when the natural dam, created by the Gros Ventre "Slide" (the mountainside dropped into the valley and stopped up the Snake River Valley, producing Slide Lake), washed away in a flood. Only two buildings remained standing—the Episcopal church and the Hilmar Bark house just north of town. Eyewitnesses claimed the waters were like "a serpent of huge size crawling down the valley... its venomous children crawling down the irrigation ditches." Six people and countless livestock died.

...9) According to the Bureau of American Ethnology, Teton County was established during 1921, named after the mountain range within its border. The government report suggested "Teton" came from a Sioux tribe and meant "dweller on the prairies." Censorship of the French meaning, maybe?

...10) Mrs. H.H. Stone holds the honor of being the very first white woman to ever visit Yellowstone National Park, a feat she accomplished in 1872. The story has it that she journeyed all the way down from Bozeman, Montana to "see the sights."

...11) Indians and mountain men floated Yellowstone Lake in a variety of canoes and rafts for centuries. However, the first officially documented "boat" on the lake was named *The Annie*. She was christened for Senator H.L. Dawes's daughter, Anna L. Dawes. Getting the boat to the lake proved something of a story in itself. She (the boat) was shipped from Salt Lake City, Utah in pieces, then assembled in Yellowstone beside the lake.

...12) "The Cornice" on Teton Pass received its name from Capt. Benjamin Louis Eulalie de Bonneville. While crossing Teton Pass, Bonneville's horse (minus its rider) went over a ledge. Bonneville gained fame in August of 1832 by leading the first twenty mule and horse team wagon train over the South Pass.

...13) During the winter of 1887, four men, including pioneer park photographic concessionaire Frank Jay Haynes, made Yellowstone National Park's first winter tour. Launched from Fort Yellowstone at Mammoth Hot Springs, they traveled through the park's four geyser basins, traversed the Grand Canyon of Yellowstone, then crossed the Washburn Mountain to just north of Tower Falls before heading back to the hot springs. The trip took a total of twenty-nine days, with the men covering almost 200 miles. On the mountain crossing, a blizzard struck, and the expedition lost its way. They wandered aimlessly for three days without food or shelter in weather that varied from ten to fifty-two degrees below zero. (The same thing can happen these days, which is why it's smart to travel the Hole well prepared.)

...14) Six mountain ranges surround the Hole—the Tetons, Gros Ventres, the Snake River Range, the Wind River Range, the Absaroka Range, and the Wyoming Range.

... 15) Pronghorns (antelope) can maintain speeds in excess of 50 mph, making them the fastest land animal in North America.

... 16) Moose are the largest group in the deer family. A full-grown bull stands seven feet plus at the shoulders and carries antlers that can span over five feet in length.

... 17) Jackson Hole is home to North America's largest wintering elk herd, known by the Indian name *wapiti* (pronounced wha pa tee) which means "white rump." Elk are the second largest member of the deer family and once grazed the open countryside of most of the current-day United States. (Early settlers to Jackson Hole estimated 25,000 wapitis in the valley.) With the encroachment of civilization, the wapiti quickly dwindled until around the start of the 1900s, over ninety percent of their original rangeland had disappeared.

... 18) The characteristic white head plumage on bald eagles, both female and male, comes with maturity at four to five years of age.

... 19) The 1800s commercial plumage trade caused the near extinction of the trumpeter swan, North America's largest waterfowl, reaching a height of five feet and with a wing span of eight feet. During the second half of the nineteenth century, trumpeter swans were hunted for food and/or the downy feathers on their breasts. By 1935 only seventy-three remained.

... 20) It can, and often does, snow year round in Jackson.

Jackson Hole Secrets

1. The Best Kept Secret in Jackson Hole

Mormon Row in Grand Teton National Park hides in the shadow of the Tetons near Blacktail Butte, quietly falling into ruin. Park officials complain of no funds for development of interpretive signage, parking areas, road improvement, and facilities such as restrooms and water fountains. In addition, they suggest that increased visitation to the Row could cause bison/people conflicts since the huge animals tend to congregate in what was once the Row's hay fields.

But Mormon Row suffers as a result of a deeper discord within the Park Service itself. A Park Service cultural review of the area has concluded the sites along Mormon Row are eligible for the National Historic Register, but bureaucratic red tape has so far delayed its nomination. Thus the Row is caught between those officials who want to see it and other historic homesteads within the park boundaries preserved and those who want Grand Teton National Park to become a "natural park." In other words, park people would rip out the century-old hay fields along Mormon Row and reestablish natural vegetation such as sagebrush. Historic buildings would be either auctioned off or destroyed, allowing nature to take over and the park to turn into pretty much a haven for hikers.

Most hikers know and understand the value of indigenous wilderness, but doesn't history, especially one as important to the area as Mormon Row is to Jackson Hole, deserve a place, too?

Currently the Andy Chambers Homestead (see Section Nine for more details) is the only site on Mormon Row listed on the National Register of Historic Places. The Moulton family (see Section One, Chapter Four for more information and the family's life on Mormon Row) spent years badgering the Park to allow them to restore the regionally famous Moulton Barn. (Incidentally, this classically designed barn is one of the most photographed barns in the West and stands as the symbol of Jackson Hole.) The Moultons support nominating the barn for the National Register, but park officials won't let them since the Moultons really have no standing to actually nominate the barn themselves. Should the barn end up in the register, it would mean the national park system would be responsible for maintaining the structure in its present condition—a difficulty in the current funding crisis.

On the other hand, the Park Service did allow—and helped fund—some restoration at the Andy Chambers Homestead in October 1995, initiated by the Chambers family. Maybe there's hope for the Row yet.

2. The Hotel That's Seen It All (Almost)

Jess and John Wort started the Wort Hotel back in 1941. Since that time, the hotel has stood the test of time and experience.

Gambling still ruled in those days, and the Wort reverberated with the click of roulette wheels and the clatter of dice. Rooms (for sleeping, if you could) cost two bucks and some change. The cow punchers who came to town to participate in or bet on the Cutter races, then held in front of the Wort, would just sleep off the celebrating that took place in the hotel bar after the races by passing out in the hallway, comfy-cozy on the red and white tiled floor.

At such wild times, the stuffed animal heads that decorated the hotel walls would grow legs and wander off to such places as guest rooms and find their way into the bed to await discovery by some unsuspecting housekeeper. A horse found its way (with John Wort's help) into the bar on occasion. One of the town's barbers committed suicide after losing all his money gambling. A disgruntled dishwasher (who had actually quit to take a job at another eatery) stole into a guest's room and murdered two little girls. He was quickly caught, tried, convicted, and executed in the state penitentiary's gas chamber. A long-time employee even found a newborn baby in the toilet, left to die by an uncaring mother.

Once the government shut down the gambling for good, dancing replaced games of chance in the bar, and things settled down—sort of. The hotel suffered from an explosion, a flood, and a tornado. Then in 1980 fire struck, ignited by some wiring creating a spark in a bird's nest tucked into the hotel's neon sign. About the only thing the hotel hasn't experienced is an armed robbery.

Rebuilt, the Wort continues to draw tourists, cowboys, and locals—whether for a cup of great coffee and a hearty breakfast, a night's lodging, or some just plain fun at the annual Wort Historic Celebration held in mid-April.

The Wort Hotel is located at 50 North Glenwood, P.O. Box 69, Jackson, WY, 83001, 800-322-2727 phone, 307-733-2067 fax.

3. A Unique Tale of Business in Jackson Hole

Horse-sitting. Not house-sitting, but *horse*-sitting.

Long-time wrangler and horse enthusiast Nancy Mortensen opened Horse Watchers in the spring of 1996. For years, people could find sitters for their setters or company for their cats and canaries, so why not for their hoofed family members?

Mortensen grew up around horses and taught basic riding and safety skills in addition to wrangling in Yellowstone.

As part of her unusual equine service, Mortensen feeds, grooms, cleans, and exercises horses for short or long term and even in emergency situations.

Contact Horse Watchers at 307-734-1886 if you find yourself in need of horse-sitting services while in Jackson Hole.

4. Red Flag, Driver's Warning

In the Jackson area it's a given that people share the highways, streets, and roads with wildlife—some of *them* much larger than folks' vehicles! During the winter when snow covers the range, spring when the wildlife migrates back to the high country, and autumn when the weather once again forces the herds to drift down into the valleys, animals and people often become more than just dark shapes that pass in the night.

The Jackson Hole Wildlife Foundation estimates that vehicles hit over 100 animals per month during December and January, the two worst encounter months of winter, and an average of fifty each in April and May.

Founded in 1993 with a mission to "promote the preservation, human respect and enjoyment of Jackson Hole wildlife and wildlife habitat through education and protection," the Wildlife Foundation has worked to lower the road kill numbers through a two-fold plan of signage and awareness. Working in conjunction with the Wyoming Department of Transportation, Wildlife Foundation volunteers have marked the most likely road kill spots with wildlife signs that also carry red flags. These "hot spots" include stretches along Highways 26, 89, 191, and Wyoming 22. In town you can see them on West Broadway from the Days Inn to the Federal Express building and from the Albertsons store to the Virginian Lodge.

The foundation has also combined with the Outfitters Association to promote driver education. When you spot a clump of willows near the road, you can bet moose are nibbling nearby. Open buttes should bring deer leaping to mind—and possibly the eye. Expanses of sage flats draw antelope and bison.

Contact the Wildlife Foundation at 307-733-9736 for more safety and awareness tips.

5. You Haven't Lived Until You've...

...made the first run of the day down Rendezvous Mountain in fresh powder.

...shared a growler of Moose Juice Stout with friends under a full moon on a snowy night.

...joined the Jackson Hole Million Vertical Feet Club.

...seen the Carl Rungius painting "The Days of Bison Millions" at the National Museum of Wildlife Art.

...floated the Snake River at dawn with the moose.

...seen a bald eagle flying across the National Elk Refuge.

...read Owen Wister's *The Virginian* while in the Hole.

...drifted over the Teton valley in a balloon.

...experienced a summer snowstorm in the Tetons.

...spread mountain huckleberry jam over sourdough pancakes at Jedediah's.

...plowed through waist-deep snow riding a sleigh through a herd of 8,000 elk.

...saddled up at the Cowboy Bar.

...gotten lost in the music of the Noteworthy Jazz Trio.

The Settling of Jackson's Hole

1

The Valley's First Year-Round Residents

Imagine standing in Jackson's Hole millenniums ago. A bank of clouds part and an unobstructed view of the Tetons emerges, their jagged summits rising a mile and a half straight up out of the valley floor. Only a few game trails beaten into a meadow of lush grasses and wild flowers present evidence of use—by prehistoric prey and hunter.

Archaeological records suggest Paleoindian hunter/gather cultural groups lived in the Jackson Hole valley between 8,000 and 12,000 years ago. From the projectile points, bone tools, and faunal remains left behind, these Foothill-Mountain Paleoindian bands led a different lifestyle from their open plains and basin contemporaries. While Plains Paleoindian families followed the mammoth and bison herds, Foothill-Mountain Paleoindians occupied caves and rock shelters and relied on bighorn sheep as the mainstay of their diet.

An 8,800-year-old net made from juniper bark provided archaeologists with an important key to Foothill-Mountain Paleoindian hunting practices. Discovered folded up in a dry limestone recess near current-day Yellowstone National Park, the net's two-strand, reinforced, "S"-twisted cordage indicates adequate strength and size for use in netting bighorn sheep, the only large animal in the area. Such hunting practices also continued into later eras.

During the Archaic period, 8,000 to 2,000 B.P. (before present), mountain dwellers constructed pit houses which offered a more sophisticated shelter from the harsh elements. Generally circular in design with conical-shaped roofs, these partially excavated pits provided adequate living space; storage or cache pits for seeds, roots, and berries; as well as fire pits for warmth and roasting mule deer and bighorn sheep meat.

In historic times, early white trappers and explorers in the region came across a group of Native Americans they called the "Sheep Eaters," a translation of *Du'kurkani* or *Tukudika* which means "mountain-sheep eater" or more properly "meat-eater." A band of the Uto-Aztekan speaking Shoshone, the Sheepeaters lived in scattered hunter/gatherer groups consisting of one to two families each in what is now the Jackson Hole valley, Yellowstone National Park, the Absaroka Range, and the upper slopes of the Wind River Mountains. Archaeologists believe the Sheepeaters had inhabited the vicinity since 1300 A.D.

Traces of aboriginal occupation have survived the high mountain environment in the form of dry-laid rock walls. Mountaineers climbing the western spur of Grand Teton discovered an intriguing circular structure of stacked rock slabs on the summit, believed to be the handiwork of the Sheepeaters. The climbers dubbed it "The Enclosure."

Other remnants remain as well. Partial structures found in the region suggest that Sheepeaters erected *wickiups*, lean-to type shelters fashioned from brush piles. In addition, they built tipi-shaped lodges, using pine poles which they covered with brush and twigs or with skins. Photographer William Henry Jackson captured one such dwelling on film

in 1871 while on a survey trip to Yellowstone. (We'll explore
Jackson's extraordinary trip in Section Eight, Chapter 3.)

A Sheepeater Indian family captured for posterity by
William Henry Jackson during the Hayden Expedition in 1872.

Photo Credit: Wyoming State Museum

Osborne Russell, a trapper, also encountered Sheepeaters in Yellowstone's present-day Lamar Valley. His book,
published in 1921, titled *Journals of a Trapper: Or Nine
Years in the Rocky Mountains, 1834-1843*, provides one of
the few documented accounts between whites and these
reclusive people.

In July of 1835 he wrote, "Here we found a few Snake
Indians [the white name assigned to all members of the
Shoshonean tribes] comprising 6 men, 7 women and 8 or 10
children who were the only Inhabitants of this lonely and
secluded spot. They were all neatly clothed in dressed deer
and Sheep skins of the best quality and seemed to be per-
fectly contented and happy. They were rather surprised at
our approach and retreated to the heights where they might

have a view of us without apprehending any danger, but having persuaded them of our pacific intentions we then succeeded in getting them to encamp with us. Their personal property consisted of one old butcher knife, nearly worn to the back, two old shattered fusees which had long since become useless for want of ammunition, a Small Stone pot and about 30 dogs on which they carried their skins, clothing provisions etc on their hunting excursions."

Unlike the other Shoshonean bands who owned horses and relied on them when hunting their main food source—the bison—the horseless Du'kurkani's diet consisted primarily of bighorn sheep. The few anthropological records in existence speculate that the Sheepeaters specialized in pursuing and trapping bighorns in deep snow on snowshoes during the harsh winters. In warmer weather the Du'kurkani ambushed bighorns with bows and obsidian-pointed arrows from blinds erected next to the herd's seasonal migration trails. Hunters also tracked individual game through the high country, utilizing dogs to help stalk, drive, and corner the prey in communal traps.

Sheepeater traps displayed an intimate knowledge of mountain sheep behavior. They included the construction of "V"-shaped wing walls of brush and stone and ramps of logs covered with dirt and rocks, leading to catch pens. The animals were driven into the upslope wing walls, then forced down the converging fence lines and onto the ramp which mimicked a steep slope. Once at the summit, the sheep had no option but to leap into the log catch pen.

Other tribes and Shoshone bands harvested sheep when they crossed the Du'kurkani lands on annual summer journeys to the Green River. Mountain men described the warmth and extensive uses of the pelage in Indian clothing. They also reported that the Wind River Shoshone grew wealthy by reselling the furs obtained from the Sheepeaters.

Yet the Du'kurkani didn't seem to benefit from these exchanges. Accounts such as the one filed by Lieutenant Gustavus Cheney Doane to the Secretary of War in 1870 described the Sheepeaters as "wretched beings." (We'll journey down the Mad River with Madman Doane in Section Four, Chapter 3.) In *Prehistoric Hunters of the High Plains*, archaeologist George C. Frison speculates that the Sheepeaters gained their "relatively impoverished, low status" because whites have historically viewed domestic sheep with everything from low esteem to contempt. Others classified the Sheepeaters as "outcasts" preyed upon by other tribes. Travelers supposedly recounted how the Sheepeaters sought refuge from their enemies by cowering around the geysers in Yellowstone. At the time, many Native Americans believed evil spirits roamed where the waters boiled and spewed out of the ground, and they refused to venture into the area. Thus the Sheepeaters were safe in Yellowstone.

Perhaps this nonviolent approach for dealing with foes led to French trappers considering the Sheepeaters to be *les dignes de pitie*—deserving of pity.

Their numbers never very large, the Du'kurkani posed no threat to anyone. Then smallpox epidemics transmitted by trappers in the 1830s and 1840s and cholera spread by pioneers from the Oregon Trail in the 1850s devastated the Sheepeater population. They, along with the majority of the Shoshonean groups, abandoned the Wyoming mountains for the reservation between 1870 and 1890.

On the one hand, life on the reservation was easier for the Du'kurkani. They needn't fear raids from other tribes. But on the other, reservation life stripped the Sheepeaters of a centuries-old lifestyle. Bighorn sheep didn't descend to the lower altitude of the reservation.

Although no ethnographic studies were made of the Sheepeaters prior to their relocation to reservations, general Shoshonean data suggests the bighorns may have supplied the Du'kurkani with more than just meat and clothing. Ram skulls found lodged in the forks of trees could hold religious significance. Mountain man Alexander Ross noted in 1824 that Native Americans treated these "medicine trees" like shrines, leaving offerings at them.

Nearly sixty years passed in which the Sheepeaters coexisted with Bannocks and Shoshones on reservations before ethnographers began compiling any information on what the French trappers called the "timid, harmless race." By then, their core beliefs of kinship systems, folklore, concepts of God and World had eroded and intermingled as they had with the more abundant tribes.

2

Place Names

Many of the place names you'll discover in Jackson Hole come from the area's early history—mountain men, Native Americans, and the first white settlers. Some locales went through a variety of designates before obtaining "official" status. Others began as and remain mangled versions of native descriptive terms.

Snake Indians, River, and Mountains

When white men first encountered the Native Americans in the valley that would become Jackson Hole, the tribes communicated through sign language. Often this led to comical misunderstanding and erroneous names, as well. One example is the "Snake" Indians. The Shoshones gestured their tribal name by waving a hand in a serpentine motion. The newcomers mistook the meaning as that of a moving snake. In reality, the Shoshones portrayed the in-and-out action they used to weave grasses together in the construction of their lodges. Others tribes knew them by variations of the name the Arapaho used, *E-wuka-wu-si*, People-Who-Use-Grass-or-Bark-for-Their-Lodges.

Members on the Lewis and Clark expedition first documented the river that would eventually be named for the "Snake" Indians in 1805. Clark called the torrential waterway the Lewis River after his partner, and that's how it appeared on early maps. But in the years which followed, French trappers denounced it as *la maudite riviere enragee*, the accursed mad river. Wilson Price Hunt's expedition of 1812 shortened it to the Mad River, an apt description of the river's cascades, whitewater and falls which made passage difficult at best and disastrous for glory seekers such as Lieutenant Gustavus Cheney Doane. Anthropological records list the Native American name for this river as *We'nerin)' gweBi*, Standing-One River-Course.

The Snake Mountain Range also derived its name from the Shoshone tribe.

Gros Ventres, a People and a Mountain Range

A culturally independent division of the Arapaho nation, the Gros Ventres (pronounced grow vonts) came by a French name in much the same manner as the Snakes. Gros Ventre Indians signed their tribal name by passing both hands over their stomachs, thus earning recognition as the "big bellies." Ethnographers catalog the Gros Ventres as the *S:ap* which translated into Paunch. The same Frenchmen bestowed their version of the tribal name on the mountain range these Native Americans frequented.

Chief Tog-we-tee and the Pass

In 1873 U.S. Corp of Engineers Captain William A. Jones called the 9,658-foot mountain pass after his Sheepeater Indian guide Tog-we-tee. The pass which led down into the valley of Jackson Hole was well known and used by Sheepeaters, as well as other tribes. Unfortunately, Jones misspelled the chief's name in the records he kept, thus Togwotee Pass. Tog-we-tee means spear or lance thrower.

River of the Wind

The Wind River and the mountain range received their designation from an English translation of the Native American term for the river which gushed from snow melt in the northern part of the mountains. Almost year round a current of wind flowed down the river, which the natives dubbed the "Big Wind" between the Shoshone and Wind River ranges.

The Three Breasts

Native Americans called the three distinctive pinnacles *Tee-win-ot* (currently the name of one of the peaks in the Teton Range). Members of the Wilson Price Hunt expedition of 1811, who used the unique, jagged mountain summits to guide their way, referred to them as "Pilot Knobs." French *voyageurs* later named the peaks (Grand, Middle, and South) *les trois tetons*, the three breasts, and the name stuck—for the peaks, the range, the river, the pass, and the creek.

Wilson

Elijah N. Wilson, better known as "Uncle Nick," led a colorful life. As a boy, Wilson spent two years with the Shoshone tribe, adopted by Chief Washakie's mother. As a young man, he rode for the Pony Express. Once it went belly-up, he turned to driving a stagecoach and even did a stint in the army before settling in Jackson Hole. Wilson began construction on a cabin on Fish Creek during 1894 and completed it on April 23, 1895. This homestead, which the family lived in until 1900, was entry No. 1490 filed at Lander Land Office on Dec. 16, 1903 and proved up on March 25, 1904. It launched what would become the town of Wilson.

Once the family moved out of the cabin, it became the schoolhouse. Nick's first wife, Matilda, became the town's first postmistress when the post office opened in 1898. In addition to owning a general store and a hotel, Elijah ran the town's post office after Matilda's death. The 1900 Census listed thirty households in what is today the town of Wilson. (We'll learn more about Uncle Nick in the next chapter.)

Kelly

William "Bill" Kelly proved up on a homestead beside the Gros Ventre River, building a ranch and operating a sawmill. Contemporaries claimed his love for and devotion to the Jackson Hole valley was infectious. Soon a town grew up around his place, a convenient stop for area ranchers herding cattle to and from the summer range in the mountains. When Kelly's wife, Sophie, started the post office in 1914, the town was named after Bill.

Moran Junction

This juncture where the road "Y"s to Yellowstone obtained its name from Mount Moran in the Teton Range. Indirectly, Moran Junction was named for Thomas Moran, an artist who came west with Ferdinand V. Hayden's Yellowstone survey party in 1871. (More about this extraordinary trip in Section Eight, Chapter 3.)

Moran Junction shouldn't be confused with the old town of Moran near Jackson Lake. Although part of the land that became Grand Teton National Park in 1929, the town of Moran continued to function as a tourist center until 1959. It was then dismantled, the majority of its buildings relocated to current-day Colter Bay.

Hoback Junction

John Hoback trapped and served as a guide for William Price Hunt's expedition through the canyon and along the river named after him. (We'll examine Hoback's life in more detail in Chapter 3 in this section.)

3

From Colter's Hell to Jackson's Hole—The Fur Trade

White trappers returning to civilization first extoled the wonders of what would become Jackson Hole, Wyoming. Their fanciful adventures and tall tales glossed over the harshness of the trapper's lifestyle. Later, the yearly rendezvous provided their main contact with the world they chose to leave behind.

Of necessity, mountain men embraced the Native Americans' way of life. Trappers adopted the natives' practical clothing—long, brain-tanned leather shirts, leggings, and moccasins, adding warm buffalo or elk coats for the winters. They let their hair grow long to protect their head, ears, and neck from the sun and wind.

While many disbelieved the stories of the legendary mountain men such as John Colter, Jim Bridger, and the others whose lives influenced the Jackson Hole area, no one doubted their courage or their love for the wilderness.

John Colter's Hell

What significant role do the French play in Jackson Hole's history? Besides forever associating a mountain range with women's breasts, a Frenchman's desire to cut his losses in the New World turned into the catalyst for the first white explorers wandering into the valley. In anticipation of renewing war with the British, Emperor Napoleon Bonaparte needed to concentrate his troops and resources in Europe. So in 1803 he sold 830,000 square miles to the United States for $15 million. Although Jackson Hole fell just outside the boundary of the Louisiana Purchase, the expedition President Thomas Jefferson dispatched to the "Far West" to gather scientific data brought the Lewis and

Clark team almost within smelling distance of the "stinking waters" of the Yellowstone region.

Which brings us to John Colter.

Born just before the American Revolution in Staunton, Virginia, Colter must have yearned for adventure. In 1803 he signed on as a private with the Lewis and Clark Expedition for a steady diet of the unknown and five dollars a month (which he had to sue Lewis's estate in 1810 in order to receive).

Described by a contemporary as a man bearing "an open ingenious, and pleasing countenance of the Daniel Boone stamp," Colter also possessed a frontiersman's drive and energy—two necessary components which sustained Colter on the arduous trek that would turn into seven straight years in the wilderness as a member of several different groups.

Colter, along with the twenty-seven other men recruited by Meriwether Lewis and William Clark, struck out for the Pacific in October of 1803, wintering on the Wood River opposite the mouth of the Missouri by St. Louis. By the following October the "Corps of Discovery," as people of the time referred to it, reached a Mandan Indian village approximately fifty-five miles above present-day Bismarck, North Dakota. Their number along the way swelled to between forty-three and forty-five (depending upon which historical account you rely on). During a blustery snowstorm, the group constructed a crude log encampment, dubbing it "Fort Mandan."

Early in April of 1805 the party struck out on the final leg of its journey into the unknown. According to W.J. Ghent's article "A Sketch of John Colter" in the *Annals of Wyoming*, "a total of thirty-three souls" participated in this section of the trip, including fur trader, cook, and guide Toussaint Charbonneau; Sacagawea, his Shoshone wife; and their infant son, Jean Baptiste Charbonneau.

Along the way, Colter earned repeated praise in the journals kept by the leaders and other members of the corps.

The men considered Colter among the most reliable members of the expedition. From this respect, he gained permission to leave the corps on the way home to go exploring and trapping with Joseph Dickson and Forest Hancock, two pelt hunters the expedition encountered somewhere along the Missouri River.

Clark wrote the following account in his trip journal. "Colter one of our men expressed a desire to join Some trappers (the two Illinois Men we met, & who now came down to us) who offered to become shearers with [Colter] and furnish traps &c. the offer a very advantageous one, to him his services could be dispensed with from this down and as we were disposed to be of service to any of our party who had performed their duty as well as Colter had done, we agreed to allow him the privilege provided no one of the party would ask or expect a Similar permission to which they all agreed that they wished Colter every suckcess [sic]... we gave Jo Colter Some Small articles which we did not want and some powder & lead. the party also gave him several articles which will be usefull to him on his expedition."

The Illinois trappers and Colter worked their way into the heart of Yellowstone country, spending the winter of 1806-07 along the Clarks Fork River and Sunlight Basin. When spring arrived, the trio dissolved the partnership and headed downstream to the Missouri River. There, Colter ran into Manuel Lisa, the leader of another fur trading venture heading into the terrain Colter had just come from. Various accounts suggest it didn't take much for Lisa to persuade Colter to join the expedition.

Lisa commissioned Colter to seek out Native Americans and barter for furs. Equipped with thirty pounds of supplies, including trade goods of tobacco, beads, knives, awls, and vermillion, Colter traversed an estimated 500-600 miles of mountainous terrain which included modern-day Jackson Hole valley, Jackson Lake, and, of course, Yellowstone National Park, before returning to St. Louis in 1810.

Although speculation abounds that European or Canadian explorers could have been the first white men to trample the native grasses of Jackson Hole and Yellowstone, Colter holds an undeniable claim. Although he kept no journals of his travels, his accounts of the "Stinking Water" River, "Brimstone," "Boiling Springs," and the Tetons and the maps he drew for Clark still stand as the first correct depiction of the Jackson Hole-Yellowstone area. Unfortunately, it seems that Clark or possibly the maps' compiler, Samuel Lewis (no relation to Meriwether Lewis), didn't believe the bizarre sights Colter labeled on his maps. In redrawing them for publication in the 1814 Biddle-Allen edition of the expedition journals, Clark or Samuel Lewis omitted many of the items Colter indicated.

Like Clark and Lewis, others refused to accept Colter's outlandish tales of plumes of hot water shooting a hundred feet into the air, rumbling mud pots, and a two-thousand-foot waterfall. People considered the mountain man a lunatic and scoffingly called the land he described "Colter's Hell."

Further controversy exists in the form of a stone of rhyolite lava plowed up in 1931 near modern Tetonia, Idaho (known as Pierre's Hole in mountain man days). Carved in the shape of a man's head, complete with facial features, the words "JOHN COLTER" were gouged into one side and the date "1808" on the other. Some people believe the stone is fake because of the Lewis sketching of 1814, which indicates Colter's "1807" route. But considering Colter had been in the western wilderness since 1804 and had traversed the Jackson Hole valley during the winter, which tends to last a good six months, his "1807" map date could easily include the winter of 1807-08, thus feasibly placing him in the area during the year indicated on the stone.

John Hoback and the Astorians

The same year Colter rejoined civilization (1810), John Hoback entered Jackson Hole from the Teton Pass side with two fellow Kentuckians, Edward Robinson and Jacob Reznor, members of the disbanded Andrew Henry trapping party. After working their way through the valley seeking "soft gold," the term for beaver pelts, the trio presumably exited via Togwotee Pass and made their way toward the Missouri River.

In 1811 the three met up with members of the American Pacific Fur Company. Organized by John Jacob Astor, the "Astorians," as they were called, planned to seize the fur trade out from under the noses of the British and French. Wilson Price Hunt, the expedition leader, enlisted the Kentuckians as guides for the incredible sixty-five-person group (including one Native American woman and her two children) and eighty-two horses. So the trio retraced their steps, moving the entourage westward. But Hoback and his colleagues' plans to guide the company along the Wind River, over Towgotee Pass, and into the Jackson Hole valley went awry.

Washington Irving chronicled the Astorians' adventures in his three-volume set *Astoria, or Anecdotes of an Enterprise Beyond the Rocky Mountains*, published in 1836. An entry dated September 14, 1811 divulged the hardships facing the group. "The scarcity of game, however, which already had been felt to a pinching degree, and which threatened them with famine among the sterile heights which lay before them, admonished them to change their course."

Turning their backs on the Wind River, the cavalcade headed southwest toward the Green River in hopes of encountering buffalo on its grassy banks. By the next afternoon, Hoback, Robinson, and Reznor pointed out the three scraggly, snow-glistening peaks on the horizon. "They were hailed by the travellers with that joy with which a beacon on a sea-shore is hailed by mariners after a long and dangerous voyage," wrote Irving. Hunt named the mountains Pilot Knobs in his journal—the first "official" name for the Tetons.

But instead of offering an oasis from peril, the Teton valley brought disaster and death.

Hoback showed the party a way into Jackson Hole via a canyon and river which the thankful group named in his honor. Osborne Russell later described it in his *Journal of a Trapper: Or Nine Years in the Rocky Mountains, 1834-1843.* "This stream [Hoback River] runs thro. a tremendous mountain in a deep narrow Kanyon of rock. The trail runs along the Cliffs from 50 to 200 feet above its bed and is so narrow in many places that only one horse can pass at a time for several hundred yards and one false step would precipitate him into the Chasm."

Upon leading the party into Jackson Hole, Hoback and his companions left the Astorians. History records that Nez Perce Indians subsequently killed all three Kentuckians in the vicinity of the Snake River.

The Snake proved deadly to others of Hunt's expedition, as well. He abandoned the horses and instructed the group to build canoes in order to float down the stream—the same waterway his men dubbed the "Mad River." One man drowned in the frigid water. The craft carrying all their meat crashed, leaving them starving and lost as they deserted the river for an overland route.

The four trappers Hunt chose to remain in Jackson Hole over winter fared no better. After spending the months trapping beaver, they began the 700 as-the-crow-flies miles to Fort Astoria on the mouth of the Columbia River. But Crow Indians attacked the men just after they crossed Teton Pass, killing one and stealing the entire winter's collection of pelts.

Despite such occurrences, trappers and mountain men considered Jackson Hole the crossroads of the fur trade. Had the South Pass not been "discovered" in 1812 by Jedediah Strong Smith, Jackson Hole would have been the main emigration route through the Rockies to the West Coast.

Legends of the Rocky Mountain Fur Company

After the Astorians came the legendary mountain men—Jedediah Strong Smith, Jim Bridger, and William Sublette. They ranked among those who answered General William Ashley's February 1822 ad in the St. Louis *Gazette and Public Advertiser* for one hundred "Enterprising Young Men. . .to ascend the Missouri River to its source, there to be employed for one, two, or three years."

Jedediah Smith dared to be different among a group who, by their very natures, rebelled against conformity. Being a very religious man, he refrained from drinking, "squaw-wenching," swearing, and smoking. Contemporary William Waldo called him "a bold, outspoken, professing and consistent Christian, the first and only one known among the early Rocky Mountain trappers and hunters." In addition to this high esteem, none doubted Smith's courage. His rifle remained as much his inseparable companion as his Bible.

Driven by a trailblazing wanderlust that would consume him throughout his short life, twenty-four-year-old Smith led a group of men across the heart of the Rockies on his first expedition. En route, a grizzly attacked him, grasping Smith's entire head between its jaws. Before his men could kill the bear, it ripped off Smith's ear and scalp. Everyone figured him for a goner. Nevertheless, Smith not only instructed his men on how to sew his scalp and ear back on, he declared himself fit to travel again within ten days.

During the autumn of 1824, Smith guided six trappers through the length of the Jackson Hole valley, personally taking 668 pelts in that season (a record for a single trapper). At the time, the British owned Hudson Bay Company, sarcastically called the H.B.C. (Here Before Christ) by American fur traders, declared the Snake River country a battle zone—the result of the unresolved issues of U.S. western expansion and proprietorship left in the wake of the indecisive War of 1812. The British designated the area "a rich preserve of beaver. . .which for political reasons we should endeavour to destroy as fast as possible." But the Americans won out, entering the valley in increasingly larger numbers.

The following year (1825) Jim Bridger (who earned $200 per annum working for Ashley and Henry) and a group of thirty trappers entered Jackson Hole from the southeast after attending the debut of the famous class reunion of the "Rocky Mountain College," as the mountain men snidely called the rendezvous. Altogether, Bridger, nicknamed "Old Gabe" by his companions, spent forty years in the Rockies, trading and trapping fur, blazing trails that would become the roads and railroad routes used by immigrants, scouting for the army, and racking up what one newspaperman called "Jim Bridger's lies" of Wyoming's strange sites. In response to his "lies" about "the place where Hell bubbled up," Bridger retorted, "That's what a man gets for telling the truth." But he continued concocting fanciful tales about his three expeditions into current-day Yellowstone National Park in the early 1840s. The wonders he spoke of received later verification by such respected travelers as Father De Smet and Lieutenant Gunnison twenty years before the official survey party set foot in Yellowstone and Jackson's Hole.

William "Bill" Sublette, along with Jedediah Strong Smith and David E. Jackson, bought the Rocky Mountain Fur Company from General Ashley in 1826. While Jackson trapped in the hole that Sublette suggested they name after Jackson, and Smith trapped and explored, Sublette took the furs to St. Louis and returned to the Rockies with supply goods. But Sublette discovered he could make more money selling merchandise to trappers than trading in fur. So the partners sold the Rocky Mountain Fur Company in 1830. That same year Sublette became one of the first mountain men to drive cattle into what would become Wyoming.

On their way to Pierre's Hole, the valley on the west side of the Tetons, for the July rendezvous of 1832, Sublette and over 200 trappers and 500 friendly Flatheads and Nez Perces passed through Jackson's Hole. Travel proved dangerous for Sublette's group. John Wyeth and Zenas Leonard, members of this group, recorded portions of the event that would prove quite dynamic for Sublette.

"We arrived at Lewis's fork [Snake River], one of the largest rivers in these rocky mountains," recorded Wyeth. "It took us all day to cross it. It is half a mile wide, deep and rapid. The way we managed was this: one man unloaded his horse, and swam across with him, leading two loaded ones, and unloading the two, brought them back, for two more, and as Sublet's [sic] company and our own made over a hundred and fifty, we were all day in passing the river. In returning, my mule, by treading on a round stone, stumbled and threw me off, and the current was so strong, that a bush which I caught hold of only saved me from drowning."

Approximately 150 Gros Ventre Indians (and possibly twenty to thirty Blackfeet) also traversed the area on a return trip from the Arapaho-held southern plains. Bad blood between the two groups brought on a skirmish that turned into a full-fledged fight. When the pelt hunters realized they and their Indian allies outnumbered the bothersome Gros Ventres by close to seven to one, the mountain men, led by Sublette, seized the opportunity to abolish their enemy.

Although surrounded, the Gros Ventres dug in, creating an earth and log entrenchment which allowed them to keep their attackers at bay throughout the day. That night, as they sang their death songs, the Gros Ventres formulated a bold strategy. Amid their singing, the warriors shouted that the rest of their party which traveled behind them, numbering between 600 and 800, would soon arrive to avenge their deaths. When the Flatheads conveyed the message to the trappers, the latter panicked.

"Every man thought only of his own security and ran for life without ever looking around which would at once have convinced him of his folly," wrote Zenas Leonard. Once the mountain men realized the ruse, Leonard declared the whites' rage "was unbounded, and approached to madness.

For my own part, although I felt much regret at the result after so much til [sic] and danger, yet I could not but give the savages credit for the skill they displayed in preserving their lives, at the very moment when desperation, as we thought, had seized the mind of each of them."

Accounts vary as to the number of men killed, but historians estimate the trappers lost thirty-two (seven whites and twenty-five Flathead allies) and twenty-five horses in the "Battle of Pierre's Hole" while the Gros Ventres only sustained twenty-six casualties and no mention of animals lost.

After the battle, a group of seven men took off through Jackson's Hole. Warren A. Ferris of the American Fur Company logged what happened next. "Five of seven men who departed for St. Louis, three days since, returned, and informed us that they were attacked by a party of Indians in Jackson's Hole, and that two of their number, Moore and Fay [Foy], [were] killed. The survivors saved themselves by flight, but one of them was wounded in the thigh."

Wounded himself, Sublette remained in the vicinity until late July. The survivors Ferris mentioned left with Sublette's group. The injured man in Ferris's account, one Alfred Stevens, died just before the trappers reached Teton Pass. Sublette's men buried him beside the trail. The party then hurried through Jackson's Hole, exiting through either Union or Togwotee Pass in order to avoid another confrontation with the Blackfeet who retreated from the battle to Hoback Canyon.

David Edward Jackson

Born October 30, 1788 (the year the government adopted the Constitution of the United States), David "Davey" Edward Jackson grew up somewhere on the upper Monongahela River in western Virginia. The son of a Revolutionary War veteran, Jackson fought in the War of 1812.

The only known picture of him is in his Ohio Militia uniform, painted around the outbreak of this war.

Jackson stood over six feet and, unlike many who answered Ashley's call for "enterprising young men," he followed adventure at the old age of thirty-three, leaving behind a business interest in a sawmill, a wife whom descendants claimed he was incompatible with, and four kids.

According to folklore, Davey favored the valley for trapping so much that Sublette, one of Jackson's partners in the Rocky Mountain Fur Company, named the place after him in 1829, thus "Jackson's Hole" came into existence.

Jackson served as the company's field manager. He, with the help of a slave named Jim whom Jackson brought west from Missouri, hunted around half a million dollars' worth of furs which Sublette took down the Missouri on annual trips to St. Louis, returning in time for the rendezvous with goods to sell to the mountain men at greatly inflated prices.

The three partners agreed to meet in Jackson's Hole on the Snake in 1829. Sublette came in with a force of trappers from the Wind River Range over Togwotee Pass. Smith arrived fresh from an arduous journey through the Southwest to California, the first white man to forge a path across the Sierra Nevada Mountain (in deep snow no less). Apparently, Jackson had been in the valley for some time. He kept no journal and drew no maps, but historians believe he lived year round in the region from 1823 until the partners sold the Rocky Mountain Fur Company in 1830.

Jackson left the range that year. Some speculate that he left under a cloud of suspicion involving missing property of his later partnership of Jackson-Waldo-Young. Other rumors theorized that he squandered the hard-earned fortune from fur trapping in a few short years. Whatever the case may be, he spent some time on the Santa Fe Trail and in California on a trip with his former partners Sublette and Smith around 1831. They bought a string of mules and drove them to New Mexico where they sold the animals to settlers. On this journey Smith died at the hands of Comanches.

But ultimately, this trip broke new ground, and Jackson received credit for opening a new route between Arizona and New Mexico. Such noted wanderers as John C. Fremont would later utilize this path. Jackson also blazed the trail across southern Arizona's Colorado Desert that the Mormon Battalion under Captain Cook would take during the conflict with Mexico and the '49ers would traipse over on their way to the California gold fields.

Accounts place him briefly in St. Louis in 1832, then a year later he returned home to St. Genevieve, Missouri. There, he acquired and ran several businesses, including ventures in five different states. On a business trip to Tennessee, he caught typhoid fever. Jackson died on December 24, 1837, and was buried in Paris, Tennessee.

Beaver Dick Leigh

Englishman Richard "Beaver Dick" Leigh ran away to sea as a child and ended up trapping in the Jackson Hole area at the tail end of the fur trading years in the late 1840s. Although he established a permanent home for himself, his Shoshone wife, Jenny (whom Jenny Lake in the Grand Teton National Park was named after), and their children on the Idaho side of the Tetons, Leigh probably knew more about Jackson's Hole than any other white man of his era. Along the way, he maintained a journal of his life in the Rockies and Jackson's Hole, written in a classically beautiful, yet small, fine script. His spelling, however, tended to be creative, and, as noted by contemporaries, Beaver Dick dropped his "h" when speaking and even in his correspondence.

In a March 8, 1899 letter to a longtime friend, Dr. Boise Penrose, who employed Beaver Dick as a guide on many hunting excursions, Leigh offered a glimpse of his early life. Born on January 9, 1831, Leigh, the son of a British navy man named Richard Leigh, and grandson of James Leigh who served in the English Sixteenth Lancers, came to America with his sister when he was seven. The family settled in Philadelphia. During the war with Mexico, he served ten months with the First Infantry, then moved westward to the Rocky Mountains. "And here i die," Leigh wrote.

Historical accounts claim the name "Beaver Dick" came from a combination of the Native Americans calling Leigh "The Beaver" because of his reputation as an excellent trapper, even though the fur trade had passed its heyday, and the fact that he sported two unusually long front teeth, making him resemble the animal.

A true frontiersman, Leigh hated the ever encroaching "civilization" and tried to keep at least some wilderness between it and his family. They camped in the Tetons during the three to four months of summer and wintered "at the elbo of the teton [river]" as Leigh called it.

Leigh, along with Jenny and their children, guided the 1872 Hayden Survey party through the Jackson Hole and Yellowstone country. The expedition honored Beaver Dick by naming two lakes after the family—Jenny Lake and Leigh Lake, both in modern Grand Teton National Park. The entourage included photographer Willam Henry Jackson, whose pictures of Yellowstone's wonders (the same marvels told by Colter, Bridger, and other mountain men for over sixty years) offered the first tangible documentation of the strange phenomenon's existence. (We'll see more of William Henry Jackson in Chapter 3 of Section Eight.) Jackson also devoted a day to taking the only known photographs of "Dick's Indians" as Jackson called Leigh's family.

Tragedy struck the family four years later. While traveling to their winter cabin, the Leighs came across the Native American wife and three-year-old child of a fellow trapper named Humphy. In a letter dated April 1, 1877, Leigh wrote to a friend from the Hayden Survey, Dr. C. Hart Merriam, describing the "little bumps" that had erupted on Humphy's mother's face and killed his father. A fellow trapper, Tom Lavering, told Leigh the illness must be measles or small pox. "...so i told my wife to give the woman some provishons and tel hur to go to the boat and i wold put her acros in the morning so she could go and tel the doctor on the Resirvation," Leigh wrote.

As Christmas neared, the entire family became sick, one by one. Leigh told of his wife's growing sickness in another letter. "...she shook all over and made a rumbling noyse...i was satisfide that hur hours was numbered and i spoke incorignely to hur but my hart was ded within me."

Jenny, soon after giving birth to their fifth child, succumbed to the disease. As Leigh never mentioned the sex of the child, it may have been stillborn or died right away. Ill himself, Beaver Dick saw each of his other children die within eleven days of his wife. He buried his family by the junction of the Teton River.

Beaver Dick Leigh, his wife Jenny, and their children.
Photo Credit: Wyoming State Museum

By the summer of 1888, when Leigh guided novelist Owen Wister and Dr. John K. Mitchell over Teton Pass so they could, as Mitchell put it, "get through the canyon without wings," Beaver Dick had met and married Susan Tadpole, a Bannock woman. In excerpts of Mitchell's journals, published in the *Jackson Hole Guide* during 1965, he described Susan as a "strapping girl." Mitchell also mentioned a daughter and "two or three small fry." He portrayed Beaver Dick as "a round shouldered, long-bearded, big nosed old man, with a clear light blue eye." Mitchell said Beaver Dick spent twenty-eight years scouting, guiding, and acting as an interpreter for the army.

In a letter dated March 20, 1899, just nine days before his death, Leigh again wrote his friend Dr. Penrose. ". . . i should eve beene ded 8 or 10 days ago. my insides is clene gone." Yet Leigh's major concern seemed to rest with Dr. Penrose's planned trip west. Leigh insisted his wife would have the lodge ready and his son Will would guide the doctor on the hunting expedition. Leigh ended with "i should ave like to see you before i crosen the line."

Richard "Beaver Dick" Leigh died at age sixty-eight.

4

Marysvale to Jackson

After men's hat fashions changed and the beaver fur trade dwindled, as did the animals themselves, Jackson's Hole hit a lull period. The nation embraced "Manifest Destiny," and thousands swarmed over the Oregon Trail to the western coastal lands, never knowing more than just rumors and mountain men's tall tales of the region that would become the northwestern corner of Wyoming.

But once again, politics in far-away places would infuse a new wave of people into Jackson's Hole. The War between the States (the Civil War) and the Homestead Act of 1862, together, acted like a powerful lure, drawing settlers westward. Nevertheless, they generally bypassed the Hole until about the 1880s, a decade when over five million immigrants entered the United States, looking for a better life as the political arena began heating up in Europe once again.

Bachelors and Other Early Homesteaders

In 1883 John Holland filed the first homestead claims on land located in Jackson's Hole—one for himself, the other for his friends John R. Carnes and his half-Ute Indian wife, Millie. Holland and Cranes trapped the Hole during winters in the 1870s and earned a living timbering in the LaBarge (Wyoming) area in the summers.

The sites they chose to settle on permanently lay a few miles northeast of present-day Jackson in the National Elk Refuge on what homesteaders called "The Flat" because the lush meadowlands sat in the drainage of Flat Creek and its tributaries. To increase production of the wild hay, the men began an irrigation ditch that would divert water from the confluence of Twin and Sheep creeks, tributaries of the Little Gros Ventre. This work also helped fulfill requirements of the Homestead Act which insisted that improvements must be made which would raise the land's value to $1.25 per acre.

Another condition of "proving up" on each 160-acre claim was to build a dwelling and live in it for at least seven months out of every year for five years straight. For safety and convenience, Holland and Carnes constructed the mandatory "cabins" on their joint property line, connecting them with a "dogtrot" and creating what could be considered a single residence. (See Cunningham's Cabin in Section Nine for more information on dogtrots.)

According to some old-timers, Holland and Carnes brought the first wagon into the Hole during 1884 via Bacon Creek and the Gros Ventre. Others claim Sylvester and Nick Wilson hold that honor. (See Pony Express Rider Nick Wilson's Covered Wagon for more details.) Holland and Carnes, however, did arrive in the Hole with farm equipment, dismantled and packed in on horseback, which the Wilsons would use upon their arrival in 1889.

Holland supposedly hosted the valley's first church service at his house on Easter Sunday 1890, led by the Mormon bishop Sylvester Wilson (see Pony Express Rider Nick Wilson's Covered Wagon). Of course this seems somewhat at odds with another claim made by a shady character called "Teton Jackson." When caught red-handed with a stolen herd of horses, the outlaw claimed Holland kept him in supplies when he holed up some place not too far from Holland's cabin. (We find out more about him and his antics in Section Four, Chapter 1.)

Holland and Carnes supplemented their income by guiding parties of eastern hunters, and at one time Holland may have brought in mail and supplies to the early residents—a two-hundred-mile round trip in those days.

At some point, Holland married a Victor, Idaho woman named Maud Carpenter. He sold a relinquishment on his homestead for a sum of $500 around 1890 and moved to Scio, Orgeon. He visited Jackson's Hole about 1898 and then disappeared from the pages of local history.

John and Millie Carnes, on the other hand, proved up, obtaining their homestead patent in 1897. At the time, they had moved to Fort Hall (Idaho) and were living on Millie's Indian allotment. Millie died in 1923, while John lived to see his ninety-second birthday in 1931.

If it hadn't been for Millie, the early settlers could have hung up a sign like the one in the movie *Paint Your Wagon* which read: Population Male. In *Jackson Hole: Early Settlement*, an unpublished manuscript housed in the Wyoming State Archives, Neillie H. VanDerveer states eighteen people lived in the valley in 1888—seventeen of them men.

Others first came to Jackson's Hole as young, single men looking to make their fortune or at least carve a niche for themselves. Out of this group would come men who would put Jackson on the map, start the conservation movement, save a pristine wilderness, and set the stage for modern life.

Men like Robert Miller, who, along with his wife Grace, would each play a large role in the development of the town (see Section Four, Chapter 2; Section Eight, Chapter 2; and Section Nine) and Stephen N. Leek, who saved the starving elk herd and with it a host of wildlife (see Section Eight, Chapter 1). Other men would come to the valley, seeking out the area's darker quality of isolation from the law. (We look into their lives in Section Four, Chapter 1.)

By 1890 the population had grown to sixty-four.

Jack Davis, a Real "Grizzly Adams"

Gold fever struck California in 1849. It spread, as does every fever, finding its way into Jackson's Hole with the Montana gold strike of 1862 and later the Idaho gold rush of 1883-86, although the 1920-30s would see most of the mining claims action in Jackson.

Prospectors panned the rivers and streams or dug holes here and there along the banks in search of more than just the teasing "color" they found. Jackson's gold, however, wasn't in its minerals, but in its awe-inspiring vistas and wildlife, as we'll see later. Therefore, most of the men struck with the fever drifted elsewhere in search of their fortune, leaving no trace of their time spent in the valley—with two legendary exceptions, the men who mined Deadman's Bar (which we'll uncover in Section Four, Chapter 3) and Jack Davis.

Davis came to the region in 1887. Repeating a story as old as gold camps, Davis, like every other miner around Virginia City, Montana, took his earnings and blew off steam at one of the saloons. One night he got drunk. Then he got into an argument, which led to a brawl. Davis, a blue-eyed, full-bearded goliath, hit his opponent a little too hard and killed him. Davis knew the town's "hang 'em fast" policy, so he fled the area. A while later he surfaced in Jackson's Hole, taking advantage of its reputation for being a place where a man could outrun his past.

Davis picked an isolated location on the south side of the Snake River on Bailey Creek. He constructed a crude log cabin with a rough-made door that hung on rawhide hinges and contained not so much as one window, an item which required a trip to a real town—something he couldn't risk.

A vegetable garden and the sluice boxes he fashioned supplied him with enough food and gold to trade for a few necessities. These he obtained from the nearest store fifty miles away at Menor's Ferry (more on it in Section Nine).

Possibly as an atonement for his crime, Davis never touched another drop of liquor or took another life—not even for food.

Over the next twenty-four years Davis lived the life of a hermit. But he was never alone.

According to Al Austin, an early forest ranger in the district and close friend of the fugitive in his later years, Davis filled his need for companionship with wild animals. Besides his burro, Calamity Jane, that bolted with him from Virginia City, Davis ran a menagerie for squirrels, birds, an old horse called Dan, a doe and her fawn (Lucy and Buster), and a couple of "cats" which Davis named Pitchfork Tillman after a prominent political personality of the day and Nick Wilson after a man who had much to do with the settling of the Hole as we'll see later. A curious note about the cat Nick Wilson: Austin claimed it was so named because of its preference for the "night life." Wilson must have led a more colorful life than the exciting one told by his descendents.

Bluebirds took advantage of the door open during the warm weather to nest behind a piece of a mirror that hung on the wall. There they raised their young. Buster, a typical youngster, liked to play on the furniture. The cats grew impatient with such antics. The squirrels complained when the bluebirds received more attention than they did, and vice versa. And through it all, Davis kept the peace and must have loved every minute of it.

He started a tiny graveyard for his beloved friends that died, maintaining a series of tidy, yet oddly sized mounts for all except Lucy, Dan, and Pitchfork Tillman who outlived Davis.

Davis had one curious habit. He kept a calendar on his wall and "x"ed off the days. Maybe he tracked the passage of time since that fateful day in Montana when his entire life changed. Or possibly, it marked his thanksgiving for another day of freedom. Whatever the case, it also told Austin the last day Davis felt well.

Austin periodically checked in to see how Davis and his animals were faring. One spring, the ranger found the old man seriously ill. The last "x" on the calendar covered February 11. Austin stayed with him until Davis joined his animals friends. Austin, with the help of a neighbor, built a coffin out of Davis's sluice boxes and carved a wooden headboard which read: "A.L. Davis, Died March 25, 1911." (How do you get "Jack" out of A.L.?)

Mary White, Postmistress of Marysvale

Just as the life of the valley's namesake, Davey Jackson, remains obscure, so does Mary White, the original mistress of the first post office in the Hole. She and her husband Fred came to the region sometime before 1892. They appear to have filed no homestead claim to the land on the northern part of the Flat Creek Flats where they built a cabin. No hint of a foundation let alone logs remain (which is unusual for permanent structures constructed during this era), which alludes to the possibility the cabin was in reality a shack erected to be disassembled and moved quickly. The fact that the Whites didn't stay long also supports this.

The "post office" itself consisted of a covered wagon. Evidently the Whites removed its wheels, for old-timers claimed that the wagon sat on the ground. Definitely no air of permanency there either. Just about everybody in the valley—and there weren't many at the beginning of the 1890s—signed a petition to get the post office at "Marysvale" (in honor of Mary), and they all took turns carrying the mail over Teton Pass that first year.

In 1893 the government hired a regular carrier. That same January, for some reason known only to themselves, the Whites switched the post office's name to "Gros Ventre." At some point not long afterward, Maggie and William Simpson took over, running the post office out of their home, and few details exist to tell what happened to Mary and Fred White. Mary did correspond at least a few times with a friend, Cora Nelson Barbar, who stayed in the valley, but Mary shed no light on why she and Fred left, what happened to him, the circumstances surrounding her remarriage to an unknown man named Tuttle, or why she signed the letters "Mae."

Pony Express Rider Nick Wilson's Covered Wagon

In August of 1856, eleven-year-old Elijah Nicholas ("Uncle Nick") Wilson ran away from his father's farm in Utah. He joined a band of Shoshone Indians and became the adopted brother of the famous Chief Washakie. Over the next thirty-three years, Nick's adventures would read more like a Hollywood script for a first-rate Western than real life. He lived with the Indians, fought "hostiles" both red and white, rode for the Pony Express, drove for a stagecoach line, scouted, trapped, and eventually found his way into Jackson's Hole around 1889 at the age of forty-seven.

While Nick was cutting wild hay in the valley, his brother Sylvester brought his family up from Wilsonville, Utah to Idaho in search of more productive land. The family planned to settle in what is now St. Anthony, until they coincidentally ran into Nick. He told them about the lush hay across the pass in Jackson's Hole and suggested they drive the cattle over and winter them there. Sylvester thought about it and decided to move the entire family, not just the cows, to Jackson's Hole for the winter.

Nick Wilson

Photo Credit: Teton County Historical Society

The party crossed Teton Pass in two groups. The first band went to lay in a supply of hay and brought a wagon with them. Even though they widened the narrow path by cutting trees along the way, they were still forced to dismantle the wagon and proceed two wheels at a time. Once they arrived, they borrowed a mowing machine (some accounts say from John Holland, others from a man named Will Crawford) and set to work.

Meanwhile, the rest of the family, along with the cattle, some horses, and six covered wagons loaded down with supplies, began the trek. It took them two weeks to travel the eighty-eight miles between St. Anthony (then Wilford) and the Hole. Along the way, they again cut trees to widen the trail over the mountain.

Six horses pulled each wagon up the steep pass. On the downhill side, the Wilsons used "roughlocks," untrimmed trees tied to the back of every wagon to act as an additional

drag to lessen the chances of the wagons becoming run-
aways.

Winter set in by the time the families arrived on November 11, 1889, allowing no time for constructing shelter. John
and Millie Carnes, who had completed a new home, offered
Sylvester's family their old two-room cabin with Wilson's
son-in-law's family sharing the other half of the dogtrot
cabin with John Holland. Nick's family stayed with Will
Crawford, and another bachelor named John Cherry housed
Sylvester's son Ervin and his family.

The following spring Sylvester's family "took up" land
along Flat Creek. Nick settled at the base of Teton Pass,
filing on a 160-acre homestead that would become part of
current-day Wilson, Wyoming, so named in his honor. The
town of Wilson celebrated its centennial anniversary during 1995.

Late in his life, Nick wrote about the adventures of his
youth. The book, titled originally *Among the Shoshones*,
first appeared in 1910. Few copies were printed. An edited
version came out nine years later under the title *The White
Indian Boy*.

Nick died on December 27, 1915 at the age of seventy-
three. His obituary in the *Jackson's Hole Courier* three days
later reflects that "Manifest Destiny" attitudes spilled over
into the twentieth century. "Uncle Nick was one of the early
pioneers of the West, coming to Utah as early as 1850, and
he has been a frontiersman ever since. His life has been
filled with experiences in connection with the reclamation
of the western wilderness."

Note: the term "Uncle" tended to be applied to many a
man around the Jackson Hole area, whether they had family
or not. The courtesy title might be equated with "Dutch
Uncle."

Mormon Row

On the east side of Blacktail Butte sits a once densely settled strip of land called Mormon Row. James I. May originally chose a homestead site in the area in 1894, but it took him two years of hard work and saving to accumulate enough resources to move his family to the valley overshadowed by the Tetons. When they moved onto the land during 1896, several other families came with the Mays.

These followers of the Church of the Latter-day Saints laid out an orderly community similar to those found in Utah and Idaho with homesteads lined up in a straight line, hence "Mormon Row," in what would become part of Grand Teton National Park. They also built the first church in the area in 1905. (See more about this in Section Nine, The Andy Chambers Ranch Historic District.)

Thomas Alma Moulton and his younger brother John left the family's holdings in Idaho and filed ajoining 160-acre claims on the Row in September 1907. Alma began construction on a barn for his livestock in 1913, a year after he, his wife Lucile, and their infant son Clark settled permanently on the homestead. This barn, with its additions and auxiliary structures, took twenty years to complete. It and John's stand today as the homesteading legacy of the Tetons, symbols for not only Jackson Hole, but the spirit of determination and perseverance necessary to survive in harsh conditions.

Clark Moulton and his wife Veda, great-granddaughter of James I. May, are the last remaining residents living on Mormon Row. At the time of their marriage in 1936, John D. Rockefeller Jr.'s Snake River Land Company had purchased quite a bit of the land around the community and was starting to buy up sites on the Row itself. But Clark wished to remain on the only home he had ever known, so Alma deeded Clark and his bride one acre south of the barn upon their marriage—the only privately owned land remaining on Mormon Row. (Get in on Rockefeller's "land grab" and

Grand Teton National Park's struggle to deal with the heritage of Mormon Row in Section Eight, Chapter 2.)

John Moulton's barn on Morman Row.

Photo Credit: Sierra Adare

Jackson, More Than a Name Change

By the turn of the century, settlers had "proven up" or purchased almost all of the open land in the Hole. Marysvale, then Gros Ventre, turned into Jackson when it incorporated in 1901. Grace Miller, whose role we'll witness in Chapter 2 of Section Four, located and platted the townsite. When the *Jackson's Hole Courier*'s premier issue rolled off the press on January 28, 1909, it claimed the town proper contained about two hundred people and a total of 1500 people lived around the Hole.

Jackson sported not one, but two general stores, a hotel, restaurant, drug store, feed and livery barn, blacksmith shop, a community schoolhouse, church, clubhouse, and, of course, a saloon. No longer was Jackson a struggling collection of pioneers determined to make a go of it. Jackson's Hole bloomed into a community, a town, a region, and the land of unparalleled opportunity, as we'll soon see.

Survival in the Hole

1

Nothing Like the Old Days?

The following tidbits from early-day Jackson Hole news-paper articles show that life in the valley isn't all that different nowadays. Well, almost!

Jackson's Hole Courier May 6, 1920

Things have been happening in Jackson during the past week that reminds us of a season we once called Spring... cars are darting to and fro like bees around a crock of sugar tree water.... In view of all these signs, symbols and activities, we wouldn't be very much surprised to hear if Spring arrived soon.

Jackson's Hole Courier June 17, 1915

"It has been decided to celebrate in Jackson on July 5th and a royal good time is planned for every one who will come. The celebration is to be principally for the children but the day will be so full and interesting that the older people will enjoy themselves to the limit.

In the forenoon there will probably be some exercises in one of the churches and immediately after dinner the childrens sports commence on the track in front of the grandstand.

There will be all kinds of stunts for the boys and girls and probably some for the men and women."

Jackson's Hole Courier February 18, 1915

A number of women met at St. John's House on Monday evening, and organized a "Women Voters' Study Club", for the purpose of preparing to exercise the franchise intelligently. The meetings are partly social in character, the members bringing sewing or fancy work to keep fingers busy, while the instruction is in progress. Meetings are held every Monday evening at 7:30. Mrs. Daniel is President and Miss Eynon Secretary-Treasurer for the season. Women voters or prospective voters are invited to join.

Jackson's Hole Courier May 21, 1914

"Word has been received at the Jackson Post office that no bid of more than $2500 will be accepted, for carrying the mail from Jackson to Moran."

Jackson's Hole Courier February 25, 1915

"Word has gone forth from forest headquarters to have the roads, trails and streams on the national forests well-marked before the camping season opens. In consequence signs conveying accurate, reliable information are being prepared, at odd times during the winter when storms and deep snow make it impracticable to engage in outside work, to be placed at points where needed throughout the forest. At every cross-road or point where there is a probability of leaving the main roads or trails a sign will indicate the direction and distance to local geographic points. If the trail is well-defined there will be no further directions until another point of divergence is reached; if, however, the trail is so dim that it is hard to distinguish it from the many game and stock trails, it will be "blazed", that is trees along it will be marked with a catface slash under a line at a height of about five feet."

Jackson's Hole Courier February 25, 1915

"A camp outfit, be it for one or a dozen, is not complete if it does not include a camp stove. The convenience and comfort in preparing the meals, the saving of both labor and wood in keeping the pot boiling, and reducing to the minimum the danger of Forest Fires, make it almost indispensable. These stoves can be bought at sporting goods and outfitting stores at a price ranging from 55 cents for a small camp broiler to $3 for a 4-hole collapsible stove weighing about 11 pounds. Good stoves, not collapsible, can be had for from $1.50 to $2.25.

To the person going camping for the first time, or to the man with whom camping has become a habit, a visit to a store that specialized in camp equipment and sporting goods will be a long step toward making his summer outing a success."

Jackson's Hole Courier February 1, 1917

"Last Friday witnessed the beginning of a violent storm which has prevailed throughout the northwest, tying up railroads and blocking traffic and mail. Jackson' Hole came in for her share of the storm being in the throes of the blizzard for many days. . . . The Hole has been without mail for five days, but telephone messages from the outside state that the storm has abated its fury and that things will be moving on schedule again soon."

Jackson's Hole Courier February 1, 1917

A report from Jackson's Hole states that the thermometer registered 59 below zero one night last week and that a great deal of damage was sustained by some of the stockmen of that section. Nineteen head of cattle, according to the report, froze to death in one herd."

Jackson's Hole Courier December 24, 1914

Flat Creek has been freezing and overflowing at the bridge in the southwest corner of town, flooding the road to a depth of a couple of feet or more, until it has become almost impossible to cross with a team. This is causing a great deal of inconvenience, but it is thought that it will soon be frozen solid, and the difficulty overcome."

Four-horse transportation used in and out of Jackson Hole.

Photo Credit: Wyoming State Museum

Jackson's Hole Courier December 24, 1914

On Tuesday of this week the mail had all upset on the other side of the hill. The box and hind bobs of the sleigh completely upset and rolled off down an embankment until they bumped into a quaking asp tree, and lodged. The team and front bobs remained on the road. Two passengers were on, but escaped unhurt. In fact, no injury of any sort resulted from the accident.

Jackson's Hole Courier June 24, 1914

Editor Courier,—

"I am glad to see you come out for strict enforcement of the game laws and against Federal control. We should do all we can to keep the State's game under State control. I want to do what I can. I think it would be well to know who the friends of game protection are. For that purpose why not publish the enclosed pledge, or another similar, with the request that it be signed and returned to you or me as you wish. You know I have some time on my hands now."

S.N. Leek

Following is the pledge as proposed by Mr. Leek:

"We, the undersigned, hereby pledge our moral and practical support to the game wardens and forest rangers in their endeavor toward forming and maintaining a game protective association for the better enforcement of the game laws."

We would be glad to hear from other valley residents on the subject of the game in Jackson's Hole. We consider that the matter is an important one, and will be glad to publish anything that our readers may see fit to offer on the subject. Some action toward preservation of our game should certainly be taken by the people here.

Jackson's Hole Courier April 29, 1915

Motoring will be permitted in Yellowstone National Park, beginning August 1st, Secretary Lane has announced, thus opening the last of the great government reserves to automobiles. Control stations are to be established at junction points throughout the park to regulate traffic. Secretary Lane's announcement added that it was expected the road through the Yellowstone would become a link in the highway to the opportunity of seeing some of the other national parks.

Jackson's Hole Courier September 18, 1919

Mr. and Mrs. R.E. Miller, Fred Lovejoy and Wm. Mercill were the guests of S.N. Leek from Thursday 'till Sunday of last week at one of his summer camps on Moran bay. They took a motorboat and trolled for macinaws in Jackson lake, but the big fellows evidently were not at home.

2

An Outfit for Everything or Survival Gear for the Hole*

There's a saying in Wyoming—"If you don't like the weather, wait ten minutes. It'll change." And it does. Snow can and generally does fall every month of the year. A hot summer's day in the nineties often starts with a heavy frost on the ground. Once the sun sets, temperatures drop or even

---

*   Much of the information found in this chapter is excerpted from *Trails & Tales: Day Hikes and Historic Sites on the Way to Yellowstone* and *Backcountry Cooking: Feasts for Hikers, Hoofers and Floaters.* See the Bibliography for details.

plummet. A summer thunderstorm might blow in over the Tetons, and you won't see it coming. In winter, the high might be somewhere BELOW zero, but the day might actually be considerably warmer up on the ski slopes.

In other words, weather conditions change fast and on occasion drastically around Jackson Hole. Coming unprepared might ruin an otherwise fantastic vacation.

Cotton is fine for shorts and T-shirts, but for Jackson Hole's varying weather conditions select sweaters, long-johns, jackets, etc. that wick moisture away from your body, such as polyester pile, synchilla, polyprophylene, and wool. Layering lightweight clothing also gives more protection and warmth than a single heavy layer.

A Few MUSTs Regardless of the Season:

Keep sunblock on. This applies to EVERY season. Just because the days feel cool or cold, it doesn't mean you won't burn to the point of blistering in the thin, high altitude atmosphere. A hat with a brim also helps protect from the strong sunlight.

Wear UV sunglasses.

The combination of altitude and sun can sneak up on you long before you notice anything more than a dull headache. Always CARRY WATER and DRINK FREQUENTLY. Try to drink double or triple the amount you normally do at home. (And no substituting coffee, tea, or sodas!) Taking a couple of aspirin as soon as you notice a headache coming on can help, too, in avoiding altitude and sun sickness.

Unless you want "beaver fever" or "backpacker's plague," when in the backcountry, bring and use water purification tablets. Most tablets take thirty minutes to effectively treat the water, more if you're dipping very cold water (as from a snow-melt-fed stream). Double the waiting time before drinking.

Lip balm is another absolute necessity in the sunny, windy climate around Jackson Hole.

Bring a camera and lots of film to catch the wonders of Jackson Hole. Or bring a video camera with spare battery packs.

Always carry an extra jacket. It helps to have one in the ever-changing weather.

Summer Biking

Shorts, T-shirt, tennis shoes, light windbreaker, wind pants, sweater, helmet, gloves, and water bottle (full of water) work well for riding bikes in the summer. Trail food is also a good idea (see Food for the Trail for suggestions).

Ballooning

In summer, wear shirt, pants, sturdy shoes with socks (your feet might get wet if there's a heavy dew in the meadow), sweater, and jacket. Gloves and a cap that covers your ears are also handy to have along. In winter, wear all of the above, plus a heavy coat.

Covered Wagon Trips

Since these trips enter into high country, nights can get quite cold, with heavy frosts in the mornings. Come equipped with layers that can be peeled off as the day warms up. Shorts and jeans with a T-shirt and long-sleeved shirt, sweat shirt, light jacket, and a wide-brimmed hat work well for daytime; you need a sweater and heavy jacket, gloves, a cap, and longjohns for evening. Wear hiking boots (and bring riding boots if you want to spend time on horseback) and wool socks, with an alternate pair of footwear (and socks) in case one set gets wet. Also bring rain gear and a swimsuit (for the brave at heart!).

If you are camping out, don't forget your personal toiletries, towel, wash cloth, flashlight, water bottle, purifying tablets, and insect repellent. Options include your own musical instrument and binoculars.

Dog Sledding

Dress in layers starting with longjohns, warm pants, a heavy sweater, boots with wool socks, a coat with a hood, and heavy winter gloves, or ski jumpsuits.

Skiing

For heli-skiing suit up in a one-piece ski jumpsuit, goggles, gloves, a hat with ear flaps (or stocking cap), and rent an avalanche beacon. The same applies to downhill.

Cross-country skiing demands layers that can be added or stripped off as body temperature fluctuates with activity. Start with pants and a heavy shirt (longjohns underneath in cold weather), sweater or jacket, a water-repellent windbreaker, wind (shell) pants and jacket, gloves, hat or cap that protects your ears, a couple of pairs of heavy socks (wool is best), and as an option, bring a pair of gaiters. Carry plenty of water and food, as well as an emergency thermal blanket (available at backpacking shops) for each member of the group.

Hiking

Summer days in the Hole get windy and often are cool. Afternoon thunderstorms develop regularly and can come over the mountains in a hurry. Therefore, in addition to shorts and T-shirts, pack a warm sweater (preferably wool) and rain/wind jackets and pants. Sturdy hiking boots (lightweights for day hiking), two pair of wool socks, and a pair of gaiters (optional) can keep your feet in good working condition. A hat helps protect from the harsh sunlight.

A standard life-saving item is an emergency thermal blanket. No larger than a couple of candy bars, the packet weighs almost nothing and has kept many travelers alive when freaky weather took them unaware. Moleskin for blisters and travel scissors really can save the day, too. In addition to your water (and purification tablets on longer hikes), carry plenty of trail food.

Horsepacking

Jeans, a long-sleeved shirt, jacket, and work gloves are a must for riding, as is a good felt cowboy hat. It guards against the bright sunshine and shields your eyes from wind-blown sand or snow. The compressed felt also repels water, and the brim's wide shape acts like a gutter, keeping frigid rain water from dripping down your face and the back of your neck. (And you thought they just looked stylish!)

The same practicality applies to cowboy boots. Their pointed-toe construction allows for quick access into the stirrup of a wheeling horse, while the heel stops your foot from slipping through the stirrup and becoming caught.

Then there's the slicker. Especially designed for horseback use, the mustard-colored 1880s Pommel Slicker, also called a "Fishskin" or "Tower" saddle coat, was made of a heavy canvas or duck material that had been waterproofed with linseed oil. Other than utilizing modern rain-repellent fabric, today's slicker differs little from the original pattern. The long split up the back allows the ankle-length coat to cover the entire saddle, as well as the rider. So you stay dry, all of you, while in the saddle.

Wildlife Safari or Guided Photo Trip

On summer trips, dress in a pair of shorts and a T-shirt under sweatpants and sweatshirt that can be removed as the day warms up (or added as the evening cools). Wear sturdy shoes or lightweight hiking boots and bring a jacket, gloves, and hat. In winter, dress as if you were going cross-country skiing (see above).

Extended Pack/Fish/Float Trips

In addition to shorts, T-shirt, pants, long-sleeved shirt, extra socks, longjohns for evening, warm jacket, sun hat, a stocking cap for the cool nights, gloves, and rain gear, take camp shoes, riding boots, sleeping bag, flashlight, and insect repellent in a duffel bag.

Day Fishing Trip

Wear shorts, T-shirt, pants, long-sleeved shirt, waders, warm jacket, sun hat, gloves, rain gear, and your favorite fishing vest and lures. And don't forget the insect repellent! Snacks are also welcome.

Whitewater Trips

Plan on getting wet! If the weather is warm, wear a swimsuit under a pair of shorts and a T-shirt. Also wear sneakers and a wide-brimmed hat. Bring wind pants and a jacket. In cooler weather, add a warm sweater and wool socks. A towel and a dry sweatshirt and pants for after the trip will feel good. You can also rent a neoprene wetsuit, gloves, and booties. Your guide will provide life preservers.

For an overnight trip, include a warm sweater or jacket, sleeping clothes, and personal toiletries.

Scenic Floats

On warm days, shorts and a T-shirt are fine, with a light long-sleeved shirt for added sun protection. Bring a hat and a light windbreaker. On cooler days, you might want to wear a long-sleeved shirt and pants and carry a jacket. Insect repellent can come in handy during the height of summer.

Mountain Climbing

For single-day climbs during the summer, shorts and a T-shirt with loose-fitting legs work well. Gloves, preferably a work variety, come in handy for rappelling. Gaiters are a great option as well. Bring a sweater, rain gear, and a windbreaker in a day pack. A wool stocking cap to keep your ears from being windblown makes a good addition, as does insect repellent during June and July. You can rent a pair of climbing shoes from the Moosely Seconds Mountaineering, 307-733-7176 or Teton Mountaineering, 307-733-3595. If your guide service doesn't include a meal, bring food and snacks in addition to plenty of water.

For two-day or winter climbs, dress in layers like you would for cross-country skiing (see above), bringing a warm parka, gaiters, and lightweight mountaineering boots. In addition to work gloves, include a pair of wool ones. Carry extra wool socks in a pack large enough to hold all your gear, plus food and water. Check with your guide to see if you need to bring your own camping equipment. Your climbing guide will supply specialized mountaineering equipment.

Food for the Trail

The bulk bins at your local supermarket provide a cornucopia of perfect trail foods. In normal hiking conditions figure on roughly half a pound of assorted trail foods per person per day. Include more salty type items such as cracker mix and corn nuts than sweets. For convenience, pre-slice the cheese to be consumed on the trail.

Pick up the following assortment:
    corn nuts
    pretzels
    banana chips
    dried papaya pieces
    dried pineapple rings or chunks
    dried apricots

dried apples
dates
assorted fruit leathers
assorted M & Ms
caramels (take individual wrappers off)
licorice
yogurt balls
walnuts
cashews
sunflower seeds
pumpkin seeds
assorted hard cheeses
Triscuts
cracker mix
assorted jerky

A Safety Tip While Driving

Drive slower around dawn and dusk. Many animals, large and small, are most active during these hours. And watch the sides of the road, as well as the road. Deer and antelope in particular seem to pop up out of nowhere. Your vehicle's headlights may cause them to stop right in the middle of the road. ALWAYS BE PREPARED TO STOP FAST. Vehicle/animal encounters don't just kill animals.

High Altitude Facts

- The air contains one-third less volume of oxygen at 10,000 feet elevation.
- Strenuous activity at altitude requires double the normal intake of water to offset dehydration.
- There are two primary kinds of snow avalanches—loose snow and slab. Loose snow avalanches begin small and grow on the way down the mountain. Slab avalanches occur when a large section of snow fractures and slides at once.

- Approximately eighty percent of all avalanches happen during or directly after a storm.
- The majority of hypothermia cases occur during the summer when temperatures range between 30 and 60 degrees.
- Most mountain sickness happens when camping out above 8,000 feet elevation.
- The thinner atmosphere at high altitude filters out fewer of the ultraviolet rays, increasing chances of sunburn—summer and winter.

Places in the Hole

1

Sleigh Rides Through an 8,000-Head Elk Herd and Other Unique Things to Do

People have been doing many of the things available to do in Jackson Hole for over a hundred years. The sense of and connection with history, such as you feel on the stagecoach ride around Town Square, overlaps with many of what would otherwise be just tourist gimmicks. On the other hand, the area's phenomenal scenery makes balloon rides or mountain bike treks uniquely Jackson.

Town Square

The Town Square, officially named the George Washington Memorial Park in 1932 in honor of the president's 200th birthday, sets the stage for stagecoach rides, craft fairs, art shows, and the annual antler auction. The Rotary Club constructed the arches at each corner of the park from shed elk antlers collected in the National Elk Refuge by the Boy Scouts. (You may recall seeing them in several movies, including the 1980 Clint Eastwood film *Any Which Way You Can*.)

Antler arches of Town Square.

Photo Credit: Sierra Adare

From 1988 to 1995 the square's best known fixture and law enforcer was Monster, the Town Square cat. He, with his owner, spent many a summer day in the square, safeguarding it from dogs, which were banned from the location by a town ordinance. Spitting and hissing, Monster licked every dog that tried to break the law. Monster died at the age of fifteen after an eight-month battle with cancer.

Surrounding Town Square is Jackson's historic downtown, complete with board sidewalks first installed by the all-woman town council (the nation's first) in the early 1920s. (Tally the votes for this council in Section Four, Chapter 2.) The Jackson Hole Museum offers a self-guided walking tour of downtown (nineteen buildings within an eight-block area) that starts at the museum with its collection that displays Jackson Hole's history from prehistoric Native American artifacts through 200 years of white colonization. Or you can choose their guided Historic Walking Tour. Catch one between May 27 and September 9. They last about an hour and are conducted each Tuesday, Thursday, and Saturday.

Historic walking tours of downtown Jackson are provided by the Jackson Hole Museum and Teton County Historical Society. Call them at 307-733-9605.

The Shoot-Out

Up until the early 1920s Jackson Hole was considered a safe haven for outlaws and assorted other hellraisers. Even today, gunfire rings out around the Town Square—usually right about 6:30 p.m. Residents gather to perform one of several twenty-minute melodramas based on some tale or actual event of western history.

The Shoot-Out began in 1957 with a bunch of local businessmen strapping on real 357s and Colt 45s (of course, the ammo wasn't real) and acting out skits in an effort to bring tourists into the downtown area. Nowadays, locals and actors in town to perform at the summer theaters play the roles of lawmen, shootists, and more or less innocent bystanders. On occasion, celebrities visiting the area participate and surprise the unsuspecting crowd. Sean, who has worked the Shoot-Out since 1990, calls it "stress relief at the end of the work day."

These shoot-outs occur as part of Old West Days over Memorial Day weekend and help officially kick off the summer season. They continue through Labor Day weekend.

The Jackson Hole Chamber sponsors this summer-long event which takes place nightly except for Sundays. For details write or call them at P.O. Box E, Jackson, WY 83001, 307-733-3316 phone, 307-733-5585 fax.

Elk Refuge Sleigh Rides

A horse-drawn sleigh ride through the National Elk Refuge highlights cold winter days around Jackson Hole. Approximately 8,000 elk (the nation's largest wintering wapiti herd) make the annual trek to the refuge, part of what has been their winter feeding grounds for centuries. Between December and March, draft horses pull either a sleigh or wagon (depending on the amount of snow) on an hour-long ride through the refuge.

Sleighs were first used to haul hay out to the herd. Passengers lent a hand by helping to distribute the feed. Before long, more visitors than hay piled onto the sleighs. Rides soon became separate from feeding. But the elk quickly grew accustomed to the sleds of people and are not disturbed these days by the visitors.

There's no exact schedule, but rides are continuous throughout the day between 10 a.m. and 4 p.m., leaving from the National Wildlife Art Museum three miles north of Jackson on Highway 26 and 191. Contact the museum for tickets and information at P.O. Box 6825, Jackson, WY 83002, 307-733-5771 phone, 307-733-5787 fax.

Teton Balloon Flights

All the guests spending the night at the Teton Tree House Bed & Breakfast (more on the Jackson Hole B&B experience in Chapter 4 of this section) decided to attend a balloon rally just over Teton Pass in Victor, Idaho—which meant everybody got up and got packing by 5 a.m. The owners, Chris and Denny Becker, packed a picnic basket full of breakfast goodies, and the group piled into three cars.

Up on the pass the rain started. Strong lightning bolts struck at the launch point, while the balloonists huddled in tents, and the B&B folks returned disappointed. The moral? Ballooning is at the mercy of weather. However, weather, along with wind and the fact that Grand Teton National Park doesn't allow balloon flights over the park itself, creates the ONLY limits to ballooning in Jackson Hole—an experience that shouldn't be missed!

Five forty-five in the morning comes awful early, but on clear mornings—every clear morning—that's the time Andy Breffeilh, the owner and pilot at the Wyoming Balloon Company, meets the day's passengers at flight headquarters at 515 North Cache Street. From there, the group heads out of town and into an open meadow. Only a few sandhill cranes and a herd of horses in a pasture across the way witness the spectacle of the propane-fueled fireball heating the air, which fans blow into the filling balloon.

Andy Breffeilh of the Wyoming Balloon Company
getting ready for an early morning take-off.

Photo Credit: Sierra Adare

Jackson Hole resident and "balloonatic" Andy sends up test balloons (birthday party-sized) to check on the wind currents. He's flown balloons for six years and planes longer still. (By the way, all balloonists are FAA certified, licensed pilots, and the balloons must pass yearly safety inspections just like planes.)

As up to nine passengers climb into the huge bamboo basket, Andy runs through his list of safety instructions— "don't mess with the propane tank" and "don't get out." Then the balloon, holding approximately 40,000 cubic feet of hot air, gently lifts into the atmosphere.

The flight lasts about an hour, with an unparalleled 360 degree view of the most spectacular scenery Jackson Hole has to offer. Watch the sunrise color the Tetons. See the Snake River slither through the valley floor, boiling with trout. Spy eagles, osprey, elk, antelope, bobcats, and an occasional moose, all from above. Only a short blast of flame breaks the silence. Andy uses air currents to steer, changing altitude to change direction.

"Flying and what you see are different every day," Andy says. "It's true flying by the seat of your pants."

At the end of the ride, Andy provides a champagne breakfast, following another ballooning tradition that Andy claims dates back to the early days of ballooning outside of Paris, France and that country's king. (The story gets a little wild from that point!)

The Wyoming Balloon Company is the only balloon out- fit which is permitted to fly in Jackson Hole, and they do it year round. Reservations are required. Contact them at P.O. Box 2578, Jackson, WY 83001, 307-739-0900.

Mountain Bike Tours

Expert or novice alike can discover the ultimate ride in Jackson Hole. Let gravity do the majority of the work by riding up the chairlift at Snow King Mountain and zooming down the dirt roads that wind through the mountain's meadows and trees with Fat Tire Tours. A guide will walk beginners through mountain bike techniques at the summit. Then you take off for Leeks Canyon and ultimately back to U.S. Highway 89.

Rent a bike from the Wilson Backcountry Sports shop and peddle along the many trails located on 8,400-foot Teton Pass. Or brave the challenge of 4,139 vertical feet peddling (with a bit of hiking thrown in) up Rendezvous Peak at Teton Village.

If you're more into natural and human history interpretive tours, try a guided expedition of either Yellowstone or Grand Teton National Park, the National Elk Refuge, or head out into the Bridger-Teton National Forest with Teton Mountain Bike Tours. David Hunger, the owner, saw a niche of interest and started these tours in 1991. "People come to Jackson Hole expecting to see Disneyland," he explains. "What they get is a chance to experience nature—wildlife, storms, mountain flowers—at a pace they can enjoy. "One of the most memorable events came on a Snake River Road Tour. A herd of sixty elk crossed the river not twenty yards in front of us. Lots of little ones swimming with their moms."

The Antelope Flats Tour is one of David's favorites. Mormon Row with its history and the Moulton barns offer insight into the homesteading era in Jackson. "It's a shame the old Joe Pfeiffer homestead burned down in 1994. It was a great example to talk about on the tours."

Teton Mountain Bike Tours offers three half, two full, and custom multi-day trips with transportation to and from the tour area and even child carriers provided on request. Contact them at P.O. Box 7027, Jackson, WY 83002, 307-733-0712 phone, 307-733-3588 fax.

For chairlift/bike rides contact Fat Tire Tours at P.O. Box 2877, Jackson, WY 83001, 307-733-5335. For mountain bike rentals contact Wilson Backcountry Sports 307-733-5228 or Hoback Sports, 40 S. Millward, Jackson, WY 83001, 307-733-5335.

Dog Sledding

Thirteen-year musher and six-time Iditarod veteran Frank Teasley cofounded the Jackson Hole Iditarod Sled Dog Tours as a "pension plan" for his race teams and a "high school" for the youngsters just learning the ropes (literally). Located in Hoback Junction, the teams trot over trails of abundant wildlife heading for either Granite Hot Springs, Grand Teton, or the Bridger-Teton National Forest in the Gros Ventres.

After an orientation session where guests get acquainted with each dog, learn basic commands (to give the dogs), and learn how to drive a team, the mush is on.

"No other method of travel over snow can compare with dog sledding," says Frank. "The only sounds are the shushing of the runners, perhaps the panting of the dogs, and the wind in your face."

Half- and full-day trips can start as early in the season as the end of November and usually run into April. Both include lunch. Custom tailored outings are also available. Contact Jackson Hole Iditarod Sled Dog Tours at P.O. Box 1940, Jackson, WY 93001, 307-733-7388.

Jackson Hole Stagecoach Rides

From every Memorial Day to Labor Day since 1985 downtown Jackson Hole has clattered with the clip-clop of horses' hooves as the old Overland Mail Stagecoach rounds the corners of the town and pulls into the stage stop next to the Square—much like it did a hundred years ago. In fact, that's how old the stage is. Its bright red, boxy, egg-shaped body rocks on leather springs called thoroughbraces. Mark Twain called the one he rode west in back in the early 1860s a "cradle on wheels."

During the summer, stages brought passengers and mail over Teton Pass to Jackson Hole, using at least a six-draft horse (or mule) team. Today, a two-horse team like Ralph and Toby, a pair of Belgium mix, draw the stage on the ten-minute rides, giving visitors a taste of what turn-of-the-century travel felt like.

For schedules and more information about the rides, contact the Jackson Hole Chamber of Commerce, P.O. Box E, Jackson, WY 83001, 307-733-3316 phone, 307-733-5585 fax.

Prairie Schooner Holidays

Fur trappers brought the first recorded wagon into the Rocky Mountains, with a four-pounder cannon mounted on a carriage and drawn by a pair of mules. When Jedediah Smith returned from exploring California, his friends (possibly Davey Jackson and Bill Sublette, his partners in the Rocky Mountain Fur Company) shot the gun in a "welcome back" salute, the only known firing of the weapon. In 1830 the partners brought a wagon train of supplies to a rendezvous in what is now Wyoming, and Sublette made the six-month return trip with the wagons loaded down with the furs Jackson had trapped in the Hole.

This Rocky Mountain Fur Company jaunt marked the beginning of opening the West to emigration via covered wagon. Today covered wagon treks follow ruts of a different kind—those made by truck tires rather than steel and wood wheels. Journeys last up to six days instead of an average of six months. But they still give modern-day travelers the feel and the awe-inspiring vistas experienced by the pioneers a century and a half ago.

Wagons appeared to sail on a sea of grass, hence the name "Prairie Schooner." Horse lovers can arrange to ride full time on the journey.

Trips take you in the National Forests surrounding Jackson Hole, allowing plenty of time for hikes, horseback rides, swimming in high mountain lakes (if you wish to brave the always cold waters), nightly campfire tales, singing, and a chance to take life at a pioneer pace.

Of course, the "roughing it" comes a bit easier. Comfortable cushioned seats, cozy sleeping bags (which you can rent), and great food sure beats the old days. Early pioneer fare consisted of the same chuckwagon-style cooking (dutch ovens over open fires) as utilized on today's trips, but earlier travelers rarely ate such delectables as barbecued chicken, fresh corn on the cob, salad fixings, and brownies. No fear of running out of food like in the olden days either!

Wagons West offers two-, four-, and six-day trips into the Bridger-Teton National Forest and Mount Leidy Highlands. You can reach them by writing to Peterson-Madsen-Taylor Outfitters, Afton, WY 83110 or calling 800-447-4711.

The Jackson Hole Bar-T-5 Covered Wagon Train travels through Targhee National Forest (between Yellowstone and Grand Teton National Parks) on four-day trips. (As a side note: Bill Thomas, one of the owners, is the great-grandson of "Uncle" Nick Wilson, who brought the first covered wagons into Jackson's Hole back in 1889.) Contact the Bar-T-5 at P.O. Box 3415, Jackson, WY 83001, 800-772-5386 phone, 307-739-9183 fax.

2

Shopping From the Out-of-Doors to the Outlandishly Trendy

Downtown Jackson stores tender everything from western art and jewelry galleries to live Wild West musical theater, bona fide soda fountain drinks at the Jackson Hole Drug since 1914, designer western apparel, and antler furniture. Unfortunately, not many of the unusual items found in Jackson's shops are created by local artisans.

Antler Art

Antler art represents the area's most unique shopping opportunity. Not only are the antlers collected in the surrounding mountains and meadows, they are auctioned and sold around Jackson's Town Square, part of the world's largest antler auction. (See below for more about this.) Many of the buyers in turn fashion an incredible number of very Jackson items which shops around town sell.

Elkhorn Designs, off the Square, carries deer antler-framed mirrors, elk antler chandeliers, buffalo bone toothpicks, antler key chains, and deer button buttons.

Elkhorn Designs, P.O. Box 7663, Jackson, WY 83002, 307-733-4655 phone, 307-654-7830 fax.

Elk Antler Auction

Each April the local chapter of Boy Scouts descends on the National Elk Refuge to gather the antlers the animals have shed during the winter (all antlered animals lose them each autumn and grow a new set the following spring, unlike horned animals such as bighorn sheep and antelope that have one permanent set).

Only scouts are allowed to collect antlers on the refuge. In turn, the funds raised at the annual auction benefit the Scout district and the refuge.

Vic Lindeburg, the antler auction chair, explains, "It all started with the Rotary Club gathering antlers for the arches in the Town Square. The Boy Scouts were looking for a way to earn money to sustain their $10,000 district membership, send Cub Scouts to day camp, purchase equipment, that sort of thing."

Once the scouts round up the antlers, a Forest Service biologist lays the antlers out and matches pairs, binding sets together, and bundling the odd assortment into loads for the auction held the third Saturday in May.

Wholesalers and individual buyers come from around the world to purchase the antlers for use in everything from

Asian aphrodisiacs to wall mounts to furniture to gun racks to candle holders to decorations in dried floral arrangements.

The annual antler auction.

Photo Credit: Sierra Adare

Cattle Kate's*

The original "Cattle Kate," Ella Watson, homesteaded and, according to some accounts, rustled cattle in the West during the 1800s. For the latter, she holds the dubious distinction of being the first woman hung in Wyoming. But the only thing that rustles about Kathy Bressler, the West's current "Cattle Kate," is the bustle on the nineteenth-century-style Prairie Dancer Dress she designed. Located in

---

*   Excerpt from *The Living West*. See the bibliography for details.

Wilson, Wyoming, Cattle Kate designs contemporary clothing with the look and feel of the Old West.

Bressler received the nickname long before she started Cattle Kate's. She lived in historic South Pass City and had a little store in back of a saloon where she designed modern-day versions of authentic western apparel for tourists and townspeople.

When she married and moved to the Jackson Hole area, Bressler began making practical, keep-your-neck-warm silk cowboy scarves for her husband and his friends. They became so popular, she started accepting mail orders, and Cattle Kate's branched out from there. Calling the company after the nickname she'd carried for years was a catchy way to market the thriving young company.

To keep the look authentic, Bressler uses lots of calico, brushed twill, cotton corduroy, wool, and handkerchief linen fabrics. Silk ribbon, cotton piping, lace, and velveteen accent the fashions. The clothing line includes turn-of-the-century split riding skirts, leg-of-mutton sleeved carriage coats perfect for a buggy ride on a cool autumn day, and romantic linen shawls. Of course, the lacy hem of a petticoat or the ruffled edge of pantaloons offer a tantalizing glimpse of yesteryear.

"Designing clothes along old themes is more creatively fun and challenging," states Bressler.

Cattle Kate's also outfits men. A frock coat with a classic four-fingered silk Sunday go-to-meetin' tie adds a real western flare to an occasion. Drover vests, horsehair suspenders, and three-in-one shirts with interchangeable button-on collars to dress up or down as circumstances warrant all add a dash of frontier spirit.

Bressler's scarves, which come in thirty colors, remain Cattle Kate's most popular item. "They are a functional, attractive western statement that anybody can wear," she explains. "You don't have to be a hard-core cowboy to wear one of my scarves. You just put one on and feel in place in

Wyoming." An interesting perspective considering she sells her creations around the world.

Nevertheless, Cattle Kate's clothing does touch people's lives in unexpected ways. Bressler often receives letters and pictures of her customers dressed in their western finery.

One that stands out in Kathy's mind portrays a Japanese gentleman decked out in a frontier vest, scarf, and buckskin Buffalo Bill fringed gauntlets, grinning big as he leans against a Japanese version of a western bar.

You can either see Cattle Kate's selection at Kathy's store at 3530 South Park Drive in Wilson, Wyoming, or send for a catalog (which costs $3.00) at P.O. Box 572-JHU, Wilson, WY 83014, 800-332-KATE (5283) phone, 307-739-0767 fax.

Other Wyoming-Style Clothing

The Black Possum Rodeo carries kids clothes from newborn to six-X (preschool). Color coordinated bibs and tees, caps, crib blankets, and pillow sets in western patterns are all designed and made by Mandy and Bryan Beverly, the store's owners.

Black Possum Rodeo, 80 W. Broadway #16A, P.O. Box 4558, Jackson, WY 83001, 307-733-8433.

Unc's Boot Shop custom-makes boots fashioned to fit each individual foot. Choose between tooled or scallop tops, finger holes, baby mule, or mule ears pull holes. Select between inlaid design and overlaid leather. Unc's uses only quality calf, kangaroo, elephant, bullhide, shark, alligator, lizard, and ostrich leathers. Of course, you can add that personal touch with your initials or brand if desired. Boots can also be dyed any color you like.

Unc's Boot Shop, P.O. Box 7944, Jackson, WY 83002, 307-733-5477.

Genuine Wyoming Cowboy Hats

Although the beaver top hat went out of style in the 1840s, felt made from beaver fur quickly became the preferred material for western cowboy hats. One hundred percent beaver felt hats fetch a high asking price these days, but they will last thirty years or so and look good the whole time. Or at least that's how Paul and Marilyn Hartman make them.

The Hartmans founded the Jackson Hole Hat Company after discovering some old hat-making machinery gathering dust in the drugstore's basement. It, plus a 1928 "how-to" book, started the customized business which serves locals and tourists alike, as well as a growing mail order trade. Beginning with felt that has been shrunk to hat size and stretched into a rough hat shape, the Hartmans use a blocking machine to shape the crown and brim. A jigger sands the brim, then they "pounce" the hat (sandpaper the crown to smooth it). Then they hand-sand each hat to finish it before setting the brim with a flanger.

Jacksonites wear cowboy hats for practical reasons—like protecting their head and neck from the sun, wind, rain, and snow. Styles change a bit, but the basics remain. The "Gus" became a popular type after the release of the mini-series *Lonesome Dove*. Fedoras showed up again with Indiana Jones and Dick Tracy on the big screen. The *Man From Snowy River* encouraged demand for the "Outback." The Hartmans make those, as well as the standbys such as the "Cattlemen's," the "Montana," the "Bullrider," the "Jesse James," and the "Revenger."

Check out a hat with your personal stamp on it at the Jackson Hole Hat Company, 255 North Glenwood, P.O. Box 1308, Jackson, WY 83001, 307-733-7687.

3

Sourdough Ain't Just for Breakfast Anymore

Due to the diverse flow of folks passing through, and especially those who sink roots into Jackson Hole's soil, the valley thrives with an international line-up of eats to satisfy any palate.

Buffalo and elk are two popular and very Wyoming menu items around Jackson Hole. The buffalo meat tends to come from a growing number of bison ranches throughout the West. On the other hand, commercial wapiti herds aren't allowed here (thus eliminating the temptation to poach elk for profit). All the elk meat available at area restaurants is imported from New Zealand where the animals have been raised on ranches. That, however, doesn't diminish its delicate and delectable taste!

The Granary

The Granary serves both elk (chops for dinner or flank fajitas for lunch) and buffalo (in the form of tenderloin) with a killer view of the Teton Range from just about every seat in the place. Dine on specialities such as rack of lamb, game chili, smoked duck quesadilla, rabbit bratwurst, pheasant and duck pate, or golden trout dipped in a jalapeno and Parmesan egg mixture, sauteed and served with a tomatillo salsa—while taking advantage of the screen-enclosed sun room if you wish.

Or view a spectacular sunrise while feasting on a traditional continental breakfast of juice, pastry or toast, preserves, fruit, and cereal. For a different wake-up twist, try the Game Hash made of hash venison, potato, onion, and peppers all fried crisp and topped with eggs; Granary Sunshine Skins featuring scrambled eggs with spinach and snow crab in three potato skins topped with jack cheese; or

Bagel and Smoked Salmon served with cream cheese, onion, tomato, and fresh fruit.

The Granary is located at the Spring Creek Resort, 1800 Spirit Dance Road, P.O. Box 3154, Jackson, WY 83001, 307-733-8833. Be sure to call for dinner reservations.

Jedediah's Original House of Sourdough

Sourdough may have came to Jackson's Hole with the early trappers. And it was a fixture on the settlers' menu as they hauled in wagonloads of supplies over Teton Pass. Today, Jedediah's Original House of Sourdough carries on the tradition with their hundred-year-old sourdough starter.

Co-owner Mike Gieran started working as a baker, but Jackson Hole's pioneer heritage beckoned. In a bold move, he decided to open an eatery with a mountain man theme. "Visitors come to get a sense of the valley," explains Mike. "They can find it here in the old pictures in this log house the restaurant is located in."

The *Mountain Rendezvous Times*, a "newspaper" published by Jedediah's, came about when the county library put old copies of the *Jackson Hole Courier* on microfilm and then got rid of the actual papers. The *Times* features "articles" based on historical events and people from Jackson's Hole's past such as "Jedediah Returns to Jackson Hole!," "Stephen Leek receives camera from George Eastman," "Beaver Tooth again eludes game warden," and "Cissy Patterson opens Flat Creek Ranch."

"I'll vouch for the paper," Mike says, "but not the articles. The whole thing started out as a limited number printing, just for fun. Now it's up to 30-40,000. People enjoy taking them home."

You can also take home some of Jedediah's renowned sourdough starter, not a modern "instant, add water" kind, but a living starter fresh from their fifty-gallon crock. They will also mail order it, or their *Jedediah's Cookbook*, which includes instructions on How to Care For Your Starter, Tips on Sourdough Cooking, and favorite recipes, or their original jams and jellies.

Mike's favorite (and a lot of other folks', too) is sourjacks pancakes. You've never tasted anything like them! Jedediah's also serves great sourdough bread sandwiches, buffalo burgers, and sourdough carrot cake.

Jedediah's Original House of Sourdough's historic log cabin.

Photo Credit: Wyoming Travel Commission

Jedediah's Original House of Sourdough is located at 135 East Broadway, P.O. Box 3857, Jackson, WY 83001, 307-733-5671.

Nani's Genuine Pasta House

In June 1990 Carol A. Mortillaro Parker opened Nani's Genuine Pasta House one and a half blocks from Town Square on a quiet neighborhood/commercial block within

Jackson's original townsite. An Italian restaurant, Nani's specializes in truly authentic regional Italian food.

"I hesitate to use the word 'authentic' since it is over-used and abused," comments Carol, "but in our case it is true. Each month we feature the food of a different region of Italy. The chef carefully researches this to be sure that we are 'regionally correct,' so all of the regular menu items of the month and also our nightly specials are from that one region.

"It's been a lot of fun and has given the local people who follow the regions an interesting and educational gastronomic tour of Italy. The tourists are very happy to find Nani's, too. They and the locals are surprised to find out how different the foods of the various regions are from one another.

"We make everything from the Italian bread to the desserts in our own kitchen from the best ingredients, never using bases, mixes, or enhancers."

And dining at Nani's is like coming home to a big family meal.

Nani's menu changes nightly, but a few samples of regional dishes you might find are "Malloreddus," a homemade saffron and flour gnocchi tossed in a fresh tomato sauce and served with Parmesan and Romano cheeses; "Coniglio all' Agredolce," pan-seared rabbit simmered in a sauce of capers, olives, red wine vinegar, and dried prunes served with greens and pasta; "Creme Caramelo," a light custard with caramel sauce; and a Cappuccino Trieste to round out the evening.

Nani's Genuine Pasta House, 240 North Glenwood, P.O. Box 1071, Jackson, WY 83001, 307-733-3888 phone, 307-733-3957 fax.

The Sweetwater

Like Jedediah's Original House of Sourdough, the Sweetwater restaurant, which opened in 1976, resides in a historic log cabin. A Mormon couple from Utah, Clarence and Martha Dow, constructed and lived in the structure for five years. Then, as many other pioneers to Jackson Hole did, they gave up and moved on to begin again some place easier.

In those days, the empty cabin invited occupation, and many families found shelter beneath its roof, which started out with an unpretentious pitch. The current gabled design was added when the cabin was expanded during the 1920s.

The Sweetwater satisfies hearty appetites with such dishes as Moussaka, the classic Greek casserole of layered eggplant and spiced ground beef topped with a cheese souffle; Chicken Grand Marnier, baked breast of chicken filled with brie and black currants served with a strawberry Grand Marnier glaze; Smoked Buffalo Carpaccio, thin slices of smoked buffalo roast served in a horseradish cream with French bread; and Roast Lamb, produced locally; or try a salad with the Sweetwater's own feta herb garlic dressing.

The Sweetwater, the site of one of Jackson's historic homesteads.

Photo Credit: Sierra Adare

The Sweetwater restaurant, the corner of King and Pearl streets, P.O. Box 3271, Jackson, WY 83001, 307-733-3553.

Blue Lion

The Blue Lion, not far from Town Square, offers a casual but elegant atmosphere and unusual treats. For an appetizer try some Croute Havartien (cheese, spinach, and mushrooms wrapped in a flaky puff pastry and baked until golden brown) or Stuffed Mushrooms. A popular Jackson item is the Grilled Elk Loin served sliced and topped with brandy and a green peppercorn sauce. Wyoming beef comes to the forefront in Tournedos Au Blue, medallions of beef tenderloin sauteed to temperature and finished with crab, artichoke hearts, and brandy blue cheese cream sauce. Then there are Pasta Primavera or Shrimp and Smoked Chicken Linguine (shrimp and smoked chicken breast sauteed with garlic, tomato, and scallions and finished with sherry and fennel, while the linguine is tossed with white wine, a dash of lemon juice, and fresh tarragon). The Blue Lion also offers a vegetarian menu, and child portions are available.

The Blue Lion, 160 N. Millward, P.O. Box 1128, Jackson, WY 83001, 307-733-3912.

SilverDollar Restaurant

Located in the Wort Hotel, the SilverDollar Restaurant serves tasty, hearty meals that bring in the locals. Breakfast favorites range from Mountain High Game Hash to Belgian Waffles with Huckleberry Syrup. Specialties of the house include Mountain Man Chili with Homebaked Corn Bread, Smoked Trout with Horseradish Coleslaw, Grilled Venison Sausage with Green Peppercorn Sauce, London Broiled Buffalo, Hunter's Game Stew, Char-Grilled Buffalo Burgers, and a "to die for" French Onion Soup—all served in a historic atmosphere.

SilverDollar Restaurant, corner of Broadway and Glenwood, in the Wort Hotel, 307-733-2190.

Gun Barrel Steakhouse

If you want to chow down in a Wild West Show ambience, look to the Gun Barrel Steakhouse. It used to be the home of the Wyoming Wildlife Museum and Taxidermy, and there are several reminders still hanging around to lend a feel of a hunting lodge to the place. An interesting collection of antique cowboy relics (saddles and such, not actual cowpokes), and an original Hayden survey map from the area that dates back to 1877, all blended with the hand-peeled lodgepole pine logs makes for a western experience even before you smell mesquite grilled steak kebabs, salmon, or chicken. But, of course, their caliber is measured by their steaks—buffalo, beef, and a variety of game.

Gun Barrel Steakhouse, 862 W. Broadway ("under the bugling elk"), 307-733-3287.

The Bunnery Bakery and Restaurant

Mention the Bunnery and O.S.M. (Oat, Sunflower, Millet) immediately springs to mind and starts the taste buds to anticipating some of the made-fresh-daily special Bunnery recipe O.S.M. breads, rolls, pancakes, hot cereal, and granola.

Dominique Yverneult, a New Yorker, loved vacationing in Jackson Hole and wanted a way to stay. When she saw the need for a restaurant that would appeal to the locals instead of catering to summer tourists, she opened The Bunnery, providing good food at a reasonable rate.

Besides breakfast, The Bunnery serves lunch and dinner, the same menu for both. "A family style works best for us," explains Dominique. "Nothing too complicated or expensive. We keep the meals simple and high quality."

O.S.M. bread came about the same way. Dominique decided to create a special food, something healthy and hearty enough to suit Jacksonites' active lifestyle. Made every morning in The Bunnery's on-site bakery, the bread's unique combination of ingredients gives the restaurant's sandwiches a rich flavor all their own.

Of course, The Bunnery didn't stay a local secret long. Visitors wandering along Jackson's board sidewalks soon discovered the restaurant tucked away in an inset square known as "the Hole-in-the-Wall Mall."

The bread and other O.S.M. products quickly were in such demand with tourists wanting to send a taste of it back home to friends and relatives, Dominique started a mail order business. Now she express ships items all over the United States. Currently she's negotiating to have O.S.M. distributed through a nationwide supermarket chain.

A Jackson Hole tradition, The Bunnery's breakfasts are "not to miss," served any time. In addition to a wide variety of omelets, there's The Grand Teton, three eggs, a ham steak, homefries, and toast; The Gros Ventre Slide, fried eggs on a bed of homefries, pilled high with green chilies, cheddar cheese, sour cream, and sprouts; Mother Earth, broccoli, tomatoes, and mushrooms over homefries, blanketed with melted cheese; and O.S.M. waffles and French toast. Favorites for other meals include the Teton turkey sandwich; The Western, lean roast beef with Swiss cheese, lettuce, and tomatoes; homemade chili; burritos; and divine desserts and pastries.

The Bunnery is just half a block north of the Town Square in the "Hole in the Wall Mall," 130 North Cache Street, 307-733-5474. Their mail order address is P.O. Box 3522, Jackson, WY 83001, 800-349-0492.

Vista Grande

Tom and Becky Shell opened the Vista Grande in 1978. And an enchanting view of the Tetons awaits you. So does South of the Border cuisine with just the right spice! Plato Tomas starts with a chicken burrito laced with guacamole, sour cream, salsa verde, and half with salsa rojo topped with monterey jack cheese and tampiquena salsa; Jalapeno

Spinach Chicken takes marinated chicken breasts and grills them with a jalapeno, spinach, cheese sauce, that's served with black bean relish and Mexican rice. Along with traditional chile rellenos and taco salads, there's a skier's special, the Teton Grande—"a meal right for a hungry mountain man." It begins with a flour tortilla stuffed with seasoned beef, beans, guacamole, and sour cream, then everything is smothered with chile con queso and splashed with salsa rojo. Round it off with some imported negra modelo dark ale! Oh, and there's also a Gringo Burger for the faint of palate.

Vista Grande is located on the Teton Village Road. Call for reservations at 307-733-6964.

Dornan's Chuck Wagon

Since 1948 five generation of Dornans have cooked up genuine chuckwagon meals in dutch ovens almost big enough to swim in. Perched on the bank of the Snake River next to the Tetons, this is outdoor cooking at its finest (which must be the reason why President Clinton ate here more than once while vacationing in Grand Teton National Park the summer of 1995). And Dornan's is all you can eat, so come hungry!

Barbecue short ribs, roast beef, vegetable beef stew, cowboy beans, and potatoes and gravy all simmer over open fires. If starved, you can add steak and prime rib specials to the menu. Each meal also comes with all the salad, sourdough bread, and coffee, tea, or lemonade you could want.

For breakfast sink your teeth into sourdough pancakes, two eggs, ham or bacon, juice, and coffee or cocoa. Lunch sandwiches offer a choice of barbecue beef, french dip bacon and avocado, grilled chicken breast, crab and avocado salad, or a chef salad.

Just look for the huge tipis, used for dining out of the sun or during bad weather (easily spotted from Highway 28, 89, and 191), that signify Dornan's Chuck Wagon at Moose, WY, 307-733-2415.

Chuckwagon and Covered Wagon Cookouts

Harnesses jingle. Wagons creak, rocking gentle, pulled up the mountain by a two-horse team. Vistas open up as you pass aspen and pine groves protected in folds in the mountains. Lupine and sagebrush splash the landscape with color. Horses snort and shake off the slight chill in the breeze. The high plains air stimulates the appetite. Good thing breakfast or dinner awaits just over the horizon.

Taste this western experience as the A/Ok Corrals Covered Wagon Cookouts round up three-hour outings in either a pioneer-style covered wagon or on horseback across the Billings Ranch. From a plateau high on the ranch, you receive an uninterrupted view of the Gros Ventre Mountains, the Teton Range, and the Snake River winding through the valley 500 feet below.

Fill up at breakfast with sourdough pancakes, eggs, bacon, sausage, ranch fries, and camp coffee. All you can eat. Or return to the past, dining in the alpineglow of the Tetons, with thick cuts of New York steaks sizzling over an open fire, beans bubbling in a big pot, baked potatoes, steaming rolls, and brownies covered with frosting, while a singing cowboy ushers in the evening.

Group rates are available. The A/Ok Corral is a ten-minute drive from Jackson near Hoback Junction on Highway 191. Get all the details and make reservations by contacting them at P.O. Box 3878, Jackson, WY 83001, 800-733-6556.

The Box K Ranch features Grand Teton Covered Wagon Cookouts for breakfast and dinner. A twenty-minute ride into Buffalo Valley to a quiet clearing in an aspen grove not only sets the scene, but builds your anticipation for a real cowboy meal of country-style (big) flapjacks, scrambled eggs, bacon, sausage, and hash browns.

Dinner rides offer tasty ribeye steak fingers, homemade barbecue beans, salad, and baked potatoes and dessert, plus cowboy entertainment. Kids four and under eat for free.

Contact the Box K at P.O. Box 110, Moran, WY 83013 or call 800-729-1410.

Bar none, the Bar J Chuckwagon Supper and Western Show is like nothing you will ever see elsewhere. From Memorial Day through September, rain or shine, the Bar J feeds up to 600 people per night, serving them all in just twenty minutes. Honest! Western hospitality never tasted better than you find on this working cattle ranch on the Teton Village Road.

Besides feeding you tender sliced beef smothered in a mild barbecue sauce, grilled chicken, potatoes, beans, home-made biscuits with butter and jelly, chunky applesauce, old fashioned spice cake, and lots of real ranch coffee, the Bar-J Wranglers will keep you laughing and stomping your feet with loads of cowboy songs, ranch style humor, yodeling, and cowboy poetry.

Reservation are strongly recommended, and "lap size" kids eat free. Contact the Bar-J Ranch, P.O. Box 220, Wilson, WY 83014, 307-733-3370.

Note: While the chuckwagon and covered wagon meals tend to run along similar lines, each setting remains unique and each encounter differs from place to place. Short of taking a wilderness trip like the ones described in Section Five, Chapter 2, these meals come closest to a genuine experience of this nation's westward surge.

Jackson Hole has many other fine restaurants. Contact the Jackson Hole Chamber of Commerce for a Dining Guide, P.O. Box E, Jackson, WY 83001, 307-733-3316 phone, 307-733-5585 fax.

4

Dudes, Guest Ranches, and Places in the Hole

> Snake River came into the place through canyons and mournful pines and marshes, to the north, and went out at the south between formidable chasms. Every tributary to this stream rose among high peaks and ridges, and descended into the valley by well-nigh impenetrable courses... Down in the bottom was a spread of level land, broad and beautiful, with the blue and silver Tetons rising from its chain of lakes to the west, and other heights residing over its other sides.
>
> Owen Wister, *The Virginian*

The idea of "dude ranching" in Jackson Hole dates back to around 1890, the vision of John Sargent and his partner Robert Hamilton. The two even constructed a ten-room log ranch house to accommodate guests, calling it Merry Mere. An ironic name for a notion that was never to be. (Walk the ill-fated path of Merry Mere's occupants in Section Four, Chapter 3.)

Others around the turn of the century also liked the concept, but getting the dudes and, more importantly, the supplies needed to accommodate them, limited the business to primarily hunters and fishermen until the JY Ranch opened in 1908, owned by Louis Joy.

The JY Ranch

The JY nestled in the foothills above the Snake River on three-mile-long Phelps Lake, where, according to a surviving brochure, the altitude is "bracing without being over-stimulating." In addition to the main lodge, used for recreation and a dining cabin with a kitchen, the JY maintained ten guest cabins.

At the JY, guests could participate in western style horseback riding, boating and swimming in Phelps Lake (where a moonlight night "is a revelation"), target shooting, bird or big game hunting, fishing the lake or the Snake River, photography, and "cowboy sports" on the Fourth of July.

The JY Ranch brochure unfortunately offers no date, but the $35-per-week price, which included the use of the laundry, a pony for each guest, and one of the boats, and the fact it listed Joy as still running the place, indicates a publication date between 1912 and 1916. So does the suggestion that women outfit themselves with split riding skirts, high boots, leggings, flannel blouses, rain gear, and a wide-brimmed felt hat. Men should bring heavy woolen underwear, flannel shirts, heavy trousers, wool socks, sturdy shoes, leggings, gauntlet gloves, rain gear, wool sweater, neck handkerchiefs, and a wide-brimmed felt hat. The discrepancy in the kind of keep-you-warm clothing suggests either women could tolerate the cold better or they were expected to do less. Of course, none of that stopped women of the caliber of Cissy Patterson from tackling all forms of the great outdoors. (Tag along on Cissy's successful hunt in Section Four, Chapter 2.)

Bar BC

"Change—Desirable and Needful But Where? Our suggestion—Do Anything you like and you will like it, riding, fishing, picnicing, packing, camping, cowpunching, nights in Jackson to see the sights and become one of them or to bed in a comfortable cabin 6,400 feet above sea level, also have Bar BC paper *The Wrangler*."

This is how the Bar BC, Jackson Hole's second dude ranch, brought the dudes in to the ranch that sprawled in the shadow of the Tetons, overlooking the Snake River.

Struthers Burt, twenty-five when he first came west from Philadelphia, and his partner, Dr. Horace Carncross, started the Bar BC in 1910, and it ran until 1986.

Guests arrived at the Bar BC by traveling to Rock Springs, Wyoming or Victory, Idaho on the Union Pacific Railroad, or via Northern Pacific to Gardiner, Montana. At first a ranch wagon and a team of horses and mules, then later a ranch vehicle met the guests at the train station.

According to a pamphlet produced by the Bar BC (again one without a date, but obviously later than the one for the JY), a short stay of one to three weeks cost $91 per week per person. Three to six weeks went for $84 a week and the season, for $77 per week. Pack trips went for an extra $10 a day.

Struthers Burt wrote in *The Diary of a Dude-Wrangler* the one item of clothing a dude or "lady dude" should include with the standard western riding garb was a snug-fitting pair of knee-length "underdrawers," because a western style saddle could "remove portions of your skin where you can least afford to lose it."

The Bar BC became part of Grand Teton National Park, but unlike the Triangle X (another dude ranch now part of the park), the Bar BC is no longer in operation. In fact, the current flow of the Snake River threatens to destroy this ranch, which is listed on the National Register of Historic Places.

In addition to the JY and the Bar BC, the Triangle X, the Double Diamond, the White Grass, Turpin Meadows, and the Circle H all wrangled dudes from Jackson Hole's early guest ranch days. (Burt's definition of a dude-wrangler was "a man who herds and takes care of dudes," the latter being strangers to the area.)

Working Guest (Dude) Ranches

Today, guest ranches offer bases from which to enjoy a variety of year-round activities. Visitors may choose hiking, climbing, scenic and whitewater float trips, fishing, wilderness horseback trips, hunting, trail rides, golf, and visits to Grand Teton and Yellowstone National Parks as part of their dude experience.

Surrounded by solitude, the mountains, and centuries-old wilderness, "relaxing" best describes a dude ranch vacation. Jackson Hole has over twenty guest ranches to chose from, and there are differences between ranches. Some offer a *City Slickers* opportunity to perform the day-to-day chores side by side with cowpunchers on a real working ranch. Other ranches specialize in certain activities such as fishing or summer wilderness horsepacking trips and fall hunting expeditions. Most operate from May through October, with a few remaining open in winter, offering snowmobile or cross-country skiing excursions into the parks or Bridger-Teton National Forest.

All guest ranches require reservations well in advance.

The Triangle X Guest Ranch, started by "Dad" Turner in the early 1900s, is still run by the Turner family (three generations later). Located within Grand Teton National Park, as a private concession, the Triangle X provides an all around Wyoming-style family vacation with horseback riding, horsepacking and hunting trips into the Teton Wilderness, and fishing or scenic floats along the Snake River.

The 1956 movie *Jubal*, starring Glenn Ford, Rod Steiger, Ernest Borgnine, and Noah Beery Jr. (Wallace Beery's nephew), as well as segments of the 1963 *Spencers Mountain*, starring Henry Fonda and Maureen O'Hara, were shot at the Triangle X Guest Ranch. (For more on Hollywood in the Hole, see Section Six, Chapter 6.)

Get all the details by contacting the Turners at the Triangle X Ranch, Moose, WY 83012, 307-733-2183 phone, 307-733-8685 fax.

Turpin Meadow Guest Ranch, located near Moran Junction just forty miles from Yellowstone and only two miles from Grand Teton National Park, began in the early 1920s with the lodge serving as a store and catering to tourists on their way to Yellowstone. Open year round, Turpin Meadow is one of the longest continuously running dude ranches in Wyoming. The family-owned and operated ranch features cabin accommodations and home-cooked buffet-style meals. Its summer offerings include trail rides and wilderness pack trips, as well as a variety of western activities. One of the more unique is the weekly "gymkhana" where kids and adults, too, can demonstrate the equestrian talents they've learned during their stay. An authentic cowboy cookout on the banks of the Buffalo River awaits you on Friday evenings, arrived at via covered wagon. In autumn, head out on a hunting expedition, and in winter, hit the snowmobile trails.

Write the Castagno family at Turpin Meadow Guest Ranch, P.O. Box 379, Moran, Wyoming 83013, 800-743-2496.

The Lost Creek Ranch borders Grand Teton National Park with a 7,000-foot view of the range. Built in the late 1920s, the lodge and cabins welcome guests after a day of trail riding, floating the Snake, swimming, tennis, or a wilderness pack trip.

Lost Creek Ranch, P.O. Box 95, Moose, WY 83012-0095, 307-733-3435 phone, 307-733-1954 fax.

Eighteen miles west of Jackson, Kelly and Roxann Van Orden outfit guests to Moose Creek Ranch for short trail rides or all-day excursions into the Jedediah Smith Wilderness Area, whitewater floats on the Snake, guided fishing, hiking, or camping trips. Delight in the Wednesday night rodeo and the cookout on Saturday night or a ride on the Moose Creek Stage.

Moose Creek Ranch, P.O. Box 3108, Jackson, WY 83001, 800-676-0075 phone, 208-787-2284 fax.

Originally a working ranch built in 1910, the Heart Six Dude Ranch customizes trips so you can "brand your heart on the Tetons." Start the day by watching the hands wrangle the horses into the corral at daybreak. Head into the high country of the Bridger-Teton National Forest on a three-day wilderness pack trip or a five-day exploration of Yellowstone country to the headwaters of the Snake. Swim the Buffalo (which automatically makes you a member of the Polar Bear Club). Take a hayride and twirl around at the country dance in the rec hall. Experience a black powder shoot. Kids can camp out in a tepee. Arrange a scenic float trip on the Snake, mountain biking, or fishing excursion. In winter, snowmobile Yellowstone.

Heart Six Dude Ranch, P.O. Box 70, Moran, WY 83013, 307-543-2477.

Nestled against the river, the Gros Ventre River Ranch has the look and feel of Jackson's history. Horseback ride along the top of Sheep Mountain, known locally as Sleeping Indian, where you can see the entire valley, then cross the top of the Gros Ventre slide that formed Slide Lake. Or paddle the lake, explore the fish streams, pitch horseshoes, or listen to stories around the campfire. In winter, the ranch wrangles snow fun with snowmobiles, cross-country skis, or snowshoes. Gros Ventre River Ranch, P.O. Box 151, Moose, WY 83012, 307-733-4138 phone, 307-733-4272 fax.

The Cottonwoods guest ranch comes closest to the early dude ranches in that it's only accessible by four-wheel-drive vehicle forty miles into the Gros Ventre Wilderness. Yes, they do generate their own electricity, and the outhouses have been replaced by a modern bath house. But no phones, radios, or TV. Unstructured activities include riding (experienced riders can head out on their own if they wish), trout fishing (with your own gear and license), hiking, or enjoy a cup of cowboy coffee by the campfire.

The Cottonwoods, P.O. Box 95, Moose, WY 83012, 307-733-0945 phone, 307-733-1954 fax.

The Diamond D Guest Ranch and Outfitters serves up all sorts of western hospitality with everything from a standard dude ranch experience with trail rides, hiking, and loafing to customized sight-seeing tours in the parks and Jackson.

Diamond D Guest Ranch and Outfitters, P.O. Box 211, Moran, WY 83013, 307-543-2479.

A Bed and Breakfast for Every Taste

The bed and breakfast experience in Jackson Hole varies as much as the activities that can fill up your days and nights.

All B&Bs require reservations in advance. Many are nonsmoking and have a minimum length stay, so check in with them first.

Several things make A Teton Tree House Bed & Breakfast Inn unique among Jackson Hole's B&Bs. First, it's located on Heck of a Hill Road (and very appropriately named, too). Owners Chris and Denny Becker wanted a "problem site" when they started looking for the perfect property for their house. What they found turned into a four-story gem of a place tucked into a forested mountainside surrounded by solitude, pines, and an incredible view of the valley—all within three-fourths of a mile of Wilson, the town at the base of Teton Pass.

Ninety-five gentle steps that lead up to the house add yet another dimension to this retreat. But the climb is more than worth it. Five guest rooms have all the comforts of home with private baths, cases well stocked with a wide selection of books (including regional history and guides), private decks, and an outdoor hot tub where you can relax amid the wilderness while sipping one of Denny's tasty fruit juice concoctions.

Western hospitality and spaciousness permeate the house—from the cozy fireplace and nearby piano to the huge handmade dining table that seats fourteen where breakfast is a very entertaining meal. Chris and Denny serve a delicious variety of healthy, homemade foods. Among their specialties, Chris's own recipe for Granola ranks right up there with Denny's Cream Cheese Coffee Cake and fresh Banana Bread.

Then there are the goats. No kidding (pardon the pun). Take an evening stroll with Denny and the herd. Or just visit them. As Denny says, "They love to be scratched under the chin." (So does Coco, the dog.) Coco and the goats won't allow other pets. For all the particulars, contact Chris and Denny Becker at A Teton Tree House, P.O. Box 550, Wilson, WY 83014, 307-733-3233.

Hans and Nancy Johnstone, both Olympic athletes, built The Alpine House Bed & Breakfast to give people who love the mountains a home away from home in the Hole. Located in downtown, the hand-hewn timber lodge resembles a Scandinavian design. Seven spacious rooms, each with a private balcony and path welcome guests after a day of outdoor activities. In the morning, there's a healthy, homemade breakfast waiting.

No pets are allowed. Contact Hans and Nancy at The Alpine House Bed & Breakfast, 285 N. Glenwood, P.O. Box 20245, Jackson, WY 83001, 800-753-1421.

In the late 1920s, Homer Richards homesteaded a place on the edge of Jenny Lake, running a general store, gas station, and some one-room log cabins which he rented out on a nightly basis. When Homer sold to the Rockefellers, he bought a place in Jackson and continued his business as the Ideal Lodge. Later he designed a home for his granddaughter, Jackie Richards Williams, which became the H.C. Richards Bed & Breakfast, named in honor of Homer. One and a half blocks off Town Square, the H.C. Richards B&B offers three large guest rooms on the main floor. All are decorated in an English manner and suggest the simpler times of the elegant bygone era. So snuggle under one of Jackie's goose-down comforters, enjoy a gourmet breakfast and, of course, tea time.

Ken and Jackie Williams can make special arrangements for children and pets. Contact them at the H.C. Richards Bed & Breakfast, P.O. Box 2606, Jackson, WY 83001, 307-733-6704.

Located at the base of Snow King Mountain, the Twin Trees Bed & Breakfast's three rooms, all with private baths, offer an atmosphere of a country home. Owner Pat Martin built the house specifically for the B&B in 1992. From the house, you can watch two of the biggest events held in Jackson—the April World Championship Snowmobile Hillclimb and the town's Fourth of July fireworks.

Pat can supply you with a "sleep-in" cat to make you feel more at home, but they won't allow other pets. Contact Pat Martin at the Twin Trees Bed & Breakfast, 757 S. Willow, P.O. Box 7533, Jackson, WY 83002, 800-728-7337 phone, 307-739-9737 fax.

Fourteen B&Bs in the Jackson Hole area have joined together to establish the Jackson Hole Bed and Breakfast Association. You can contact them for all the details on area B&Bs by calling 800 JHBandB (800-542-2632), or write them at P.O. Box 6396, Jackson, WY 83002.

What's Inn in Jackson Hole

The Spring Creek Resort began as the 1893 homestead of William Preston Redmond. He brought a wagonload of building supplies in from Bozeman, Montana and constructed a cabin at Spring Creek Gulch eight miles from the current town of Jackson. The resort sits atop East Gros Ventre Butte, overlooking the Teton Range where you get a "view with a room."

Choose from hotel rooms, studios, suites, and condominium lodges, all with fireplaces (which the concierge will be happy to light for you if you prefer), executive refrigerators, rustic but very comfortable lodgepole furnishings, and your own private deck or balcony where you can sit and absorb the landscape 1,000 feet above Jackson Hole.

Spring Creek also offers horseback rides, cookouts, four-star cuisine at The Granary, nature trails, tennis courts, and a Jacuzzi with a waterfall.

The resort also provides a shuttle service to and from Jackson, the airport, and Teton Village.

Spring Creek Resort.

Photo Credit: Sierra Adare

Spring Creek Resort, P.O. Box 3154, Jackson, WY 83001, 800-443-6139.

Minutes from downtown Jackson, the Wyoming Inn offers Old West charm in modern comfort. Decorated with Wyoming-made furnishings, many of the rooms come equipped with fireplaces, kitchenettes, and even Jacuzzis. A continental breakfast starts the day, and a cuddly stuffed moose or antelope and a fleecy terry robe await the end of a fun-filled evening.

Wyoming Inn of Jackson, 930 W. Broadway, P.O. Box 30505, Jackson, WY 83001, 800-844-0035.

Of course, if you're camping out and only want a hot shower, head for The Bunkhouse, Jackson's own Hostel, located at the Anvil Motel, 215 N. Cache, P.O. Box 480, Jackson, WY 83001, 307-733-3668 phone, 307-733-3957 fax.

For the kids, there's the Teton Valley Ranch Camp. It supplies boys and girls (in separate five-week sessions) between the fifth and tenth grades the opportunity to experience a wide range of western activities such as backpacking, fly tying and fishing, archery, horsepacking, and lapidary.

Teton Valley Ranch Camp, P.O. Box 8, Kelly, WY 83011, 307-733-2958.

For a full listing of places to stay in the Jackson Hole area, contact the Jackson Hole Chamber of Commerce, P.O. Box E, Jackson, WY 83001, 307-733-3316 phone, 307-733-5585 fax.

5

Watering Holes

According to the Hollywood version of the Old West, saloons defined the towns. Catch an episode of "Gunsmoke," and you'll see community life evolved around the Long Branch Saloon! While no historical evidence substantiates this as far as Jackson Hole goes, it's a safe bet the town's watering hole drew cowpokes fresh off the range like flies to. . .you know, that stuff crusted all over their not-designer-made cowboy boots.

Not much is known about Jackson's earliest saloons. The only one listed when the town incorporated in 1901 was named Foster's. At some point, an enterprise called the Crane Saloon appeared a couple of blocks off the Town Square, later becoming a lady's hat shop. Then along came Joe Ruby's Saloon directly across from the square.

Million Dollar Cowboy Bar*

Ruby's Saloon, which would become the Million Dollar Cowboy Bar, personifies an authentic western watering hole.

On some unrecorded date before the mid-1930s, Ruby drifted into Jackson. Eventually he decided to open a saloon—a shed actually—on the west side of the tract of land that would become the Town Square. In keeping with other western saloons of the era, gambling chips changed hands as fast as the whiskey flowed. Cowboys could sit in a poker game, spin the roulette wheel, or even try their hand at a "one arm bandit." (Remnants of gambling memorabilia lingers as a historic backdrop in the bar today.)

---

*   Excerpt from *The Living West*. See the Bibliography for details.

If a cowpoke preferred, he could twirl a girl around the dance floor to live music or play a game of pool in the back. Business boomed—literally. When things got rowdy in the bar, patrons tended to shoot up the place, with stray bullets whizzing through the wall into Berta and Jack Moore's cafe next door.

Along about 1936, Ruby sold out to Berta and Jack. They built a new cafe beside the old one—most likely with thicker walls!—and expanded the bar into the original eatery.

But this wasn't the end of Ruby, at least not yet. Three years later, Ruby sat in on a card game at his old bar. An argument broke out, and it turned ugly. As the story goes, Ruby shot one of the other players. And as pioneer justice went, folks told him to get out of town and not come back.

Some years elapsed quietly. The Moores decided to put the saloon up for sale. Ben Goe, a rancher wishing to invest the money he made from selling his spread to the Elk Refuge, purchased the place and renamed it the Cowboy Bar. Under his ownership, the saloon received quite a unique facelift that's still visible today in the interior's pine burle wood and painted murals. The bar's notable neon light came onto the scene shortly after the end of World War II under the ownership of a Casper man, Pres Parkinson.

But one old fixture remained throughout—gambling. The clinking of genuine silver dollars and the clatter of the roulette wheel continued quite openly until the 1950s. Nevertheless, the state attorney general resolved to rid the state of this widespread, though illegal, menace.

Jacksonites, however, loved their sporting and devised a plan to foil any of the government's attempts. They set up lookouts at the base of Teton Pass, and whenever they spotted "revenuers" headed over the pass, the sentinels flashed a series of mirrors, signaling back toward town. Every stick of gambling paraphernalia mysteriously disappeared into cracks in the woodwork, rematerializing once things cooled down again.

Still the Cowboy Bar didn't content itself with just being a characteristic western saloon. Something happened in 1952 that made the place the stuff of modern-day legend. A gas heater in the basement went out. Parkinson and Lew Bartholomew, a staff member, trotted downstairs to check things out. Both men must have had a cold or had lost their sense of smell in the bar's smokey atmosphere, because neither caught a whiff of the leaking gas before Parkinson made the mistake of striking a match to relight the pilot. The place really blew! The entire building blasted right off its foundation, oddly enough all in one piece. An instant later, it dropped back into place again.

Both Parkinson and Bartholomew received severe burns. A rubber mat lying next to a support post wound up under the log and a chair mysteriously got stuck in the ceiling. The explosion also threw a gambler sitting at one of the front tables through the window. He landed in the street, still clutching a hand of cards. Passersby heard him say, "It wasn't a very good hand anyway. I think I'll go down to the hotel," and he departed. Miraculously, no one died. After a short closure, the bar was up and running again. However, gambling disappeared for good thereafter.

Nowadays customers can "belly up to the bar" and step into real saddles (in leu of bar stools), call for a draft of "genuine Cowboy Bar Beer," and maybe spend a little time elbow to elbow with the locals or other travelers, swapping a few lies about experiences in Wyoming's wonderland or just listening to them. Or better yet, get the bartender to tell you why it's called the Million Dollar Cowboy Bar.

It's located at 25 N. Cache Street in downtown Jackson, across from the Town Square, 307-733-2207.

Otto Brothers' Brewing Company

When the Sheridan Brewery closed down in 1954, Wyoming-brewed beers, ales, and stouts became nothing more than a tasty memory—until a revival in 1988 by Charles and

Ernest Otto, two brothers of German-Austrian descent, living in Jackson Hole. Taking advantage of the Teton County Home Occupation Law, which allowed for a business based out of the home, or the backyard as in this case, the brothers turned a portion of their sixty-eight-year-old log cabin into a brewery. The 210-foot brewery, small even by microbrewery standards, produces 760 barrels of beer each year. Compare this to the government definition of a microbrewery which produces 15,000 barrels per year or less.

Their flagship brew, an amber "Teton Ale," went out to local taverns and restaurants by the keg and instantly grew popular. Patrons wanted to take some home with them. Yet the size and scale of the backyard brewery made individual bottling unfeasible. The solution came in the form of a long-forgotten European-style container called a "growler," a metal pail with a lid in vogue in the days before the six-pack. The name stems from the growling noise the beer would make as it sloshed around in the tin pail. Updating it, the Otto brothers' growler is a glass jug that contains sixty-four ounces of beer. It satisfied consumer demand, and growlers proved beneficial to the environment. Just wash them out and take them to one of the "refill stations" around town or the brewery and say fill 'er up. You save forty percent of the cost of beer purchased at the store that goes to packaging, and refills cost less since you aren't buying the bottle. Later, the brewery came out with a twenty-two-ounce refillable bottle, continuing their tradition of commitment to the environment.

Beer brewing began as a hobby for Charlie and Ernie. Both loved the full flavor and finish of the freshly brewed, locally produced beers readily available in Europe. Subscribing to the German purity law known as *Reinheitsgebot*, which dates back to 1516, the Ottos refrain from using chemical preservatives or adjuncts that can compromise the beer's natural flavor.

While patterned after Old World beers, Jackson Hole nevertheless inspired all three of the Otto brothers' brews—Teton Ale, Old Faithful Ale, and Moose Juice Stout. The "English" style Teton Ale holds the coppery color of a mountain sunset and is as distinctive and robust as its namesake. The light gold of Old Faithful Ale follows the tradition of pale ales as American as this Yellowstone National Park symbol. Moose Juice Stout, on the other hand, is "the beer a moose would drink on a bitter cold winter night, if a moose drank beer."

Arrange to take a tour of the brewery and sample the brew at the Otto Brothers' Brewing Company, located at 1295 N. West Street in Wilson, WY 83014. Their mailing address is P.O. Box 4177, Jackson, WY 83001, 307-733-9000.

Jackson Hole Pub and Brewery

The Jackson Hole Pub and Brewery (known locally as the Brew Pub) "double brews" their beers to maintain a consistant quality and taste. You can watch them make everything from pale ale to stout in their glass-enclosed, two-story brewery.

Brews on tap carry local names like Wapiti Wheat, a malted wheat with a touch of clove styled lager; Custer's Last Ale; India Pale Ale; Buffalo Brown Ale full of American malts; Bald Eagle Bock, Bavarian-style lager; and of course, Snake River Lager, a festive Oktoberfest style. If you have trouble deciding, they offer a sampler's size glass.

And don't forget the woodfired pizzas and pastas and soft pretzels with a fantastic mustard seed sauce!

Located on the corner of Millward and Hansen (265 South Millward), Jackson, WY 83001, 307-733-BEER (2337).

More Taverns

Other watering holes carry a variety of names you'll recognize from Jackson Hole's colorful past. There's Beaver Dick's Saloon, the Virginian Saloon, and SilverDollar Bar & Grill in the Wort Hotel to name a few.

An interesting note about SilverDollar Bar, other than its 2032 real, uncirculated silver dollars embedded in the bar (all minted in 1921), is that it was cut apart and carried out of the burning Wort Hotel building to safety (the 1980 fire was one of the worst in Jackson Hole's history). When the Wort was rebuilt, they had to construct the room to fit the bar. The SilverDollar also displays an impressive collection of Jackson Hole historic pictures and newspaper clippings about the fire.

SilverDollar Restaurant, corner of Broadway & Glenwood, in the Wort Hotel, 307-733-2190.

Then there's the Mangy Moose in Teton Village, a huge open-spaces kind of bar with an unbelievable view of the mountains from several levels, inside and out. Plan to spend some time there, gaping at all the stuff hanging from the ceiling! They also serve up a full menu of food.

Mangy Moose, Teton Village, 307-733-4913.

Hole Characters—Legends, Dreams, and Nightmares

1

Outlaws and Mountain Law

Around the turn of the century, folks considered Jackson's Hole the "most talked-of outlaw rendezvous in the world." But at the same time, the valley's residents maintained a reputation for minding their own business in the extreme. So long as any man, outlaw or otherwise, left his neighbors and their property and livelihood alone, no one cared who the man was to the outside world.

"Teton" Jackson

About an hour before midnight in the spring of 1892, a tall, brawny man strolled into view against a backdrop of the abandoned adobe ruins of old Fort Caspar, Wyoming, a revolver in his hand. The Casper newspaper reporter who agreed to such a late-night rendezvous at what had become a hideout for criminals, expected to interview an outlaw, but probably not Harvey Gleason, the recently escaped felon the

Chicago Herald called, "the premier horse-thief of the mountains" and the man who had gained (rightly or wrongly remains unclear) the reputation for leaving a trail of murdered U.S. deputy marshals behind him.

As the correspondent approached, Gleason, who sat beside a small fire that lit his fiery red hair and beard and give-away-nothing black eyes, began to talk. Here's part of what the reporter wrote:

"I am the fellow they call Teton Jackson... I make my home up south of the [Yellowstone] Park, near what is known as Jackson's Hole... We are looked upon as horse thieves, and every horse that is stolen in the West is laid on me or my gang. There are lots of these stories gotten up by men who have no horses to steal, and if we stole all the horses that they say we do, we would be shipping two carloads a day... Although I suppose I handle stolen horses, I get them from fellows who are respectable, and steal horses to keep from working.

"All I ever do is to act as a go-between. That is, I run the horses out of one locality and exchange them, and take back others, and I get half what the horses bring when they are sold.

"I am an outlaw for an affair that happened in the early days in Joplin, Missouri. There are a number of boys up in the Hole with me, and we don't fear anybody and the boys kind of feel better when they know that people know where they are, and that they dare not come and get them."

In the interview, Jackson dared the "Pinkeys" (Pinkerton detectives) to come after him and his gang, admonishing them to "bring along their overcoats." Brave words? Not hardly. Neither he nor the prominent gang members mentioned by Wyoming sheriff Frank M. Canton, the man who sent Jackson to prison prior to the Fort Caspar interview, were ever captured while in the Hole. And the boldness of this interview serves as a perfect illustration of how Jackson Hole obtained its "outlaw haven" status.

"Teton" Jackson

Photo Credit: Teton County History Society

Depending on the source, Teton Jackson's mob numbered anywhere from a dozen to three hundred. The latter sounds iffy, considering the mere handful of people living in the entire valley at the time. That many men around at once, doctoring the brands on an estimated eight hundred to a thousand head of horses, waiting for the hides to heal before herding the animals off to sell elsewhere, not to mention the amount of provisions a camp that size would need, would have been noted in some early pioneer's journal or shown up in the stories handed down through the generations.

More likely between ten and twenty thieves carried out the raids. Canton and another sheriff named Malcolm Campbell both outlined Teton's slick operation. The band scouted Idaho for decent horseflesh, stealing a dozen or so at a time, figuring the owner would think they had just wandered off. The gang would keep the ever-growing herd in Jackson's Hole, which provided plenty of wild forage and hay supplied by the bachelor homesteaders. More than one account names John Holland and his partner John Carnes as the source for feed, as well as food for the whole lot.

Once the thieves had a sizable herd all fixed up with new brands, they drove them to central Wyoming or South Dakota to market. On the return trip they raided ranches, picking up riding stock and colts which they turned around and sold in Idaho.

This continued for about a decade between 1876, when Teton Jackson, at the time a scout for General George Crook's campaign against the Sioux, escaped after an incident involving some missing pack animals and the murder of two soldiers, and his arrest in 1886 or '87.

Famous novelist Owen Wister learned of Teton's outlaw ways on his trip through Jackson's Hole in 1887. Meanwhile, does Chapter 33 of Wister's novel *The Virginian*, published in 1902, sound familiar?

"Somewhere at the eastern base of the Tetons did those hoofprints disappear into a mountain sanctuary where many crooked paths have led. He that took another man's possessions or he that took another man's life, could always run here if the law or popular justice were too hot at his heels. . . . Not many cabins were yet built there; but the unknown rider of the horse knew well that he would find shelter and welcome among the felons of his stripe."

Accounts of how Teton Jackson ended up range from mending his ways by marrying, having a family, and becoming a respectable cattle rancher or a bank director to once again finding himself behind bars in 1893, dying during a failed escape attempt. Maybe, like countless others, he just disappeared into the recesses of the Hole to live out his days peacefully.

Edwin H. Trafton

Edwin H. Trafton, alias Ed Harrington, had a passion for stagecoaches—robbing them, that is. He held up approximately forty during his career, with a record-breaking count of between fifteen and nineteen in a single day—July 29, 1914. Normally, this feat would have seen Trafton's name plastered across every newspaper in the country, especially considering the victims he relieved of their wallets, jewelry, and other valuables happened to all be very well-to-do visitors who could afford the $130-per-person package excursion to Yellowstone National Park. (We'll ride along on one of these trips in Section Eight, Chapter 3.) However, fate robbed the bandit. Something with slightly larger ramifications transpired at the same time. World War I broke out in Europe.

His capture for this crime a year later suffered a similar destiny. The headlines were filled with the *Lusitania*'s demise. But Trafton should have been used to such things. When he and his wife, the daughter of a man he stole some cattle from, went to prison in 1910 for stealing $10,000 off Trafton's mother (a life insurance payment when her husband died, no less), Halley's Comet blazed across the sky and the headlines.

Not much occurred to light up the newspapers in Trafton's earlier criminal career—it lacked his later sensationalism—with the exception of his stint holding up a Union Pacific train with members of the Hole-in-the-Wall gang. Remember that scene in the movie *Butch Cassidy and the Sundance Kid* where they use too much dynamite on the safe? Well, guess what? That actually happened in 1887. Not only did they blow up the train, the blast took out forty feet of track and nearly killed the would-be robbers. For their trouble, the bandits got no loot.

But Trafton's chance to be immortalized possibly came in the form of Owen Wister. The two men crossed paths at Colter Bay on Jackson Lake, currently in Grand Teton National Park, where Trafton lived at the time. It may be coincidence, but striking similarities appear between the villainous, would-rob-his-own-mother Trampas in *The Virginian* and the actual deeds of Trafton, more than just the closeness of their names.

But Trafton wanted more recognition for his lifetime of unusual crimes. So he went to Hollywood in the early 1920s to "sell" his life story to the silver screen. Hollywood, however, found his story too far-fetched. (See the steps he took to change this and how Trafton's story could have been one of the first of many movies filmed in Jackson Hole in Section Six, Chapter 6.)

Unsuccessful at gaining attention once again, he wandered into an ice cream parlor, had a heart attack, and died at the bar.

Tuskers and Vigilantes

An incredible irony exists over "tusking," the removal of the two ivory teeth found at the back of an elk's upper jaw. The reason the blackmarket business for "tusks" commanded up to $100 a pair came about because of the Benevolent Protective Order of the Elks (BPOE).

The organization adopted the elk tusk as its emblem, and the members utilized tusks for all sorts of things like cuff links, lapel pins, watch charms, and even hat pens for their wives. This created quite a demand for the teeth, which in turn precipitated the illegal slaughter of elk solely for their ivory.

Detecting "tuskers," the term applied to elk ivory poachers, proved a big problem by 1904. Elk starved by the thousands every winter, compounding the situation because Jackson Hole residents earned extra cash by extracting the ivories from these carcasses—all completely legal. (Learn why the elk were starving in such numbers in Section Eight, Chapter 1.)

A combination of concerned individuals and a series of events in the first decades of the twentieth century led to the downfall of tusking. A.A. Anderson of the Yellowstone Forest Reserve, the forerunner of the National Forest system, ranger Rudolph "Rosie" Rosencrans, and wildlife guide turned photographer and conservationist Stephen N. Leek became major players, spearheading the effort from diverse fronts.

Ridding the forests of poachers, and especially tuskers, headed Anderson's priority list after he became the Special Forest Superintendent over the Yellowstone Forest Reserve during 1902. (For his other priority which caused Buffalo Bill Cody to warn Anderson not to return to Wyoming unless he wanted to die, see Chapter 4 of Section Eight). In an article he wrote in the *Annals of Wyoming* in 1927, Anderson told how one of his rangers arrested a man named Rogers for poaching elk. Among the hunter's possessions, the ranger found twenty-five fresh tusks and no meat. "Proof enough that he had been shooting bull elk for this one trivial reason alone, leaving carcasses to remain rotting upon the ground."

Up until 1905 the citizens of Jackson Hole followed their usual policy of live and let live. But too many reports such as the one from a settler, who, while snowshoeing through a remote section of the valley, discovered eighteen elk bulls slaughtered for their tusks, unsettled residents.

Citizens formed a "citizens' committee," a nice term for a vigilante group.

Concurrent with these events, ranger Rudolph "Rosie" Rosencrans had spent three years pursuing the worst of the offenders, the Binkley gang. One effort to catch the outlaws red-handed brought together a posse of federal and local law officials. But Binkley himself showed up at the meeting with a plausible story which pointed the finger at another man, who not only poached elk, but planned to kill Judge Pierce Cunningham, one of the area's early residents. (Check out Section Nine for details of a shoot-out over stolen horses on Cunningham's ranch.)

So the hunt was on. Binkley said the villain worked out of Yellowstone Park. The posse spent days scouring the backcountry for signs. They found a huge pile of rotting elk, minus their ivories, but no poacher. The mysterious tusker had vanished—because it was all a ruse cooked up by the Binkley gang. With the game wardens led astray, Binkley and his partner Purdy shipped $10,000 worth of contraband out of the country. Rosie reportedly laughed about the whole incident in an interview with Helen Payne sixty years later, saying, "We felt pretty cheap."

Meanwhile the citizens' committee had calmed down from their "necktie party" attitude and appointed a group to go to Binkley's place, unarmed, and order him and his gang to leave the country. After threats and lots of raging around, Binkley agreed. Witnesses claimed the outlaws packed up five pounds of elk tusks and scalps and left on the mail stage. In Idaho the Binkley group boarded a train and were arrested when they arrived in Los Angeles.

Rosie testified at their trial and must have felt repaid for the hoodwinking he suffered at Binkley's hands when the judge handed down felony convictions for Binkley and Purdy in 1907. (More about Rosie's role in Jackson Hole in Section Nine.)

Things began to wind down at that point, but tusking didn't disappear until two final punches rendered the death blow.

First, Anderson wrote to the Order of Elks, who were conducting a convention in Salt Lake City, Utah. In it, Anderson made a plea for the organization to live up to its name and help prevent the wanton destruction of this noble animal. The letter was read at conference, and, according to Anderson, the members passed a resolution to abolish tusks as their official emblem.

Second, Stephen N. Leek, the elk's biggest fan (as we'll see in Section Eight, Chapter 1), won a seat in the Wyoming House of Representatives. In 1909 he succeeded in pushing a bill through the State Legislature which made it a felony to kill elk for their teeth. To augment Anderson's letter to the BPOE, or maybe because not all the members complied, Leek also got a memorial passed by both houses of Wyoming Congress, requesting that the BPOE ban the use of elk teeth by their members.

Thus demand dropped, tusking finally faded, but sensational events didn't.

2

The Women

Up until this century, both genders considered women ill-equipped to cope with a rigorous life. But from Jackson Hole's earliest days, women proved more than equal to the task of carving a niche for themselves in the harsh environment, far removed from even the illusions of civilization. They adapted, found their own compromises with the prescribed ideals of "society," and often left an indelible mark on the valley.

Marie Wolff

Marie Caroline Bettendorff came to Jackson's Hole about 1893 as the bride of Emile Wolff, a Belgium who took part in the ill-fated Lieutenant Gustavus Cheney Doane expedition on the Mad River. (We'll ride along on this bizarre boat ride in the next chapter.)

Born in Viandan, Luxembourg during 1873, Marie spoke only French. Emile taught her English after they settled on land that would become the original townsite of Jackson. She learned how to survive the arduous conditions of homesteading in Jackson's Hole through experience, being one of the first white women to pioneer the valley.

The Wolffs brought a milk cow and a team of draft animals with them. Crossing Teton Pass into the Hole, they had to dismantle their wagon and pack it and their goods in on the horses and mules. During their first year in Jackson's Hole, the Wolffs lived on the Buffalo River, but it didn't take long to spot and claim the site of their permanent home five miles from Spread Creek. Digging one mile per year, Emile eventually brought irrigation water from the creek to the ranch where the family raised hay. President Theodore Roosevelt signed the Wolffs' homestead patent.

A fine singer herself, Marie raised four musically inclined children. When the opportunity arose to purchase a piano, one in serious need of repair after falling into the Buffalo River while being moved, Maria took it. She completely reconditioned the instrument and then taught her children how to play it. Originally the piano belonged to John Sargent. He brought it to Jackson's Hole by ferrying it across Jackson Lake in a raft. But we'll explore Sargent and his wife's strange musical proclivities in the next chapter of this section.

Marie's contemporaries noted her dark, sparkling eyes and tireless energy. Not long after moving to the valley, she nursed a young man who had been attacked by a bear. It took the entire winter for the youth to recover from his bear encounter. The animal had ripped the man's throat until his tongue could be clearly seen in his neck. In addition, his left ribs were laid bare and his left arm had been practically severed at the shoulder. Marie also tended Mrs. Sargent in her final illness.

As if Marie didn't have enough on her hands, she acted as postmistress for fourteen years, the ranch housing the post office for the upper part of the valley.

Her December 30, 1954 obituary read "Pioneer Mother Is Called By Death." It's ironic that the eulogy the newspapers ran insisted "the important part she played in local history cannot be appreciated without reviewing the career of her husband" rather than praising the individual contributions of the "Pioneer Mother" herself.

Grace Miller and Her All-Woman Town Council

Jackson Hole made national, and quite possibly international, news during the summer of 1920 with the election of the first all-woman town council in the United States. Newspapers heralded it the "Petticoat Government," suggesting the town only voted the five women into office in order to glean publicity for the area. But all of the hoopla started well before the May 11, 1920 election day.

At the time, newspapers around the country classified Jackson Hole as a "bad men's town," or a "rendezvous for western outlaws" where the perpetrators of any serious crime committed between the Mississippi River and the Pacific coast could take refuge. Of course, the fact that the town sat seventy-five miles from the nearest railroad and winter clogged the mountain passes with enough snow to make it virtually impossible to get into or out of Jackson Hole for months at a time helped perpetuate this "outlaw haven" image.

Nevertheless, townswomen nominated the all-woman slate of town officers at a caucus meeting in April of 1920. According to Fern Nelson's article "A Look at Jackson Hole's history: Bicentennial perspective on women" in the *Jackson Hole Guide*, the reason behind this bold move stemmed from residents growing "impatient with excuses" offered by the then-current town council with regards to "cleaning up the town and other reforms." Yet Pearl Williams (later Pearl Hupp), who would be appointed marshal by the woman council, offered an alternative possibility in a newspaper interview sixty-nine years later. "The men were so busy in the summer, they didn't have time to deal with city problems like stock running loose and developing a city water system."

Whichever the case, the men challenged the women to "do a better job of getting things done" as Hupp put it. The 300-500 plus residents of Jackson (depending on which newspaper you read) thought the women could indeed improve the town government and elected them—by a two-to-one victory in the mayoral race. And as one flippant but anonymous poet wrote, "And Hoyle must now/Revise his lay,/That four Queens are/The limit of the play:/In this new deal/of winning hands/Five Queens now rule/Our Ordered land."

On June 1, 1920, Grace Green Miller assumed the reins as mayor with her council of Faustina Haight, Mae Deloney, Rose Crabtree, and Genevieve Van Vleck. In addition, Marta Winger became the town clerk; Viola Lumbeck took over as treasurer; Edna Huff served as town health officer; and Pearl Williams became the marshal.

The 1920 Jackson town council and mayor.
Left to right: Rose Crabtree, Genevieve VanVleck,
Mayor Grace Miller, Mae Deloney, and Faustina Haight.

Photo Credit: Teton County Historical Society

Finding the town coffers down to an anemic $200, the newly elected, truly all-woman government initiated a plan to collect long overdue debts owed the town. Within two weeks the treasury contained $2,000. But the money didn't remain there long. The mayor and council spent some of the funds on the construction of culverts over ditches in the roads. Purchasing title to the forty-acre tract of land that had been used as a cemetery for years but was in the public domain and could be filed on at any time, Miller's team established a good road up the steep hillside to it and set aside monies for the installation of a new fence around the perimeter and saw to it that stones marked the graves.

By November 4, 1920, the *Jackson's Hole Courier* ruled in an article entitled "Women Officials Make Good" that the women-run government was "an intelligent, efficient administration." When reelection time came, the *Courier*'s headline said it all. "Women are Re-Elected by Vote of Three to One."

In a letter dated July 18, 1921, Edwin Trafton, the very same stagecoach bandit of the previous chapter, wrote a letter to the Honorable Mrs. Grace Miller, congratulating her on her "mayorality" reelection. In the text, he expressed an interesting viewpoint—for an outlaw who victimized travelers to the area and whose antics helped create the "outlaw haven" town image—reprinted here by permission from the Teton County Historical Society:

"I have always contended that the mountain people of WYO. and Idaho. are a long ways ahead of the festive tenderfoot, good breeding, philosophy, wisdom, and clean politics," Trafton pronounced. He also claimed the reelection proved his argument about the community. "IT not only shows the confidence placed in its Intelligent Women, but the progressive intelligence of its citizens. HURRAH, for Jackson WYO." Trafton signed off with "your old friend."

Over the course of their three years in office, the "lady mayor" and council passed ordinances that prohibited milk cows, pigs, and other livestock from running loose in the town's streets. They outlawed the use of "torpedoes," firecrackers, and other such explosives within town limits. Dogs had to be licensed, as did pool tables. It became a misdemeanor to throw garbage in the roads or in vacant town lots. Furthermore, they established a permanent town dump site, built the first board sidewalks (a feature retained by the current downtown area), had the streets graded, and got pools of stagnant water drained off.

Although Mayor Miller and her councilwomen declined to run again in 1923, their governing skills rebuked the fluke theory and fulfilled the prophecies made by the few newspapers that suggested the town would "enjoy and benefit from one of the best administrations she [Jackson] has ever known."

Cissy Patterson, the "Countess of Flat Creek"

Eleanor "Cissy" Patterson first wandered into Jackson Hole during 1916. She was thirty-five, divorced in an era when that "simply wasn't done," and bored with life. Her fairy-tale marriage to a Polish Count and cavalry officer, Josef Gizycki, whom she met during a visit to her uncle, the American ambassador to Russia (then under the rule of the Czar Nicholas), ended in disaster with the Count abducting their daughter, Felicia. Cissy regained possession of Felicia only after President Taft sent a letter to the Czar.

On a whim, Cissy decided to travel to the wilds of Wyoming to the Bar BC "dude" ranch, owned at the time by Struthers and Katherine Burt and their partner Horace "Doc" Carncross.

And wild it was. The Burts sent a wagon to pick up their guests, bringing them across Teton Pass. Felicia, then eleven, described the wagons as "crude homemade affairs" pulled by a team of horses. The "brake" consisted of a post with a rope affixed to it. Passengers were forced to get out and walk up the steep sections. The lucky ones missed being rained or snowed on and just arrived in the dark of night all coated with dust and no hot bath in sight.

City slicker Cissy must have found the Bar BC very primitive as it had no running water, indoor plumbing, or electricity. Supposedly she shipped her French maid and six of the seven trunks she brought with her back to civilization on the following morning's wagon. But Cissy and her daughter stuck it out.

In fact, Cissy went elk hunting with the Bar BC wrangler, Cal Carrington. They packed in with ten horses and hauled out the young bull Cissy bagged. She was also good with horses, and in an age where independent women were frowned on, she found peace in the mountains where people applauded strong women. Cissy eventually staked her claim in the Hole, as well.

Carrington owned a homestead in an isolated section of Flat Creek Canyon. Rumor had it he used the locale to hide the horses he and some partner thieves stole from time to time. But Cal was never caught in the act. Cissy bought his place from him in 1923, turning it into a ranch.

Once Cissy returned to her back East life, she took up newspaper reporting, then publishing, but she never forgot her visits to Jackson Hole, where people accepted her as a person, not for her position in "society."

When her health failed her, she decided to return to Jackson Hole and arranged for a private railroad car. Unfortunately, she died before seeing the plan through. She was sixty-seven. At the time of her death, Cissy owned and was the publisher of the successful *Washington Times Herald* (the result of two failing newspapers she had purchased and merged into one). A colleague described her as "imperious but gentle, hard-boiled but sentimental, malicious but charming, exasperating but lovable. Friend and foe agreed that never was she dull."

In Celebration of Women

Each year, Jackson Hole informally celebrates women's contribution to history and life in the valley during March as part of nationally observed Women's History Month. Although not "organized" by any group or individual, observances often include a chance for women to tell stories—theirs or others—sing, participate in midnight ski trips, or share their work with others in as many as thirty events, collectively called "In Celebration of Women."

Women writers take the stage at an open mike night hosted by the Teton County Library. In ten-minute segments, they read poetry, excerpts from original works of fiction, essays, or entries from their journals.

Various sites around town provide the setting where historians and authors discuss pre-twentieth-century female adventurers such as the infamous "rustler" Cattle Kate, frontier guide Sacajewa, missionaries Narcissa Whitman and Eliza Spaulding, and others.

Dornan's puts on a night of music by local women. Galleries show the works of western women artists. The local chapter of National Organization of Women sponsors films on women's history and rights.

Since events change from one year to the next, contact the Jackson Hole Chamber of Commerce or the Teton County Library for a current listing of activities that celebrate women's frontier community spirit.

Jackson Hole Chamber of Commerce, P.O. Box E, Jackson, WY 83001, 307-733-3316 phone, 307-733-5585 fax. Teton County Library, P.O. Box 1629, Jackson, WY 83001, 307-733-2164.

3

Sensationalism and the Bizarre in the Hole

While "back East" settled down into "modern," "civilized" twentieth-century life, Jackson Hole's rowdiness was just getting started—for all the reasons that appeared in Chapter 1 of this section, and possibly a few more. Not everybody can handle isolation as well as men like John

Edith Sargent playing her violin at Merry Mere.

Photo Credit: Teton County Historical Society

Deadman's Bar

Deadman's Bar (a favorite put-in spot for float trips) received its name from a triple homicide of some gold miners searching for the stuff along the banks of the Snake River during the summer of 1886.

Deadman's Bar

Photo Credit: Wyoming Division of Tourism

The Sunday, April 17, 1887 *Cheyenne Daily* reported the following testimony of the confessed slayer John Tonnar:

"We were building a dam, and had a quarrel on the 15th of July about dumping the dirt high enough on the willows. I and Henry Welter carried dirt with a hand barrel. The other boys, [T.H.] Tiggerman and [August] Kellenberger, were throwing rock with their hands on the willows. In some way the barrow tipped over, Tiggerman struck me, and held me under the water a long time. He told me that I couldn't be a partner any longer; that I was a lazy and a bossing cuss or dog, or something like that. When Welter and I started to load again he told me he didn't want me any more as a partner. He rushed up and took the shovel away from me, jerked it out of my hand and raised it up to strike me over the head. I warded it off with my hand, and got hold of his

legs, and shoved him on his back so that he could not strike
me. As he fell over I got my hand in his mouth, and the mark
is there on my finger. He got his two arms around me and
shook me for a long while choking me. I felt my face swel-
ling, and my eyes getting all black, and I could see nothing.
Something struck me on the head. I don't know what it was
but think it was a rock. Then he let me up. I struggled away
but I felt in my throat as if something was broke. I then went
down home and changed my clothes which were all wet, and
laid down in bed. I was feeling sick. It was between 3 and 5
o'clock when I got up to fix the fire for supper. I thought to
make friends with them and do the same as before. We had
supper all together but there was not a word said to me that
night. Henry Welter cooked the breakfast the next morning.
Tiggerman went to a box outside the tent and took out some
tools that belonged to me. Kellenberger went to water the
horses. A little after breakfast we all got ready to go to work.
Tiggerman told me that I was not to be a partner. Kellenberger and Welter were there. I asked them, 'Boys, can I go
along to work this morning?' I asked them to forget about
the quarrel the day before. They told me they didn't want
me any more in partnership, and Tiggerman didn't want me
any more as a partner. Henry Welter was putting on his
boots and I told him, if I couldn't work in partnership any
more them boots belonged to me; that he could not have the
boots any more. I got hold of them and told him I paid for
those boots, they belong to me. He came up to me and tried
to get hold of me and called me a s---of a b---. I backed up
and says you can't have them. He got hold of my shoulder
and tried to throw me down. I threw the boots away, got hold
of him and we clinched. He tried to strike me on the head,
but I guarded the blows off. Then Kellenberger kicked me in
the rear, and he swore he would kill me if I touched anything
in the camp, break my neck. We were clinched together
about two minutes when I heard Tiggerman cry, 'Kill the s--
of a b--.' He had just come up from the river. As soon as he
hollered out 'Kill the s-- of a b--,' he ran to a shovel lying

there in camp and tried to come up to us. I jerked loose, rushed away and ran for the gun to hold him off. The gun was lying at the foot of the bed in the tent. When I got the gun he was up to me within five or six steps. I turned around quick to hold him off so that nobody could get hold of me. Tiggerman was up close to me with the shovel raised to strike me, when I raised the gun and shot him in the head. Kellenberger came towards me with an axe in his hand, and when he was seven or eight steps from me I fired and shot him in the neck. Henry Welter was a little ways behind and tried to get hold of me and knock me down. I shot at him to stop him and hit him in the breast. I fired four shots, one going off accidentally.

"I ran away as soon as the last shot was fired in the brush and stayed there about an hour and a half or two hours. I was thinking about killing myself, but came back and threw a gunny sack over Tiggerman's face. I didn't want to see the flies in his mouth, and I didn't like to look at him. I didn't like to bury them there, or let them be there, as somebody might find them out before I got to an officer. i took Kellenberger first and loaded him on the horse. When I got him on the horse I went upon a high bluff about a mile down the river and threw him over. I thought that was the easiest place to put them and nobody would find the bodies until I got to an officer."

But Tonnar never "got to an officer." Instead he showed up at Emile Wolff's where the killer stayed for three weeks, helping with the haying and other chores, saying his partners had gone hunting. A conductor for the Southern Pacific Railroad chanced upon the bodies, and Tonnar was arrested.

The *Cheyenne Daily* reported that "when he [Tonnar] lied about killing the partners he says it was to protect him from the wrath of the people in that country, and until he could get the protection of the officers of the law."

Several things about Tonnar's testimony didn't add up—such as Tiggerman's head being crushed and Kellenberger shot twice in the back and the axe cut in Welter's head. But since there were no eyewitnesses to the crime, the jury acquitted Tonnar, and he immediately left the country. The verdict shocked many, including the newspaper reporter who described Tonnar as "a small, wiry man, about 40 years of age, a little over five feet in height, and weighing 135 or 140 pounds. He has a rather abnormally developed forehead, with small, dark, restless eyes, a corrugated brow and small features. In general appearance he would make a picture of an ideal anarchist."

Lieutenant Gustavus Cheney Doane, Madman on the Mad River

Lieutenant Gustavus Cheney Doane came West seeking fame. And he accomplished this in 1876, although not in the way he intended, by ignoring his commanding officer and forcing six men (a sergeant and five enlistees) to tackle the Snake River with him during winter. This insanity nearly cost the men their lives—all for Doane's imagined glory.

For sixty-eight days Doane's men starved, almost died of exposure in subzero temperatures, grew sick from repeated soakings, and teetered on the edge of lunacy—a place Doane himself had already crossed. Somewhere along the way the boat capsized and Doane lost the journal he kept of the trip. Because he wanted a record of his "accomplishments," he tried to make his men take the trip all over again so he could rewrite his journal. Fortunately, this was not allowed.

In the end, the expedition achieved nothing. The territory was already known, mapped by the Hayden Survey four years previously. Doane abandoned the boat, thus making the attempt an incredible failure of what he set out to do; and to top it off, Doane later blamed this disaster on his commanding officer, suggesting the man had sabotaged the expedition.

President Arthur's "Cavalcade" Through Jackson Hole

In 1883 President Chester A. Arthur traveled two thousand miles to remote Jackson Hole to fish, drink, and have a good time—minus reporters, who were at the time poking holes in his administration. (Arthur had assumed the office after the assassination of President James A. Garfield in 1881, the first year into his term, and Arthur only served out the remainder, not succeeding on his own.)

The president's party, which consisted of several prominent men of the day, such as Abraham Lincoln's son Robert and Civil War hero Philip Sheridan, decided to "rough it" in the wilderness. They limited the gear to enough tonnage to weigh down an unprecedented 175 pack horses and mules (although one account ranges in the outrageous count of 300 pack animals). In addition, the cavalcade only allowed an escort of seventy-five cavalrymen armed to the teeth, and some Indian guides to insure their safety (beside keeping them from the embarrassment of becoming lost).

With no press along and the "official" releases sketchy at best, what actually transpired remains cluttered with fictitious accounts generated by unhappy tabloids. But it's safe to say a rousing, whisky-drinking, fishing grand time was had by all!

President Clinton

President Arthur holds the record for the first president to visit Jackson Hole, but every commander in chief, starting with his successor Grover Cleveland, has come to the area on vacation or business or both—the latest Bill Clinton in August of 1995 and again in 1996.

Unlike Arthur's press blackout trip, Clinton arrived amid a flurry of media fanfare. Reporters and photographers tracked the first family's every move, from golfing to hiking in Grand Teton National Park, to seeing the wolf pups in Yellowstone's Lamar Valley, to what the Associated Press called the "boatercade" down the Snake River.

While in the Hole, Clinton entered the fray between environmentalists and big business by announcing a two-year moratorium on mining claims on public land near Yellowstone National Park, saying the federally controlled land is "more priceless than gold." The president's action won't end the proposed New World Mine, a Canadian company's controversial gold mining project just two and a half miles from Yellowstone, but it will limit its growth potential.

Clinton's trip also did what other presidential excursions to Jackson Hole have accomplished. It created good press for the Hole.

Sports in the Extreme

The Sportsman's Paradise of America

Jackson's Hole is fast becoming the most popular resort for camping, hunting and fishing of any other section of America. We know of no other region similarly endowed that can surpass it for erea or diversity of game. It's myriad of swift, clear streams and deep, blue lakes are teaming with snappy, gamy trout—native, brook, salmon, rainbow and macinaw. Our undulating mountains, with their great, green mantles of fir, balsam and spruce, hold great herds of the last of America's once immense band of Elk. While the swift-footed deer darts there and here among the fallen timber and thick under-brush, and baffles the hunter's wits and skill. The lion and the lynx, the wolf and the coyote vie each with the other for the highest pitch of their piercing notes. Bears there are a plenty—black, brown and grizzly—to be stalked or trapped in the proper season. In the fields and on the sage grouse feeds; on the mountain slope and near the base the pine-grouse has it's home, and in the evening drums it's mate-call; while higher up, on the very tops of the mountains, a large specie still, known as the blue-grouse, holds full away, and mingles with the Clark's crow and the horned Jay.

Jackson's Hole is entirely surrounded with lofty, rugged peaks, the highest and most famous of which is Teton Peak, 13,747 high. Far up these rugged, ragged cliffs, feeding peacefully upon the small plateaus, which are watered by the eternal glaciers, the eager, ambitious hunter who is not afraid to exert himself, finds the wily mountain sheep at home.

For the true sport, who wants to fish and hunt, the soul that loves nature unpinted and unaltered, or the man or woman with or without a family, who is looking for a cool, quiet, beautiful mountain retreat, to rest and recreate, Jackson's Hole has a call.

The valley can be reached with a car from the north via Yellowstone Park; from the northeast, via Dubois, Wyoming, and Two-guo-to-ee Pass; from the southwest via Lander or Rock Springs and the Hoback canyon road. Or, cars coming from the west can strike a good government built road at Victor, Idaho, and climb Teton Pass with most any kind of a car that's working good.

For further information write Community Club, Forest Supervisor or the county, Jackson, Wyo.

This article appeared in the *Jackson Hole Courier* on July 17, 1919. Think things have changed in the Hole since then? Decide for yourself.

1

Skiing the Lows and Bowls in the Hole

In 1895 Captain H.M. Chittenden wrote in his book *Yellowstone National Park*, "The art of traveling by snowshoe [the reported term for skis at the time] is about the most difficult method of travel known and is rarely resort to except from sheer necessity."

The reason for this stemmed from the crudity of the equipment. The first winter expedition into Yellowstone during 1887 equipped themselves with Norwegian wooden skis made of ash. They weighed in at thirteen pounds a pair and measured nine feet nine inches in length. A leather thong loop or strap tied the foot in place. They used a stout stick six to eight feet long for a pole—no disc. On steep grades, skiers wrapped a piece of rope around the left ski to prevent backsliding. When faced with an abrupt rise, they negotiated it by the corduroy step, side-stepping their way up.

Early information about skiing and other winter transportation methods in Jackson Hole relate to mail delivery via snowshoes (Canadian web shoes) or wood skis. Wyoming's first ski resort, Snow King, came into existence in 1939 but really didn't start taking off until 1946 after World War II ended. Nowadays, Snow King, which rises up out of the heart of downtown Jackson, and the Jackson Hole Ski Resort, twelve miles from town over in Teton Village, offer everything from the easiest of bunny slopes for beginners to extreme black diamond. Pick your passion—downhill, cross-country, telemarking, snowboarding, heli-skiing, snowshoeing, or snowmobiling. Or experiment with a combination.

Shops around town rent and repair every piece of equipment you'll need to try any of these activities, provide instructions or clinics, and in some cases, furnish guided tours for what skiers claim is the "best skiing in the world."

Snow King Ski Resort

Snow King's season opens in late November and closes around the first of April. Besides being the first ski resort in the state, it is the only one that offers the uniqueness of night skiing. Its convenient position of only six blocks from Town Square allows the locals such unheard of privileges as skiing on their lunch hour or taking the lift to the summit just to catch an unforgettable view of the valley.

In addition, Snow King carries a complete line of rental equipment, offers ski repairs, runs a full-service ski school for alpine and nordic skiing, conducts a complimentary ski clinic every Sat. at 9:30 a.m. with director Bill Briggs, and provides a ski shelter with food service on the mountain.

Snow King stats:
- Base elevation 6,237
- Top elevation 7,808
- 400 acres of skiable terrain
- Half of the terrain available for night skiing
- 300 acres of machine-groomed terrain
- Longest run 9/10 of a mile
- 2 lifts
- 1 surface tow
- 15 percent of the terrain suitable for beginner
- 25 percent of the terrain suitable for intermediate
- 60 percent of the terrain suitable for advanced

Snow King Ski Resort, P.O. Box SKI, Jackson, WY 83001, 800-522 KING (5464) outside Wyoming, 800-533-SNOW (7669) inside Wyoming.

Jackson Hole Ski Resort

Jackson Hole Ski Resort, known locally as "Teton Village," opens early in December and closes at the beginning of April. Other than an undescribable, bird's-eye view of the Teton Mountains and an unrivaled skier's dreamland of runs, the resort contains the nation's greatest vertical rise—4,139 feet. The resort's terrain encompasses two mountains, Apres Vous and Rendezvous, the location of some of the filming of a Rosalind Russell/Darren McGavin movie *The Unexpected Mrs. Pollifax*. (Spy on this CIA thriller in Section Six, Chapter 7.) Overall, Teton Village

n to day runs, three- to seven-day packages
ınique, experience-building adventure from
rough mid-April. Each day includes six runs,
on of additional runs, transportation to and
pad, and a famous Heli-Deli lunch with snacks
keep you going during the day.
information contact the High Mountain Heli-
. Box 173, Teton Village, WY 83025, 307-

nd Camps

s around Jackson Hole include alpine, nordic,
and snowboarding for all class levels from
ost pro. Learn about skiing on all types of
fast, skiing hard, in a group, or individually.
s little as two hours or up to a full day (six
advanced skiers can hit the slopes for moun-
on powder and steeps, utilizing infrequently

ructor might be Olympic gold, silver, and
ist Pepi Stiegler or gold and sliver medalist
who bases his Olympic training program out
le. Or it might be Doug Coombs, the two-time
e Champion or his wife, Emily Gladstone
a world Extreme Champion who coaches a
amp.
tion might be to try snowboarding. Clinics
, bumps, and off-trail steeps. There are also
rograms for the physically challenged, and
nch" that provides infant and child care, plus
the older ones. Pick lessons that fit your
e it to improve your skills or to learn some-

ow King or Teton Village (numbers listed
he clinic and rental details.

receives a yearly snowfall average of thirty-eight feet (approximately 400 inches) of mostly dry powder. Valley temperatures average about twenty-one degrees, while a temperature inversion tends to make the upper slopes about ten to twenty degrees warmer.

The characteristic red and white aerial tram, the ski area's symbol, carries skiers to an altitude of 10,450 feet. Jackson Hole's range, with its incredible array of traverses, ridges, bowls, gullies, couloirs, and chutes, bewilders new-comers to the mountain. As with Snow King, every path carries a name associated with the area's history—many related to the Hole's fur-trading days. But just as a guy named Charles may go by "Chuck" and Elizabeth's friends call her "Libby," ski runs, as well as the landmarks near them, carry nicknames, too. More often than not, these unofficial names get used when the ski patrol goes in search of lost or injured skiers.

The ski patrol also uses a group of stones beside Rendez-vous Bowl to predict avalanches. Once the locally known "Indicator Rocks" disappear under snow (which means the coverage ranges around fifty to sixty inches), it signals the possibility of an avalanche. Then the ski patrol kicks into overdrive on avalanche watch.

Radiation Woods sits above Avalanche Run. The patch of ground received its unlikely tag from a "Danger! Radiation" sign the National Forest Service posted to keep skiers out of a study area. The sign has long since gone, but the designa-tion lives on.

Goldmine Chute can trace its origins back to the gold fever days the likes of Deadman's Bar. Prospectors combed Rendezvous Mountain in search of the mother lode. The terrain situated north of Laramie Bowl received quite a bit of attention, but there's no record of anyone striking it rich. And if you yearn to try your hand, think again. This area is closed to skiers.

The regulars at Teton Village can fill you in on all the mountain's quirks. There's also an excellent ski school, run by

Olympic gold medalist Pepi Stiegler. Plus, the resort has all the necessities in rentals, clothing, maps, food, and lodging.

Jackson Hole Ski Resort stats:
- Base elevation 6,311
- Top elevation 10,450
- 2,500 acres of skiable terrain
- Longest run 4.5 miles
- 10 lifts
- 22 miles of machine-groomed terrain
- snow-making capabilities
- 10 percent of the terrain suitable for beginners
- 40 percent of the terrain suitable for intermediate
- 50 percent of the terrain suitable for advanced

Jackson Hole Ski Resort, P.O. Box 290, Teton Village, WY 83025, 800-443-6931 central reservation, 307-733-2292 main switchboard, 307-733-2660 fax.

Cross Country

Jackson Hole has more cross-country skiing options than you can shake a ski pole at. And if that's not enough, there's telemarking at both ski resorts. Explore among the pines of the Bridger-Teton National Forest or glide past the area's diverse, breathtaking winter landscape in either of the national parks.

Instruction, advice, and recommended routes await you. You can also rent all the nordic gear necessary to experience the backcountry with a guide or on your own. Check with Grand Teton National Park or the Bridger-Teton National Forest before heading into those areas for any restrictions and for permits you may need.

The Jackson Hole Ski School and Nordic Center offers a getaway from bustle of Teton Village with twenty-two kilometers of quiet, groomed trails or a self-guided nature trail. Or just take to the gently rolling terrain alone. In addition,

they offer telemark lesso
tours. Contact them at 76!
Village, WY 83025, 307-739
307-733-2292 for the Nordi

The Spring Creek Nord
ski tours, has fourteen kilo
or individual guided tours i
Box 3154, Jackson, WY 830

Teton Pines Nordic Ski
golf course with approximal
and diagonal tracks. They
Hole Racquet Club, 307-73!

Heli-Skiing

If leaping out of a helic
der snow sounds exciting, d
in Jackson Hole!

Full day helicopter skii
pickup at Teton Village. The
fly to terrain of fresh powd
anything else. Heli-skiing
experience, starting at the
outright quiet, and from 12
skiing opportunities. Take
the Teton, the Palisades, o
describes it as an "undeterr
able experience" than downl

And you don't have to be
capabilities either. "Fat b
designed for extreme condit
intermediate skier, regardles
ter the mountains. Twice as
are shorter, permitting easie
provide better balance. In otl
wind up planting your face o
also have more maneuverabil

In additi
allow for a
December tl
with the op
from the hel
and drinks t

For mor
Skiing at I
733-3274.

Ski Clinic

Ski scho
telemarking
novice to a
terrain, ski
Classes las
hours). Mo
tain trainin
used runs.

Your i
bronze me
Tommy M
of Jackson
world Ext
Coombs, a
Steep Skii

Anothe
cover free
race clini
even a "ki
ski lesson
desired go
thing new

Conta
above) for

Getting Conditioned

Work out at home to get into shape before the season starts. A good aerobic program used in conjunction with stretching exercises and some supervised weight training will limber up your muscles, strengthen your cardiovascular system, and increase your stamina. And don't forget to warm up your muscles with a few light stretches before a workout or skiing. Flexible muscles are less likely to get injured, especially in cold weather.

In addition, give your muscles plenty of energy by eating a well-balanced diet. And take time to acclimatize to the higher altitude before over-exerting yourself. (For more ski- and winter-related safety tips, turn to Section Two, Chapter 2.)

Races

Snow King hosts the Jimmy Huega Ski Express in mid-March. The event, part of the largest charity ski series held at twenty-seven resorts around the nation, raises money for multiple sclerosis research. Beginners and pros alike join the fun. Forming coed teams of three skiers each, teams raise a $1000 minimum in pledges. For details call 307-733-9292.

Since 1974, the annual Jackson Town Downhill rallies around Snow King in early March. After a race billed as the "hog of all town downhills," there are training runs on Saturday, more races on Sunday for both women and men, pros, Skinnies and Snowboard.

Late February 1990 marked the first annual Teton Mountaineering twenty-five-kilometer Moose Chase. Starting from the Jackson Hole Nordic Center, an average of 200 skiers race cross-country to Teton Pines.

Winter 1991 heralded the beginning of the annual Jackson Hole Cowboy Ski Challenge. Held at Teton Village during late February, the weekend event includes a pack scramble, novelty ski races and rodeo, teamster events, a Dutch Oven Cook-off, western music concert, a barn dance, and cowboy poetry. So if you've ever wondered what cowboys do in winter, here's your chance to come and see.

Celebrity and Cowboy Skiing

Want to ski with the stars (in person, not in the sky)? Here's your chance. The Celebrity Ski Extravaganza, which began in 1989, gives folks a chance to mingle and actually ski with the stars. Held during mid-March, the weekend kicks off at the Jackson Hole Ski Resort with the Celebrity Ski Classic. Nightly entertainment and the ski events all go to benefit the community Entry Services. Call 307-733-7637 for who's hosting the extravaganza and how you can get involved.

Snowshoeing

You may have skied or even raced at night, but on a pair of snowshoes? This unique annual race started in 1995. During mid-March the Moonlight Snowshoe Romp challenges you for the benefit of the Friends of Pathways. Races get underway at 7:00 p.m. at the Cache Creek parking lot. Call 307-6094 for more details.

Numbers to Keep Handy

- Snow Conditions 307-733-2291
- Forecast and Avalanche Conditions 307-733-2664
- S.T.A.R.T. Bus Line (Jackson/Teton Village run) 307-733-4521
- Hole in the Wall Snowboard Shop, Teton Village 307-739-2687

- Overnight Storage Ski Locker, Teton Village 307-733-8715
- Aerial Tram, Teton Village 307-739-2753.
- Bridger-Teton National Forest 307-739-5500
- Grand Teton National Park 307-739-3399
- Yellowstone National Park 307-344-7381

2
Hiker's and Hoofer's Heaven*

Whether you like to walk, ride, or drive, the Hole offers stunning vistas as easy or as hard to reach as you could possibly want. Ecosystems range from sagebrush deserts to aspen or lodgepole pine forests to subalpine and alpine meadows.

On summer backcountry expeditions expect to see an array of wildflowers such as the alpine sunflower, often called the "old-man-of-the-mountain"; fireweed; Indian paintbrush, the state flower; elephanthead; columbine; prairie smoke; death camas; showy daisy; and glacier lilies.

Over fifty types of bird species take up residence in Jackson Hole during the year, from the rare peregrine falcon and whooping crane to the more common gray jay and western tanager. Animals come in many forms, from the smallest pika, yellow-bellied marmot, or pine marten to the biggies—mule deer, moose, antelope, elk, bighorn sheep, bison, black bear, and grizzlies.

---

*   Some information from this chapter is excerpted from *Trails & Tales: Day Hikes and Historic Sites on the Way to Yellowstone* and *Backcountry Cooking: Feasts for Hikers, Hoofers and Floaters*. See the Bibliography for details.

Wildlife Etiquette and Encounters

How many time have you heard "pointing is rude"? Well, when it applies to wildlife, it's more than that. It's downright harmful. Tom Segerstrom, senior biologists and director of the Great Plains Wildlife Institute, teaches how wildlife succeeds in the Hole's often harsh environment and how visitors can avoid hindering their survival. The first human trait Tom discourages is pointing at animals. It upsets them. To escape what to them could be a possible act of aggression or a threat, the animals move. Each time they move, they burn up energy—energy in the form of stored calories they need in order to endure the winter months. (And with the Jackson Hole valley seeing only about thirty frost-free days, life gets rough for animals without people adding to the problem.) Anything that disturbs wildlife from their primary function in the short summer months, eating in order to put on enough weight to see them through winter, contributes to their mortality rate.

This in mind, Tom suggests observers stay in their vehicle, viewing wildlife through spotting scopes, binoculars, and camera lens. Avoid direct eye contact and don't stare at one animal for long periods of time. Remember, many animals, especially species such as antelope and deer, can see as well as we can with the aid of binoculars! (Learn more about the Great Plains Wildlife Institute in Section Six, Chapter 5.)

Since the Jackson Hole area houses large land animals from buffalo to bears, a few safety precautions will allow for enjoyable wildlife encounters. First of all, buffalo ARE NOT overgrown, lumbering cattle! Ask anyone who works on a bison ranch. They will tell you a buffalo bull the size of a one-ton truck can spin around, kicking straight up over his head with deadly accuracy, faster than you can blink. As one bison wrangler puts it, "If you walk up too close on a buffalo, trying to get that great picture, you're invading their space, which buffalo see as a definite threat. You'll wind up gored and on the ground before you realize that half-asleep, lazy-looking creature just ruined your whole month—if you were lucky."

Likewise, give bears a wide berth. They aren't any more "tame" than buffalo. Never approach bears with the idea of feeding them or taking their picture. When traveling through designated "bear country," let them know you are coming by talking or making noise. Given a choice, bears prefer to evade people. They generally attack when people startle them at close range. Travel in a group rather than alone. Don't hike at night. In bear areas, it's wiser to not camp with pets along.

Should you encounter a bear on the trail, back away slowly, avoiding direct eye contact, while talking in a soft monotone. NEVER turn your back on a bear and NEVER run. Climbing a tree doesn't make for a good escape either. Instead, stand your ground if a bear charges. Often this is a "mock charge" to test the adversary. As a last resort, play dead. Tuck yourself into a ball, using your arms and hands to cover your head and neck, and stay that way until you are certain the bear has left the vicinity.

One final note for bear country. Jogging can be hazardous to your health. Think about it. You're doing all the wrong behavioral things. You're running; you're alone; it's early morning or evening; you aren't making noise; bears use the same trails you're jogging on; strong scents such as sweat attract bears. Therefore the potential to attract or surprise a bear, especially running around a blind curve, is greatly enhanced.

Trails and Day Hikes

Short hikes in the Jackson Hole area last anywhere from a couple of hours to all day. Trails come rugged and steep with excellent vistas of peaks or ridgetops, or gentle grades lush with water and wildlife.

Snow King Mountain offers the most accessible hiking trail direct from downtown Jackson. Part of the Bridger-

Teton National Forest, Snow King's nature loop trail takes you through a sagebrush meadow and patches of forested area with a ridgetop finale. Or you can follow the service road up the face of the mountain. Either last between two and four hours.

For details, contact the Snow King Ski Resort, P.O. Box SKI, Jackson, WY 83001, 800-522 KING (5464) outside Wyoming, 800-533-SNOW (7669) inside Wyoming.

A longer taste of mountain hiking around the Hole can be found at the Jackpine Creek trailhead across from the Granite Creek Road (just past the hot springs) out from Hoback Canyon. The trail turns sharply south and wanders through a forested sideslope before heading east on a dissected bench at the base of the Gros Ventre Mountains. An incredible view of Shoal Falls and Deer Ridge make this four- to six-hour hike well worth the effort.

Contact the Bridger-Teton National Forest for detailed day hike information, forest regulations, and maps. BTNF Supervisor's Office, P.O. Box 1888, Jackson, WY 83001, 307-733-2752. Or try the Jackson Ranger District located at 140 East Broadway, P.O. Box 1689, Jackson WY 83001, 307-733-4755.

For a twist on the standard day (or overnight camping) experience, take the aerial tram at the Jackson Hole Ski Resort up to the top of Rendezvous Mountain. Aerial trams run two and a half miles straight up a 4,139-foot rise in twelve minutes during the summer (faster in winter to accommodate the influx of skiers).

The view from the summit of Rendezvous Mountain affords a top-notch perspective of Housetop Mountain (10,537 feet), Marrion Lake, Grand Teton National Park, Fossil Mountain (10,916 feet), Mount Bannon (10,966 feet), Granite Canyon, Prospectors Mountain (11,241 feet), Mount Hunt (10,783 feet), Grand Teton Peak (13,770 feet), Buck Mountain (11,938 feet), Static Peak (11,303 feet),

Jackson Lake, the Teton Wilderness, the Absaroka Range, Mount Leidy (10,326 feet), Blacktail Butte (7,688 feet), Lower Slide Lake, Gros Ventre River, Sheep Mountain (11,190 feet), the Bridger-Teton National Forest, Gros Ventre Range, Jackson Peak (10,707 feet), Cache Peak (9,730 feet), the town of Jackson, Snow King Mountain (8,005 feet), the Snake River, and the Snake River Range. From this zenith you can wander the easy Summit Loop, a twenty-minute trek around the nob where the tram sits. More moderate hikes take you on the Teton Village to Granite Canyon trailhead (one to two hours), the Green River Overlook (two to four hours), or Cody-Rock Springs Loop (four to six hours). For those seeking a bit of a challenge, check out the Rendezvous Mountain to Teton Village (7.2 miles down), the Rendezvous Mountain to Granite Canyon trailhead (11.5 miles), or the ultimate Rendezvous Mountain to Marion Lake (12.0 miles loop).

Overnight camping requires a backcountry permit, obtained free from the Grand Teton National Park. Officials won't allow dogs on the tram, the trail, or in the backcountry. Other no-nos include picking wildflowers, collection fossils, or feeding wild animals.

More hiking information and maps can be obtained through the Jackson Hole Ski Corp., P.O. Box 290, Teton Village, WY 83025, 307-739-2753.

Hiking and Backpacking

Mountain hikers may contact The HOLE Hiking Experience for hikes geared to all levels of physical ability and with knowledgeable guides. You may choose an interpretive day hike, an all-day trek, or four-hour walks at sunrise or sunset. Private hikes and overnight backpacking trips may also be arranged.

Contact the HOLE Hiking Experience at P.O. Box 7779, Jackson, WY 83002. Or call them twenty-four hours a day at 307-739-7155.

Llama Packing

If your idea of hiking fun is NOT carrying a sixty-plus-pound backpack, consider letting llamas do the heavy work. Llama packing allows minimum impact camping with the pleasures of fresh food and other comforts.

Llama packing

Photo Credit: Wyoming Travel Commission

Black Diamond Llama Expeditions make easy work of minimum three- and five-day treks into the Gros Ventre Wilderness and the Bridger-Teton National Forests.

Contact Black Diamond Llama Expeditions, Star Route Box 11-G, Jackson Hole, WY 83001, 307-733-2877.

"Llama Louie" (Lou Centrella) founded Jackson Hole Llamas, which offers four- or five-day expeditions into Yellowstone or the Jedediah Smith Wilderness of the Tetons.

Write Jackson Hole Llamas, P.O. Box 7375, Jackson, WY 83002, or call 307-733-1617.

Trail Rides

After a few hours in the saddle on a trail ride, you begin to sample a bit of Jackson Hole from the early settlers' perspective. They entered the valley on worn game trails, not knowing what lay beyond the next bend, viewing nature's wonders amid the steady rocking motion of the horse's gait.

Ward Whitman's family came to the valley via horseback in 1889, trailing a herd of horses and cattle, and they continue the tradition today. Ward and his wife, Betty, provide guided horseback or wagon rides, leaving from the corrals at Spring Creek Resort. Choose between one- or two-hour rides, half- or all-day trips or a one-hour ride with a breakfast or dinner cookout of hearty pioneer foods and plenty of camp coffee (tea or hot chocolate). Rides with breakfast must be reserved by 8:00 a.m. (and 2:00 p.m. for dinner) of the previous day.

W.W. Guides is located at the Spring Creek Resort. Contact Ward at P.O. Box 3154, Jackson, WY 83001, 307-733-8833 phone, 307-733-1524 fax.

Step into the saddle of a ranch-raised horse suited to whatever your riding skill, or lack thereof, happens to be at the A/Ok Corral. Owned and operated by Ray Billings, a fourth-generation Wyomingite, and his wife, Bertha, the A/Ok Corral will instruct you in western horsemanship before you head up into the high country on a one- or two-hour trail ride, or a half- or full-day trip.

Guides, well versed in local history, lead you past Horse Creek, an old homestead, and a variety of interesting geological features before looping back to the ranch. Longer rides cover the upper plateaus for an unparalleled perspective of Jackson's Hole.

Reserve your mount at the A/OK Corral, P.O. Box 3878, Jackson, WY 83001, 800-733-6556.

Moose Creek Ranch borders the Targhee National Forest near the Jedediah Smith Wilderness area on the western slope of the Tetons. Guests enjoy cabin or log ranch house accommodations with family-style meals and cookouts. The ranch features mustang horses, and its riding program gives instruction in proper riding methods and basic horse care. Write Moose Creek Ranch, P.O. Box 3108, Jackson Hole, WY 83001. Call 800-676-0075 phone, 208-787-2284 fax.

The Box K Ranch offers Jackson Hole Trail Rides in August with the option of races, campfire entertainment, and socializing. Box K Ranch, owned and operated by the Walt Korn family, also offers summer pack trips and fall hunting camps. Write Jackson Hole Trail Ride or Box K Pack Trips, P.O. Box 110, Moran, WY 83013 or call 800-729-1410.

For unguided day-long horse and raft rentals at Alpine, Wyoming (about 30 miles south of Jackson), call Riding & Rafts at 307-654-9900 or 307-886-3356.

Wilderness Horsepacking Trips

Wilderness pack trips by horseback offer exciting opportunities for several days of sightseeing, photography, and fishing. Outfitters provide horses, equipment, and guides and always assure excellent food.

The Triangle X Ranch, located in Grand Teton National Park, run by four generations of the Turner family (Harold, John, and Donald), offers a true "roughing it" style vacation in the Tetons. They'll tailor the daily itinerary to accommodate special interests such as photography, wildlife watching, fishing, exploring, or riding. Mountain-wise horses trek through some of the nation's most scenic wilderness—the Tetons, Absarokas, and Gros Ventres, in addition to Yellowstone's backcountry.

Starting in mid-June, summer pack trips continue through early September with a four-day minimum. Most run about a week. You do need to make reservations ahead of time. Contact the Triangle X Ranch at Moose, WY 83012, 307-733-2183 phone, 307-733-8685 fax.

John Henry Lee Outfitters provide personalized pack trips into Yellowstone National Park and the Bridger-Teton Wilderness. Write to John Henry Lee Outfitters at P.O. Box 8368, Jackson, WY 83002 or call 800-3-JACKSON (800-352-2576) or 307-733-9441 for more details.

Outfitter Paul Gilroy personalizes destinations and lengths of time for pack trips. Write Paul Gilroy, Box 222, Wilson, WY 82104 or call 307-733-4314.

High mountain pack and hunting trips are offered by Granite Creek Outfitters. Their Granite Creek and Flat Creek camps are located in the Gros Ventre Wilderness in the Bridger-Teton National Forest. Pack trips are for five days and four nights. Fall hunting camps offer access to elk, deer, moose, bear, and bighorn sheep. Write Jason King, Granite Creek Outfitters, P.O. Box 8264, Jackson, WY 83002 or call 307-733-2468.

Tent Camping

GREYSNEST Mountain Retreat Tent-Camp, located fifty-two miles south of Jackson Hole in the Salt River Range, accommodates those who want wilderness solitude without having to pack in by horseback. Accessible by vehicle, guests are welcome for day-long or monthly stays. Each tent has four beds, a wooden floor, and a wood-burning stove. Propane-heated water for the shower tents is piped in from a nearby stream. Guides make daily photography and fishing excursions and lead trail and pleasure rides.

Write to GREYSNEST, Jackson Hole Outfitters, Box 117, Grover, WY 83122, or call 307-886-3356.

Flagg Ranch Village and campground is located between Yellowstone and Grand Teton National Parks, two miles south of Yellowstone's south entrance. Full campground services are offered, as well as those of a grocery store, gift shop, dining room, saloon, and gas station.

Contact Flagg Ranch Village, P.O. Box 187, Moran, WY 83013. Call 307-733-8761 or outside Wyoming 800-443-2311, 307-543-2356 fax.

Sight-Seeing and Photography Trips

Sight-seeing tours allow you to concentrate fully on your surroundings, while professional guides enhance your experience as they share the history, stories, and geology of the area. Jackson's Hole Adventure offers one-day mini-van tours of Grand Teton National Park and the Gros Ventre Mountains.

Contact Jackson's Hole Adventure, P.O. Box 2407, Jackson Hole, WY 83001, 800-392-3165.

During the summer season, Callowishus Park Touring Company provides professional tour guides for day-long trips through either Grand Teton Park or Yellowstone Park. In the winter, horse-drawn sleighs take guests through the middle of the famous Jackson elk herd on their winter refuge.

Call 307-733-9521.

Day tours of either Grand Teton and Yellowstone Parks for individuals and groups are provided by Gray Line. To see both parks, overnight tours of either four or five days are available. These include accommodations and western activities.

Write to Gray Line of Jackson Hole National Park Tours, P.O. Box 411, Jackson, WY 83001, or call 800-443-6133, 307-733-2689 fax.

Jackson Hole's spectacular scenery and abundant wildlife are a photographer's dream. Wilderness Exposure Photography Expeditions offer a half day in Grand Teton National Park or a full day in both Grand Teton and Yellowstone Parks. Hike or canoe for two to five days into the Yellowstone backcountry. Professional photographer Greg Winston gives personalized instruction at all levels.

Contact Wilderness Exposure Photography Expeditions, P.O. Box 505, Wilson, WY 83014, or call 307-733-1026.

Firehole Photographic Expeditions provides one-day photo tours of Yellowstone and Grand Teton Parks with professional photographer-instructor D.J. Bassett.

Write Firehole Photographic Expeditions, P.O. Box 7395, Jackson Hole, WY 83002, or call 307-733-5733.

3

Fishing Hole

A steady stream of snow-melt water tumbles over a bed of rock. Gentle swishing sounds connect the action of the fly to the hand holding the rod. In the flow a brook or brown trout waits for a tasty morsel to drift its way. Then the sport is on for catch and release, a trophy mount, or for supper.

During the early 1900s, Easterners (mostly the gentried well-to-dos) started coming to Jackson Hole to vacation. Arriving by train at the Victor or Driggs, Idaho station, they would cross Teton Pass and spend summer in the Hole, doing the things tourists do today—fishing, wandering the countryside on horseback, hiking, and roughing it in cabins scattered around mountain lodges.

While these folks could fish the waters of home, the West offered (and continues to) a dazzling array of fishing opportunities, spectacular rivers, and mountains that overwhelm the senses. Nowadays, a slower pace, western hospitality, no phones in rooms, and a place where the staff tease guests who receive too many faxes encourage people to relax.

The Big Ones That Don't Get Away

Fly fishing enthusiasts claim the South Fork and the Snake rivers teem with trout. "Three times as many per mile as other areas," contends one fisherman. Of course, everybody who picks up a pole has their favorite fishing spots.

Fly fishing.

Photo Credit: Jackson Hole Chamber of Commerce

Even better, some sites around Jackson Hole hold record-breaking catches. Doris Budge pulled a forty-five-inch lake trout (mackinaw) from Jackson Lake in 1983. It weighed fifty pounds! Dennis Jennings caught a twenty-one-inch whitefish in the Snake River during 1977. It scaled in at four and a quarter pounds.

Of course, the Jackson National Fish Hatchery helps to keep area streams and lakes well stocked. Located just four miles north of Jackson, near the National Elk Refuge, the hatchery is one of over seventy-five operated by the U.S. Fish and Wildlife Service. Producing eggs and stocking fish in the country's lakes and streams are the hatcheries' primary goals. Each year, the Jackson hatchery raises approximately a million fish, ranging from one to eight inches, of the native Snake River strain of cutthroat and lake trout—the varieties best suited to this locale. One angler swears that "Snake River trout are smarter, more aggressive, and more selective" than other species. They live for approximately seven years and provide a rewarding challenge to hook. These trout are displayed in the hatchery's aquaria, which is open to the public.

Catch sight of them at the Jackson National Fish Hatchery, located at 1500 Fish Hatchery Road. Check with the Wyoming Game and Fish Department, Cheyenne, WY 82002, 800-654-1178, for license information, regulations, and seasons.

Jackson Hole One-Fly Event

People from around the world come to Jackson Hole in the fall to participate in the One-Fly Event. Teams consisting of four individuals apply a year in advance for the thirty-six openings. Each team splits up, fishing the Snake and South Fork rivers with a guide/judge and a member of a different team. In an effort to keep the event fair, the contest utilizes twelve separate sections of the rivers, with team members fishing diverse stretches.

Every angler creates (or has tied) one fly to be used throughout the contest. Should they lose it, or if it gets destroyed, the angler is out of the contest. Skill and luck combine to make the winning team.

Run by the nonprofit One-Fly Foundation, funds from the entry fees go to benefit water conservation projects and fly fishing education.

Jackson Hole One-Fly, P.O. Box 4158, Jackson, WY 83001, 307-733-3270 phone, 307-733-4540 fax.

A "Dude Ranch" for Anglers

Originally built in 1927, the Crescent H Ranch became the first Orvis Endorsed Lodge in the 1970s when Scott Albrecht and his partners took over the guest ranch and began advertising in the Orvis newsletter. "The idea was to create new Orvis fly fishermen and new products," Scott explains. "Now there are Orvis endorsed lodges all across the country. The programs mimic the Crescent H even down to the Friday night barbecue."

The Crescent H focuses on twenty to twenty-five guests per week between June and the end of September. "Jackson Hole has gotten so hectic," Scott says, "it's easy to get swept up in it. Here, Jackson Hole is like the way it was fifty years ago.

"When we first opened, we were almost entirely fly fishing. We wanted to mimic old English hunting and fishing lodges. At first, we mainly got 'scotch drinking' fishermen who came on 'men's vacations.' Then husband and wife teams started coming, then they brought their family. Now, two families will come together so the men can fish together while the families horseback ride or hike. We do the whole fishing trip, with guests staying a week from Saturday to Saturday."

For the beginner, the Crescent H stocks 50,000 wild Snake River cutthroat hatchling every year in the pond next to the lodge. "There's a high mortality rate," tells Scott, "and we are doing everything we can to insure survival rates. Snake River cutthroat, the native trout, isn't as big or aggressive as other trout. It likes the slower water, likes to hide behind structures in the water. There's a lot of pressure to stock rainbow or brown trout, but we're working hard to maintain the integrity of our trout."

The pond also makes a fun fishing experience for kids. The Crescent H staff were teaching how to catch and release years before it became in vogue. (However, they will cook up guests' catch for breakfast if desired.)

For more about the Crescent H Ranch, contact Scott at the Crescent H Ranch, P.O. Box 730, Wilson, WY 83014, 307-733-3674.

Anglers' Angles

Anglers' shops offer full day and overnight trips, as well as multiple day package excursions to fly and spin fishermen. They will arrange fishing trips to other U.S. locations and exotic, worldwide fishing trips. Advance booking is recommended.

In addition, Jack Dennis Fishing Trips will provide rental equipment, hourly fly casting instruction, and one-day fly fishing seminars. Write Jack Dennis Sportsman's Travel Service, P.O. Box 3369, Jackson, WY 83001 or call 307-733-3270.

Fishing Expeditions

Combining fishing with serene non-whitewater float or horsepacking trips, the Forty Rod River and Fishing Guides owners/operators Bruce and Mary Cahill customize each trip to accommodate fishermen and families.

"Our float trips are not only fun but educational," says Bruce, a retired wildlife biologist with thirty years of experience in the field. "We usually give a running account on the geology, history of the Native Americans' and pioneers' influences, and, of course, information on the plants and mountain wildlife."

Contact Bruce and Mary at P.O. Box 1747, Pinedale, WY 82941.

John Henry Lee Outfitters supplies transportation to and from the put-in point, river boats, rain gear, and fly and spin rods. You'll need to bring any special fishing equipment you want along, and, of course, don't forget to bring your Wyoming fishing license and conservation stamp. Specialty fishing/photography trips of five to ten days in Yellowstone National Park or the Bridger-Teton Wilderness can be arranged, as well as short scenic float/fishing excursions along the Tetons. Or you can head in to camp with mountain-wise saddle and pack horses, on your own or with a guide.

Write John Henry Lee Outfitters, P.O. Box 8368, Jackson, WY 83002 or call 800-3-JACKSON (800-352-2576) or 307-733-9441.

Trout fishermen from beginners to experts may concentrate on catching "the big one" in the Snake River or from many other mountain streams with Joe Allen Fishing Trips. Joe grew up in Jackson Hole and has fished the Snake River for over forty years. As a result he designed the acclaimed Double Humpy Dry Fly. Experienced guides instruct you on how to "read" the river and how the water affects fishing conditions on either half-day or full-day trips. They also provide one-on-one or one-to-two instruction in fly or spin fishing.

Contact Joe Allen Fishing/Scenic Float Trips at P.O. Box 2950, Jackson, WY 83001. Call 800-400-3174 or 800-807-2920.

Mangis Guide Service offers half- and full-day trips to fly and spin anglers, two per trip. All equipment is provided. Contact Mangis Guide Service, Klay Mangis, P.O. Box 3165, Jackson, WY 83001, 307-733-8553.

Westbank Anglers also offers half-day trips and provides equipment. Instruction is available in half- and full-day clinics plus two- and three-day schools. Westbank Anglers, P.O. Box 523, Teton Village, WY 83025, 800-922-3474. In Wyoming: 307-733-6483.

Scenic fishing trips offered by Lazy B River Company limit each boat to four passengers. Anglers may choose half- and full-day fishing trips with professional guides. Lazy B assures only two fishermen per boat. The Lazy B River Company, part of Drui Enterprises, is located at 1915 W. Bunkhouse, P.O. Box 8909, Jackson, WY 83002. Call them at 307-733-0759.

Coy's Wilderness Float Trips are custom designed for any combination of fishing, scenic or whitewater fishing, and may include all day or overnight trips. Experienced guides find the fish, which you can get to by horseback or boat. Anglers may find secluded fishing on a four-day horseback pack trip into a Yellowstone Lake. Write to Tom Coy, P.O. Box 3356, Jackson, WY 83001, or call 800-368-0957.

With Fort Jackson River Trips, continue the tradition begun by Boots Allen in the early 1940s with an army surplus raft and a Model A Ford. Scenic and fishing raft trips of varying lengths are available, as well as customized float and guided fishing trips to other Wyoming fisheries.
Get in touch with Fort Jackson River Trips, P.O. Box 1176, Jackson, WY 83001, 800-735-8430.

4

Mountain Climbing and Rock Jocks

Thanks to the fact no foothills obstruct the view of the Teton Range, you can gaze straight up at all 13,776 feet of Grand Teton, rising a mile and a half out of the valley floor.

This irresistible sight has beckoned to mountaineers since at least the time of the Sheepeater Indians, credited with building "The Enclosure" on the summit of Grand Teton's west spur. Of course, another climber, Nathaniel P. Langford, himself a controversial figure associated with the Grand (see below), assumed the circular stone structure was the handiwork of a French trapper named Michaud (most likely Michaud LeClaire, an employee of the Hudson's Bay Company). Langford based this assumption on a comment made by Beaver Dick Leigh, the guide on the Hayden Expedition of which Langford was a member. Leigh, who spent the majority of his life in the valley, told how Michaud tried to climb Grand Teton during 1843—the first actual date attached to official records about climbs. (Explore Yellowstone with this survey group in Section Eight, Chapter 3)

Most of the climbs in the Tetons range between a difficulty of 5.2 to 5.10, offering a broad spectrum of challenges for all skill levels. Points along the route often carry descriptive names like Symmetry Spire, Disappointment Peak, The Corkscrew, Caveat Emptor, and Teepe's Pillar, a "needle" of red granite and a glacier named after Theodore Teepe, an ill-fated mountaineer who died while descending the ice field that bears his name.

Of course, whenever climbing is mentioned, Grand Teton instantly springs to mind—the granddaddy of all climbs in the range. Referred to as the "American Matterhorn," mountaineers approach it with caution and respect. Beginners should look to taking basic classes at a climbing school before tackling the mountains. And remember, since the Tetons are part of Grand Teton National Park, several regulations and park permits apply to climbs. Check with the park at P.O. Drawer 170, Moose, WY 83012, 307-739-3399, for more details.

Getting yourself in shape is strongly recommended by the area's mountain climbing schools and guide services. Participation in sports and aerobic exercises help build strength and stamina needed for mountaineering.

Who Got There First?

Jackson Hole grew up amid controversy and tourism, the two usually going hand-in-hand. You've seen it in everything from early exploration to the town government to the fight over land use and animal conservation to the establishment of Grand Teton National Park. Why should the peak itself be any different?

William O. Owen claimed to have been the first person to successfully ascend Grand Teton to its summit on August 11, 1898, after three aborted attempts. He based this on what he described as a "most diligent search for evidence of a former visit" once his party reached the top. According to the *Wyoming Annals* article "The First Ascent of the Grand Teton with a Little of its History," written by Owen himself, they found "not a stone turned over nor displaced—everything just as nature left it!"

Historians, however, pointed to accounts written by members of the 1872 Fredinand V. Hayden Expedition into Yellowstone. Seventeen-year-old Bedfordshire England youth Sidford Hamp kept a journal of his adventurous first trip to the United States. In it, he recorded an accurate, detailed description of Grand Teton's terrain future climbers would verify.

Monday [July] 29. Twelve of us started at 5/30 AM to climb the Tetons. First we ascended a mountain 10000 feet high, and came to snow over which we walked about 3 miles, till we came to a high ridge of rocks, over which we got. But it was a case of hands and knees, and somewhat dangerous too, then we descended on the other side and in getting down the snow, I sliped, and slid on my sitter, about 60 yards, which didn't hurt me, and give me a good start. Then we walked 2 miles over the snow, and came to a small, frozen lake, and saw some bear tracks, then we climbed another ridge, much harder than the first, where if you missed your footing you would either break your bones, or slide down into the lake, in either case, very unpleasant. In getting down the snow on the other side, I missed my footing and slide down about 150 yards on my seat. I should think I went as fast as any stone ever went down the "Hole" at Bisopstone (don't I wish I was there now.) After that we walked 1 1/2 mile, over the snow, till we came to the Teton. Then began the hard work. I was with a gentleman named [Nathaniel P.] Langford, and his nephew, named Charlie Spencer, who was only a month older than me, and we three began the ascent. It was an auful hard climb and very dangerous. We crossed a snow slide once and I knew that if I sliped, I should be smashed, so I was very carefull, but just about 1 yard from the rocks we were making for, I did slip, but I turned over onto my stomach, and stretched open my legs, and turned myself into the rocks. After that we had to climb over loose rocks to the saddle between two of the Tetons, and jolly glad we were to get behind some big stones to eat some bread and bacon that we had with us. There we met Mr. [James] Stevenson (who was the only one besides ourselves and Prof Bradly who tried the Teton at all) and went on higher up, but we came to a place where the snow had seperated from the rock about 2 feet, and one could see between to the depth of 40, 50, or sometimes 100 feet, so as we were very tired, and the ascent got so dangerous, Spencer and I stop on a ledge and rested whilst the other two got to the top, then we began the descent, and Mr. Stevenson got a long way ahead (for he is very active,) and left us three to ourselves again. Mr. Langford had to let us other two down one place by a rope, and in another place we had to cross a small stream where there was about 2 inc[h] foothold and no hand hold, but we got down all right, and then had to walk all the way back that we had come in the morning. By the time we got to the 2nd ridge the sun set, and we had to walk up a ridge of snow about 6 inches broad and 500 feet high on one side, but in the pine wood, and wandered about, jumping ditches, and we saw the camp fire, and then got into camp at 10 oc. PM having travelled on foot for 17 hours.

Nathaniel Langford, another of the Hayden party, wrote an account of the Grand Teton climb which appeared in the June 1879 issue of *Scribner's Monthly*. In addition to describing Hamp's unfortunate slide to the edge of the glacier and down a bank of snow, Langford related an accurate depiction of the view from the summit. "... the emerald surface of Pierre's Hole... far off... the cloud defined peaks of the Wind River mountains, and the peaks surrounding the great lake of the Yellowstone."

Owen called the 1872 ascent an "attempt" on the Grand and didn't credit Stevenson and Langford with reaching the top.

In an effort to assure his position at "first," Owen managed to get it brought before the Wyoming legislature. After "investigating" the matter, the two Congressional houses passed a joint resolution "declaring the first ascent of Grand Teton Peak, in Teton County, Wyoming, to have been made by William O. Owen, Franklin S. Spalding, Frank L. Petersen, and John Shive, on August 11, 1898, and providing for a public record of the achievement."

The "public record" came two years later with the placement of a bronze tablet on the summit of Grand Teton, commemorating the "achievement of the Owen party," as part of the dedication ceremony for Grand Teton National Park. But, sometime during 1977 the Owen plaque disappeared from the summit.

Nevertheless, Owen was, beyond any doubt, party to a definite first. His wife, Emma Matilda, and Jennie Dawson, the wife of Owen's partner during their initial attempt in 1891, became the first known white women to tackle the climb. The first successful ascent by a woman came in 1923 when Eleanor Davis reached the Grand's rocky apex.

Jackson Hole Climbing Schools

Jackson Hole Mountain Guides & Climbing School is year round and geared to small groups. Learn rope systems for safe team climbing, belays, rappelling in one-day basic climbing courses. No age limit. Intermediate one-day classes concentrate on preparing for a high peak ascent. Some prior experience required. One-day snow courses teach you how to travel safely on summer mountain snow—how to use an ice axe, self-arrest techniques, and glissading. A more advanced one-day class hones experienced climbers' skills for protection placement, belays, and other practices necessary to lead climbs.

In addition, the Jackson Hole Mountain Guides and Climbing School offers guided climbs for day trips on non-technical climbs of an ascent or cirque or a technical climb appropriate to your skill level. On two-day climbs on one of the Teton's major peaks, they supply all gear and food for an arduous but doable climb for any experience level. Extended trips of two to twelve days offer a variety of mountaineering and climbing adventures, as does their sixteen-day summer climbing camp for fifteen- to eighteen-year-olds.

Located one and a half blocks off Town Square, you can get all the details by contacting the Jackson Hole Mountain Guides & Climbing School at P.O. Box 7477, Jackson, WY 83002, 307-733-4979.

During the summer of 1931, while still a teenager, Glenn Exum made his first and famous solo ascent of Grand Teton on the route that now bears his name. Out of that experience and love for mountaineering grew Exum Mountain Guides.

Exum guides all peaks and routes in the Teton Range throughout the year on one- to four-day climbs. You need not be experienced before attending their basic school. They limit classes and climbs to small numbers and will provide private guides and porters for climbing programs.

In addition to basic instruction, Exum offers courses for intermediate, advanced, expeditions, and basic snow climbing. Women guides also teach a class geared toward women interested in the sport.

Write Exum Mountain Guides, Grand Teton National Park, P.O. Box 56, Moose, WY 83012. Call 307-733-2297 in winter or 307-733-9613 in summer.

Rock Gym

The Teton Rock Gym provides a year-round indoor climbing experience. Even if you're a novice, the staff can teach you the skills needed to make a safe climb. Instruction on their specially designed climbing walls, whether individually or in a group, promotes concentration, fitness, and balance. They devise new routes weekly, challenging every skill level. Walls simulate a variety of surfaces from steep slabs to overhangs. Beginners find easy verticals, while more experienced climbers seek the multiple leads walls.

The gym can also help you get in shape for a mountain expedition with their free weights, acrobic machines, and finger boards. They carry all the latest equipment and clothing, too.

Rates include a harness, climbing shoes, and instruction. Group and family rates are also available.

They are located at 1116 Maple Way. Contact them at P.O. Box 45, Jackson, WY 83001, 307-733-0707.

5

River Runners

> July Friday 12. We got up at 4 oc. before sun-up, and packed our beds, clothes, and mules, saddled our horses, and started at 9/30 oc. for the region of bears, Indians, and worst of all the region of Musquitoes. I am much more afraid of musquitoes, than of Indians, or snakes, or anything else, and so is everyone else.
>
> July Sunday 14. We camped on the Snake River, which is very swift and deep, and if anyone gets into it he is sure to be killed.
>
> Sidford Hamp, 1872

The Mad River

At the beginning of the 1800s, French trappers called the Snake *la maudite riviere enragee*, "the accursed mad river," because of its cold, swift flowing water, shifting course, and serene stretches which led, with little or no warning, to treacherous rapids. One historical account after another told of the hardships and deaths associated with crossing this dangerous obstacle.

Today, the Snake flows at an average rate of 3,000 cubic feet per second and a typical depth of four feet. However, during the "spring" (in reality usually early to mid-summer) run-off, this increases to around 15,000 cubic feet per second. A summer current speed of six miles per hour carries scenic floaters down river, not counting the wind slowing you down.

River trips on the Snake River are geared to every visitor's desires, from screaming whitewater adventures to quiet scenic and fishing float trips. Professional guides enhance each water journey. (Be sure to ask the minimum age for children to participate.)

Scenic Raft Trips on the Snake

Scenic floats present unsurpassed opportunities to increase your tally of wildlife spotted—from bald eagles and osprey that fish the waters, to elk herds that swim at sunrise, to moose and deer that feed along the banks. Many nature films and wildlife programs are shot along the scenic sections of the Snake, including those by Walt Disney film crews which the Triangle X outfitted.

Jason Wright has guided Triangle X Float Trips on the Snake since 1987. He reads the river as easily as you do the pages of this book, sighting changes in the river's course such as the "maze." The run-off from the heavy 1994-95 winter snows cleared most of it out.

Floating the Snake

Photo Credit: Wyoming Travel Commission

Jason makes three to four trips down the river each day. "That's over 900 river miles a month," he calculates. So what does he do in his off time? "I'm headed up to Glacier National Park. I hear the water is great up there."

For wildlife watchers, the Triangle X offers a ten-mile sunrise or evening float (with a supper option of good mountain cooking on the banks of the river, and you can't beat the view of the Tetons while you enjoy dinner). In addition, they provide a shorter, five-mile scenic float, perfect for when you have small children along (kids must be at least four years old to be properly fitted into life preservers). Daytime ten-mile floats, group charters, twenty-mile floats, and special fishing floats (don't forget your Wyoming fishing license) are also available.

For information and reservations contact the Triangle X Float Trips, Moose, WY 83012, 307-733-5500 phone, 307-733-8685 fax.

National Park Float Trips are leisurely ten-mile scenic jaunts, taking less than three hours. Get a chance to watch moose, elk, antelope, beaver, herons, geese, ducks, shorebirds, osprey, and bald eagles. Contact National Park Float Trips, Moose, WY 83012, 307-733-6445 or 307-733-5500.

Ten-mile scenic float trips and cookouts are offered by Barker-Ewing Scenic Tours, which run from Deadman's Bar to Moose Village. Contact Barker-Ewing Scenic Tours, P.O. Box 100, Moose, WY 83012, 800-365-1800 phone, 307-739-1800 fax.

Boating on the Lakes in Yellowstone and Grand Teton National Parks

Among the many diversions in turn-of-the-century Yellowstone, "Grand Tours," started during the summer of 1889, was a sailing excursion on Yellowstone Lake aboard a steamboat. Yellowstone Lake Boat Company steamer *Zillah*, a forty-tonner measuring eighty-one feet long and fourteen feet at her beam, ferried 120 passengers between the stagecoach lunch station at Thumb Bay and the Lake Hotel—with a short stop-over on Dot Island to view the animal enclosure where *Zillah*'s owner, E.C. Waters, had corralled elk, deer, and buffalo. The entrepreneur also served a fish dinner.

The name "Yellowstone Lake" first appeared on a map published in 1838 by Captain Washington Hood. (He passed through the country in 1837.) Before that the body of water went by many names, among them Lake Eustis and Lake Riddle.

Nothing unusual about that. Much of the Jackson Hole area sported aliases. But Yellowstone Lake does hold one bizarre secret—the "music of the Lake." Journal entries dating back to the early days of the area's exploration occasionally speak of eerie, unearthly noises that haunted the dawn. Some who witnessed it compared the discharge to a pipe organ's reverberating tone. To others, it sounded more like the vibration of "talking wires" (telegraph) or bees or something moving through the quiet. It generally starts from the north and travels south, starting soft, then growing in intensity until it reaches overhead. Almost immediately, it disappears in the opposite direction.

Scientists who have observed the sound have no explanation for it. They have proposed everything from escaping volcanic gas to electrical currents to flocks of birds. Yet the mystery remains.

Willing to dare a Yellowstone Lake experience? The Snake River Kayak and Canoe School offers rafting, kayaking, canoeing, and seakayaking trips in the park, with some of them overnight. They also provide rentals, sales, and repairs.

Snake River Kayak and Canoe School, 155 W. Gill, P.O. Box 3482, Jackson, WY 83001, 307-733-3127 phone, 800-529-2501 fax.

Tom Coy, Coy's Wilderness Float Trips, P.O. Box 3356, Jackson, WY 83001, or call 800-368-0957.

The Colter Bay Marina in Grand Teton National Park supplies a full service marine for Jackson Lake. In addition to boat rentals, guides for trips, all the licenses and tackle you could need, groceries, fuel, lodging, and even a restaurant, they offer scenic cruises between May 6 and September 24.

Contact the marina at Colter Bay, Grand Teton National Park, 307-543-2811 phone, 307-543-2869 fax.

Boating on Jackson Lake in Grand Teton National Park is offered by Signal Mountain Lodge. Canoes, deck cruisers, pontoon boats, pleasure/ski boats, and fishing boats may be rented. Signal Mountain Lodge, P.O. Box 50, Moran, WY 83013, 307-543-2831.

For a wondrous jaunt to Hidden Falls or around Jenny Lake in Grand Teton National Park, try a scenic trip with Teton Boating. Of if fishing is more your passion, they rent fishing boats, as well. The dock is located at the south end of Jenny Lake.

Teton Boating, P.O. Box 1553, Jackson, WY 83001, 307-733-2703.

Whitewater on the Snake

Eight miles of whitewater action with site names like "The 'S' Turns," "Cutbanks 1 & 2," "Lunch Counter Rapids," "Three-Oar Deal," "Holey City," "Champagne" and "Big Kahuna," insure that daring rafters will get wet! Mad River Boat Trips makes only whitewater runs, some of which include meals. The crew has been consulted for many TV ads and movies, including *A River Runs Through It*, and performed whitewater stunts in the 1980 film *The Pursuit of D.B. Cooper*.

Contact Mad River Boat Trips, P.O. Box 2222, Jackson Hole, WY 83001. 800-458-RAFT (7238) phone, 307-733-7626 fax.

Sands Wild Water River Trips will add eight miles of a scenic trip and lunch before tackling whitewater. Overnight trips are also available. Write Sands Wild Water River Trips, P.O. Box 696B, Wilson, WY 82014 or call 800-358-8184 phone, 307-734-9064 fax.

Lewis & Clark River Expeditions also offer scenic and/or whitewater trips with meal options. Write them at P.O. Box 720, Jackson, WY 83001. Call 800-824-5375 phone, 307-733-0345 fax.

All of the Lone Eagle Expeditions have meals, including their daily seven whitewater runs. Call 800-321-3800.

6

Snowmobiling

Around Jackson Hole snowmobiles mean far more than just winter recreation. Folks rely on them to get to and from home, because drifts and just plain deep snow force them to park their four-wheel-drive vehicle some distance away on a more or less plowed road. The fun aspects simply supply a bonus!

Depending on snow conditions, snowmobiling season runs from November through April, peaking around February or March. Later in the season, the snow becomes firm, making it a great environment for beginners.

Visitors to the Jackson Hole area can take advantage of these lush snowmobiling opportunities with guided or unguided expeditions into Yellowstone National Park, Grand Teton National Park, and the Gros Ventre Mountain Range. Many businesses offer everything from half-day to week-long trips which include gear (helmets, boots, and snowmobile suits), lessons, gourmet meals, and, on longer trips, even lodging.

Togwotee Pass, just forty-eight miles northeast of Jackson on Highway 26 and 287, gives enthusiasts their earliest chance to hit the trail, as it receives snowfall sooner than the Tetons or Gros Ventres. Its powder conditions are internationally renowned.

From any of these trails you may see elk or deer browsing in a meadow, moose grazing in a river bottom, bighorn sheep darting across a mountain slope, or bison plowing through the drifts. Routes range in elevation from below 7,000 to over 10,000 feet, so come prepared for a constantly changing, cold weather environment. Easy enough with today's well-equipped machines.

Of course, back in the early days, snowmobiling took real strength, fortitude, and lots of guts. Prototypes lacked anything close to such modern comforts as padded seats, electric starters, and cushiony suspension for all those trail-blazing bumps, not to mention built-in hand warmers. Furthermore, those old snowmobiles tended to leave their riders in some of the most remote backcountry.

Old-timers tell many a tale of being stranded miles from nowhere. If they were lucky, they had the wherewithal to make a fire and had some food along. If not, they faced one long, cold, hungry trek back to civilization. Not all wind up as fortunate as a local group from the Togwotee Pass area who decided on a holiday adventure.

One New Year's Day in the early 1970s, thirty-two snowmobilers decided to spend the day out in the Gros Ventre Range of the Bridger-Teton National Forest. It would be an easy day, especially considering a few of the gang had broken around twenty miles of the trail in preparation for the ride the day before. They would be there by mid-afternoon.

But during the night two-and-a-half feet of fresh snow fell. Still, it didn't discourage the snowmobilers who ranged in age from young children accompanying their parents to a seventy-year-old. A hardy bunch, they revved up the engines and plowed through the soft powder.

Only they didn't make it to their destination that New Year's Day.

All thirty-two spent the night on the north fork of Fish Creek with two fires blazing to keep away some of the bitter thirty-nine-degrees-below-zero temperature. Disaster loomed as a real possibility with only a few candy bars to share among the group and very little extra clothing to protect against the continued extreme cold.

But even this paled when faced with the snow-covered creek crossing the next day.

After a few machines made it over, the snow caved in and the next snowmobile sank into the icy water. The tracks instantly froze. The group ended up leaving seven machines at the creek. Doubling up on the remaining machines, the weary snowmobilers finally made it to the Goosewing Ranger Station, two days late, with the mercury continuing to plunge to forty-three degrees below zero.

Nevertheless, the group was extremely lucky—only a couple of mild cases of frostbite and exposure and a few pounds lost in the process.

But the story didn't end there.

Using the radio at the Goosewing Ranger Station, one of the group hired a helicopter to get his machine out of Fish Creek. The following morning several of the men stayed behind at the creek to chop the abandoned machines out of the water. They tied a rope around one of the snowmobiles, but it proved too heavy, being totally encrusted in ice, for the helicopter to lift. So the men began pulling the machine out of the water in order to chip the ice off. The helicopter landed in a nearby field, and the pilot came to help. Once they were ready to try again, the temperature had dropped to the point the helicopter wouldn't start. The men ended up leaving it and the frozen snowmobiles until the next day when more help and warmer weather allowed them to get all the equipment out of the mountains.

With such incidents as those which occurred on the Goosewing and more beginning snowmobilers coming to experience the wide open spaces and spectacular scenery of the National Forest trails, safety has moved to the forefront.

Thirty minutes of travel on a snowmobile will take you into the wilderness farther than you can walk out in several days. Good preparation, therefore, makes all the difference between a fun and a potentially disastrous trip—especially on unguided trips.

On such journeys travel in a group if at all possible. Let others know where you plan to go and stick to it. Learn how to make basic repairs to your machine, and carry tools. Take along a first aid kit, extra clothing, matches, candles, snowshoes, and food.

And don't forget the trail maps—even though many national forest trails are well marked with international snowmobile signs. Maps contain more than just information on where the trails lead. They show gas stations, restaurants, lodging, and pit stops along the way. Also consider how big the area for snowmobiling is in this region. The Continental Divide Trail alone incorporates over 300 miles of groomed, marked trails. Sort of makes the drift buster inside all of us dream of gliding though untouched snow, doesn't it?

Granite Hot Springs

Granite Hot Springs ranks as a favorite destination, probably because you get to go from all bundled up in a snowsuit to lounging around in a bathing suit, soaking in a cozy 110-degree natural hot spring, then snuggling back into the snowsuit again for the return trip. A ten-mile ride, guided or unguided, leads to the springs through the groomed Bridger-Teton National Forest access trail in the Gros Ventre Range where a hot lunch rounds out your sojourn. Treks embark at the unplowed Granite Creek road approximately ten miles south of Hoback Junction on Route 191.

Grand Teton National Park

Grand Teton Park invites winter exploration through several designated, unplowed roads, among them the Jenny Lake Loop road, the Signal Mountain road, sections of the Moose-Wilson road, and a number of Forest Service access roads. This glacier-formed district means a rollercoaster ride of inclines and dips through rugged, majestic mountain valleys. And for the very brave at heart, the icy surface of Jackson Lake beckons to snowmobilers when weather conditions permit for a little "ice skating" snowmobile style.

Note: If you're taking an unguided snowmobile spin around Grand Teton National Park, you'll need a winter park permit, and you must pay a Wyoming registration fee. Contact the park headquarters for more on the requirements.

Grand Teton National Park, Moose, WY 83012, 307-733-2880.

Togwotee Pass

The Continental Divide Trail connects snowmobile thoroughfares in Yellowstone and around Jackson Hole to those in the vicinity of Togwotee Pass. Considered some of the nation's best terrain, to say nothing about the scenery, for premiere "powder" riding—on and off-trail—Togwotee Pass's two million acres serve up snow excitement for every skill and age level. The region's average 600 inches of snowfall over the course of the season draws everyone from the first-timer to the pros, and even snowmobile manufacturers. Guess where all those fantastic shots of powder spraying over machine and driver against a virgin wilderness backdrop get filmed? Right here.

In Yellowstone

Nothing matches Yellowstone for a journey through some of nature's most unique natural wonders. Cold air amplifies the explosion of steam belching forth from every geyser, mudpot, and thermal vent in the park. The 309-foot lower waterfall on the Yellowstone River sends up clouds of frost-laden mist and ice that look like smoke signals that retell ancient stories of olden times and races.

Many winter sports enthusiasts combine snowmobiling with skiing, traveling in by machine, then switching to skis. This affords them the opportunity to experience more of Yellowstone's incredible variety, silently gliding through the park's pristine wilderness recesses it would otherwise take days to reach.

Snowmobile Hillclimb Racing

Jackson Hole hosts a world class championship snowmobile hillclimb each spring. For three days, the rev and roar of snowmobile engines saturates the air as contestants try to conquer Snow King's 1,571-vertical-foot Exhibition Slope.

Approximately 130 racers gather to compete in a variety of modified and stock classes, with the ultimate goal to be crowned King of the Hill. The overall winner receives this title following Sunday's races.

Although some spectators bring out the binoculars and watch the race from the base of the slope, the choice spot for catching the hottest action comes up top. You can ride the ski lift up and practically stare the competitors in the face as they claw their way up the steepest pitch on slope to "put their machines over the top." And since MTV started filming the race in 1995, who knows who else you might come face to face with.

Jackson Hole Snow Devils, the local snowmobile club, began hosting the hillclimb in 1975, using the event to raise money for several regional charities. Since it's all for a good cause, you can increase the exhilaration of the race by placing a wager on riders at the Snow Devils' Calcutta, held at The Virginian on Friday and Saturday nights at 8 p.m.

To enhance your observation enjoyment, take along a lawn chair and a pair of binoculars. Dress for cold, windy weather. And whatever you do, don't forget your ear plugs!

Rentals

Togwotee Mountain Lodge offers daily guided and unguided getaways through untracked mountain meadow, challenging mountainsides and snow cornices. Besides concentrated excitement, they provide a great lunch and interpretive tours. Contact the Togwotee Mountain Lodge, P.O. Box 91, Moran, WY 83013, 800-543-2847.

Located just two miles south of Yellowstone National Park, Flagg Ranch Snowmobile Tours delivers guided and unguided trips into Yellowstone, with transportation from town and Teton Village available. Included in package tours are appropriate outer clothing, insurance, park entrance fees, and your first tank of gas. Discount packages and snowcoach adventures are also available. Flagg Ranch 800-443-2311.

Old Faithful Snowmobile Tours creates first-class excursions within Yellowstone National Park. Day trips include ground transfers, breakfast, lunch, outer clothing, and top quality snowmobiles. Four-day itineraries incorporate all the major attractions of Yellowstone National Park, in addition to gourmet meals and rustic lodging.

Old Faithful Snowmobile Tours, Box 7182, Jackson, WY 83002, 800-253-7130.

Rocky Mountain Snowmobile Tours outfits everyone from beginner to expert for daily or overnight tours through deep powder or on packed trails. Miles of unsurpassed landscape waiting to be explored promise a memorable winter vacation in either Yellowstone or the Jackson Hole area. Continental breakfast, lunch, and snowmobile clothing come as part of the package. Group rates are offered, too.

Rocky Mountain Snowmobile Tours, Box 820, Jackson, WY 83001, 800-647-2561.

Fort Jackson Snowmobile Tours offers complete package, custom trips filled with lots of off-trail riding for half or full days or overnight.

Fort Jackson Snowmobile Tours, Box 1176, Jackson, WY 83001, 800-735-8430.

Cache Creek Snowmobile Tours, Box 7014, Jackson, WY 83002, 307-733-4743, heads out to Granite Hot Springs, Togwotee Pass, or into Yellowstone with custom trips available.

Others include National Parks Adventures at 800-255-1572, High Country Snowmobile Tours at 800-542-0130, Wyoming Adventures at 800-673-7147, Elk Ridge Snowmobiles at 307-733-1450, and Yellowstone Snowmobile Tours at 800-558-0063.

Information

Maps outlining the region's trail systems are available at the Parks and Recreation office in Teton County Courthouse at 181 South King Street or reach them at Jackson-Teton County Parks and Recreation, Teton County Courthouse, Box 1727, Jackson, WY 83001, 307-733-4340.

For Continental Divide trail information and maps, contact the Wyoming Continental Divide Snowmobile Trail Association, 240 Lincoln, Lander, WY 82520, (307) 332-2224.

For the latest trail condition information, call the Wyoming Recreation Commission HOTLINE at (307) 777-6503.

Section Six

Culture in the Hole

1

Jackson Hole Art and Artists

The Teton Range has enticed artists to draw, sketch, paint, and photograph its abrupt, jagged, often cloud-enshrouded lines since the mid-1800s when artists and later photographers accompanied expeditions and fur traders into this valley.

Currently Jackson sports over forty galleries, offering art for any taste and price range. Many carry the works of local artists. A great way to learn about what's available and to meet gallery owners and the artists whose work they carry is to take the annual mid-September Gallery Walk, a self-guided tour of the downtown area.

The Galleries

Five local artists' work are represented at the Center Street Gallery, in addition to pieces from all over the world. Owners Beth and Jamie Overcast feature bold, modern portraits of the West. Stylized, rough-looking bronze horses vie with regional craftsman Denny Simpson's unique inlaid wood furniture. Very modern beadwork contrasts Indian motifs, and pet lovers can take home a comic moose fisherman or a pig cowboy.

Beth has been in Jackson for twenty-five years, the last eight at the gallery. She suggests matching art to personality. "Art really enhances life, and there is art here for every taste."

Center Street Gallery, 172 Center St., P.O. Box 4049, Jackson, WY 83001, 307-733-1115, fax 307-733-1192.

The Silverthorn began during 1994 and presents the work of local landscape artist Robert Rudd. They also feature bronze, sculpture, and stylized Indian art such as ink drawings on elk hides.

Silverthorn Gallery, 20 W. Broadway, P.O. Box 7958, Jackson, WY, 83002, 307-733-8708.

Images of Nature Gallery holds Tom Mangelsen's photos from around the world, representing the serious to the outrageously funny in wildlife and nature photography. Mangelsen's polar bear "Bad Boys of the Arctic" poster is one of his most popular.

Images of Nature Gallery, 170 N. Cache, P.O. Box 2935, Jackson, WY, 83001, 307-733-9752.

New West carries Thomas Molesworth style furniture, Danny Edwards bronzes, Bob Haper oil paintings of the Tetons, and photo gravaure plates of Western historic photos (like the ones seen at the National Wildlife Art Museum, Chapter 4 of this section), from 1918 through the 1930s, and moose antler wing chairs.

New West 125 N. Cache, P.O. Box 3658, Jackson, WY, 83001, 307-733-5490.

The Martin-Harris Gallery features baskets designed by local weaver Susan Stone and Jan Lindsley's 3-D watercolors (see below) all on Native American themes.

Martin-Harris Gallery, 60 E. Broadway, P.O. Box 3987, Jackson, WY, 83001, 307-733-0350.

Several local artists display their work at the Moynihan Gallery. Katharine Wipfler's ranch scenes and landscapes in oil hang in handmade frames decorated with gold leaf. Jean Halverson paints Western lifestyle watercolors. Kay Northup uses oils while her husband, George, utilizes bronze to portray the sporting life of Jackson Hole, including a life-size fisherman with a casting rod and black Lab at his side. Sara Mossman Victoria DuPont's jewelry and the glassware of blower Laurie Thal round out the local talent.

Moynihan Gallery, 126 E. Broadway, P.O. Box 3477, Jackson, WY, 83001, 307-733-0870.

The Shadow Mountain Gallery features oil painter Richard Miles's Wyoming summer landscapes. Miles likes to backpack in the Winds and the Tetons and uses what he sees as inspiration for his paintings.

Shadow Mountain Gallery, 10 W. Broadway, P.O. Box 1677, Jackson, WY, 83001, 307-733-3162. 800-726-1803.

Since 1978 Light Reflections has revealed the photos of local photographer Fred Joy. His "Cathedrals" of the Tetons' most famous grouping remains a popular portrayal of photogenic Jackson Hole, as does "Lupin Panorama," "Moulton Barn," "Tetons and Aspens," "Thunderhead Farm Country" and "Sea of Flowers" to name but a few of the 400 color and 250 black-and-white images found at Light Reflections.

Light Reflections, 35 E. Deloney, P.O. Box 1681, Jackson, WY, 83001, 307-733-4016, 800-346-5223.

Buffalo Trails carries three local artists. Scott Nickell captures the West's past in bronze (see below). Gail Moore creates impressionistic watercolors of the Tetons and other area scenes. Mark Mansanarez draws from the abundance of the valley's wildlife to produce accurately detailed paintings.

Buffalo Trails Galleries, 98 Center St., P.O. Box 1447, Jackson, WY, 83001, 307-733-1457.

Jack Dennis' Wyoming Gallery features the Wyoming oils of Ruth Rawhouser, in addition to pottery created in Wilson and unique woodcarved trout, kilim rugs, and handcrafted canoes.

Jack Dennis' Wyoming Gallery, 50 E. Broadway, P.O. Box 3369, Jackson, WY, 83001, 307-733-7548.

Under the Willow Photo Gallery features the stunning work of wildlife and landscape photographer Abi Garaman, Jackson's current mayor. His Moulton Barn photos are some of his most popular and best known.

Under the Willow Photo Gallery, 50 S. Cache, P.O. Box 36, Jackson, WY 83001, 307-733-6633.

Jackson Area Artists

Scott Nickell, always fascinated with bronze, attended a workshop in 1988 and produced his first piece—a cowboy with a branding iron which Scott refers to as a "boat anchor." But he was hooked. His next piece, "Strikes at Night," a Blackfoot warrior of which Scott made a limited edition of twenty-four plus the proof, sold out in eleven days. The woman companion piece, "Waterbird," sold out in two weeks. Scott takes advantage of the extensive Native American collection at the Buffalo Bill Historic Center in Cody, Wyoming, to research the detail that brings life to figures such as his "Araphoe Ghost Dancer" and his "Wild and Wooly" cowgirl decked out in a pair of woolly chaps.

Jan Lindsay turns molded rag paper and watercolors into three-dimensional visions of Native American culture. Lindsay, a Jackson resident since 1985, makes an annual pilgrimage to the Colter Bay Indian Arts Museum in Grand Teton National Park (see Chapter 4 of this section) each autumn to study the exhibits and get inspired. "I've always been fascinated with everything Indian," she admits. "And I want to push the limits." This she does by painting the paper sculptures she creates to make them appear like tanned leather, beadwork, and fringe.

Katharine Wipfler believes in painting from the source. Her landscapes depict ranch life directly from her own experiences of putting up hay, cow punching, and "cowboying" on area ranches since 1978. "I work from the soul rather than from a picture, and I've learned here from the people who do the work." Kathy lives in a log cabin near Flat Creek, and regardless of what the weather decides to do, she sets up her easel and paints the scenes of everyday living around Jackson Hole and the parks.

Kay Northrup started painting and drawing at an early age. An accomplished cartoonist and designer in stained and etched glass, oils have remained her main focus. From her home near the Snake River, the outdoors provides a large influence on her work. So do the people of Jackson Hole. "They are wonderful resources for learning." The area's natural beauty also inspires Kay's work. "Everything is so direct with color. It comes by being in this part of the world. The colors are so clear here, the light strong. This affects my use of colors."

2

Dance and Drama

When you mention dancing in connection with the West, types such as country swing and line or square dancing come instantly to mind, and you can certainly find all those forms in Jackson Hole. As an example, the Million Dollar Cowboy Bar invites you to participate in their free Western Swing dance lessons every Thursday night between 7:30 and 9:00 p.m. taught by the Dancers' Workshop. Then there's more traditional forms.

Dancers' Workshop and the Three Rivers Dance Company

Just like something out of a folk tale, the Dancers' Workshop (DW) began in 1972 as simple dance classes taught in a log cabin. Today creativity can be explored through formal educational programs for Ballroom and Country Western dancing, classes for children and adults or events such as the spring Barn Dance held at the Teton County Fair Building and the annual July Arts on the Hill Summer Dance Festival. This month-long series of workshops and performances are held in DW's tent set up at the bottom of Snow King Mountain. Kids Hour from 6:00 to 7:00 p.m. precedes Thursday, Friday, and Saturday evening's performances. Puppeteers, storytellers, and dancers amuse and delight. So pack up some deli sandwiches and a blanket for a picnic to enjoy while you sample local and regional dance and music.

If strutin' your stuff is not for you, get tickets to a performance of the Three Rivers Dance Company, DW's professional touring group.

For information or tickets, contact the Dancers' Workshop, 49 W. Broadway, P.O. Box 1500, Jackson WY 83001, 307-733-3810.

Jackson Hole Playhouse

The Jackson Hole Playhouse building, constructed in 1916, really sets the stage for Jackson's oldest original live theatre. Old West theme Broadway shows like *Seven Brides for Seven Brothers*, *Paint Your Wagon*, and *Unsinkable Molly Brown* contribute "good musical theatre for a family experience," insists Scott Finck, the playhouse manager, an actor, and whatever else is needed at the time. "We keep it light, simple, and heartfelt. The Jackson Hole Playhouse is a place where families can have fun together."

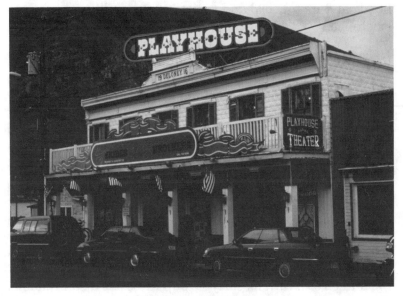

The Jackson Hole Playhouse.

Photo Credit: Sierra Adare

Back in 1959 Paula Jeffries, staying with friends Ed and Vera Cheney, came up with the idea of a live theatre for Jackson. At the time gambling had just been truly shut down, leaving visitors and locals little to do during the cool to downright cold evening hours. So the three of them turned the forty-three-year-old building into the "Pink Garter Theatre."

Jeffries actually wanted to name the playhouse the "Red Garter," but Vera suggested that might be too risqué. (Remember the conservative time frame here.) As soon as their premier play opened, Ken Booth's melodrama *Brother Against Brother*, the playhouse of live theatre was a hit. People loved to hiss the villain and cheer the hero. (They still do. Which is why the playhouse is so much fun.)

In 1969 Jeffries pulled out of the old building, taking the "Pink Garter" name with her. Thus the Jackson Hole Playhouse and its musical and variety show tradition came into existence.

After the 1995 season the playhouse started renovations to create another first for Jackson Hole—a dinner theatre. They plan to feed 150 people and perform two shows nightly.

Sarsaparilla and popcorn add a warm welcome to the nineteenth-century lobby (or parlor as they call it, and it does resemble one)—complete with the building's original tin ceiling. Tintypes of actors who have performed at the playhouse over the years line the hall leading to the auditorium, including one labeled "Conway Twitty."

Hobnob with the actors at the pre-show, filled with singing and at times even a talking moose, bighorn sheep, and antelope (whose heads hang on the lobby walls). You have to see them! Performances take place every Monday through Saturday between Memorial Day and Labor Day.

Make reservations early. Group rates are also available. Contact the Jackson Hole Playhouse, 145 W. Deloney, P.O. Box 2788, Jackson, WY 83001, 307-733-6994.

Dirty Jack's Wild West Theatre

Built in 1929, Dirty Jack's Wild West Theatre started out as the Rainbow Theatre, also known as the Rainbow Dance Hall. The lobby still contains the old greasepaint feel (and smell!), maybe because of the squeaking floorboards muffled by well-worn carpet. Or maybe it's the popcorn, corn dogs, and fudge puppies at the concession stand where the cost of said goodies changes "according to attitude of customer."

As you may have guessed, Dirty Jack's, around more or less in its present form since 1972, serves up a platter full of original, slightly off-color, good ol' western style humor. "It's all slapstick and old, old jokes," says Dirty Jack actor Tom DeWester. "Fans of the Beverly Hillbillies to the Three Stooges will love Dirty Jack's."

Kathy Stainbrook writes a new show each year, so there's always something different to keep you laughing. Or as Tom explains, "You can come in in the worst mood and guaranteed you'll leave happy."

Dirty Jack's seats 350 per night between June 1 and Labor Day, starting at 7:30 p.m. The show lasts two hours, and seats fill up fast. It's a good idea to get reservations.

Dirty Jack's Wild West Theatre, 140 North Cache, 307-733-4775.

3

Jackson Hole's Writers

A "sense of place" means more to a writer than just the setting for the story, novel, play, or poem. Often, the place where authors actually do their writing influences what they write. And a few even swear it affects how well they write. Just as the Tetons have inspired generations of artists, the Hole's atmosphere, or maybe the altitude, emancipates the creativity of the written word.

Owen Wister

The summer before Owen Wister was to enter law school, his health took a bad turn. His physician, Dr. S. Weir Mitchell, advised Wister to come West, and it changed the course of his life. Wister's trip in 1885, the first of many, not only helped him regain his health, but stirred his imagination. The result would be a revolution in Western fiction. Wister's novel *The Virginian* pulled the Western genre out of the "dime novel" state and placed it in the modern mainstream.

Owen Wister (the one pouring from the flask) on his research trip through Jackson Hole. The people, lifestyles, and terrain Wister came across became the story of The Virginian.

Photo Credit: Teton County Historical Society

In the preface of the 1928 collectors edition of *The Virginian*, Wister claimed his main character developed out of a composite of several men. However, he told his daughter Fanny Kemble Wister of a man he met only once at a stagecoach overnight stop his first night in Wyoming on his first trip to the state—a man with a Virginian's gentle voice and manners.

As a side note, according to another daughter, Frances Stokes, the only known pencil manuscript pages (two in all) of *The Virginian* still in existence are housed at the University of Wyoming in Laramie along with Wister's pencil-written diaries of his life in Wyoming.

Wister actually did become an attorney, being admitted to the bar in 1889. However, the bug to write had definitely bitten Wister while in Wyoming, and by 1891 he started his writing career. His first novel, *Jim McLean*, came out in 1897 and the celebrated *The Virginian* during 1902. Produced as a play, *The Virginian* ran for 138 performances. Cecil B. DeMille turned it into a movie in 1914. Nine years later a new movie version appeared, produced by the Preferred Picture Company (and again in 1929, 1935, and 1946). *The Virginian* then became a long-running TV series for NBC between 1962 and 1970.

In a letter Frances wrote on January 29, 1958, she talked about living in Wyoming. In it, she described coming to Jackson Hole with her parents, sister, and brothers during the summers of 1911 and 1912. "In 1912 we built a 2 story log cabin in the 100 acre ranch my Father bought not far from the JY." Supposedly Wister used the cabin as a summer home for many years.

Jackson Hole Writers Conference

The University of Wyoming offers an annual four-day writers conference in Jackson Hole every July. The conference features leading authors of fiction, nonfiction, and screenplays, as well as editors, publishers, and agents. Workshops guide participants through sessions that focus on story structure, character development, narration, plus various business aspects of writing. Drawing from a diverse group of the guest speakers, panelists, and faculty, the Jackson Hole Writers Conference imparts information valuable to writers at every skill level.

Furthermore, the faculty, comprised of authors who live in the Jackson Hole area, encourage participants to submit a fifteen-page sample of writing for evaluation. Manuscripts are then critiqued in a one-on-one session. Or for an additional fee, up to forty pages of a book manuscripts can be submitted for an hour-long, detailed one-on-one discussion with a professional writer.

College credit and scholarships are available from the University of Wyoming.

Contact the University of Wyoming, Office of Conferences and Institutes, P.O. Box 3972, Laramie, WY 82071-3972, 307-766-2124 phone, 307-766-3914 fax.

Modern Authors Carry on the Past

Robert M. Utley, renowned Western historian, moved to Jackson Hole in 1992. Winner of numerous awards for his Western nonfiction, including two National Cowboy Hall of Fame's Wranglers and a Western Writers of America's Owen Wister Award (which recognizes a lifetime of achievement), Utley knows the West, present and past. Among his titles are *The Lance and the Shield: The Life and Times of Sitting Bull*; *Billy the Kid: A Short and Violent Life*; *Cavalier in Buckskin: George Armstrong Custer and the Western Military Frontier*; *The Indian Frontier of the American West, 1846-1890*; and *The Last Days of the Sioux Nation*.

Yet Utley's connection to the West even exceeds this tiny listing of his work. He spent twenty-three years with the Park Service, serving in the capacity of historian, a director of the Office of Archaeology and Historic Preservation and as a deputy executive director on the President's Advisory Council on Historical Preservation, prior to retiring to write full time.

He has this to say about Jackson Hole and how it affects how and what he writes:

"Jackson is a tourist mecca thirteen miles down the road, a place of motels, boutiques, art galleries, and upscale restaurants. The entire valley, as enclosed by mountains on all sides, is 'Jackson's Hole,' one of a number so configured named by or for trappers of the fur-trade era. Since I am writing about mountain men—about their contributions to geographical knowledge and national expansion—Jackson Hole is a fitting place to live. We live in a big log house built by the CCC in 1933, and so I look over the top of my computer at the Grand Teton herself. That is very fitting and very inspirational, but for a historian the place is close to crippling in its lack of a university library closer than Utah State at Logan. The Teton County Library in Jackson is very helpful in securing interlibrary loans, but that is no substitute for the University of Texas Library I accessed in a 45-minute drive before we came here. On the other hand, I could not have written this book elsewhere because it depends on a thorough command of the heartland of the Rocky Mountain fur trade, which also happens to be the most complex geography in the United States. Three years here have enabled me to master these mountains, passes, and rivers, and how they go together to form the stage on which my mountain men acted out their roles.

"Fortune smiled when we came here. Despite the lack of an adequate library, drama and stage set came together with fine timing.

"I suppose I started writing for the reason most writers start: they like to see their names in print. From that initial motivation, I progressed in addition to the desire to reach as large a reading audience as possible with history that is also a good read. That remains my principal goal as a writer. It produces satisfaction and, if one is lucky, a modest financial return.

"As for the National Park Service, I was principally a central-office bureaucrat. I began with the Service in 1947 at Custer Battlefield, which then had an administrative connection with Yellowstone. As Chief Historian and later Assistant Director in Washington, my responsibilities encompassed all the units of the National Park System where historical values were present, and of course that included Yellowstone and Grand Teton. For example, I well recall the battle, about 1967, to save the last soldier station in Yellowstone from the wrecker's ball. It is now the ranger museum at Norris. But not until I came actually to live here, and without any official duties to distract me, did I come truly to appreciate both these parks."

Ann Kreilkamp moved to Jackson Hole in 1982. Holding a Ph.D. in philosophy, she has over sixty published essays and has founded three publications. *OpenSpace*, a community magazine of full, free individual expression, ran from 1978 through 1980. From 1982 to 1984 she published *Heartland*, a networking journal for peace activists in the "Deep West" which grew out of a tri-state (Wyoming, Idaho, and Montana) peace conference held when then President Ronald Reagan wanted to house MX missiles in Wyoming. This publication promoted her move to Wyoming as it provided a central place to network the region by car. Then since 1989 *Crone Chronicles* has presented the voices of women who are consciously coming of age, or as Kreilkamp defines it, "We are shifting from an exclusively biological understanding of being female to one which speaks to the mind and heart and soul."

Kreilkamp shares a different perspective on Jackson Hole and its effect on her life and work:

"I've lived in the Jackson area since the fall of 1982, and in Kelly most of that time in a 20-food diameter yurt in a yurt community which exists in the middle of Kelly, directly across from the Grand Teton. My husband, Jeffrey Joel, joined me in 1990, and together we also run the Jackson Holistic Center in Jackson.

"All the little towns in the Hole have their own peculiar atmospheres. Kelly is more remote than the others (except for Moran), and seems to be a place which attracts reclusive artists and thinkers.

"I find that living in this valley affects my mental and spiritual work enormously. I love living in high mountain valleys. I write almost continuously here. My focus is not so much on writing as it is on ideas. I have long felt that new ideas are seeded here in the headwaters of the mountains; that they are then disseminated and popularized along the coasts."

Tradition of Storytelling

The Snake River Institute (details in Chapter 5 of this section) celebrates western writing through readings and discussion groups. The public meets, listens to, and gets to know local and regional authors. (More about their programs in Chapter 6 of this section.)

4

Museums

As you have seen in previous sections, Jackson Hole's history connects not only the area's past to its present and future, but forms the life's blood of the valley. Therefore, museums play an important and growing role in the Hole. Area museums also offer bite-size (or should that be byte?) information that gives visitors a more overall understanding of the community and life found in Jackson.

Grizzly Discovery Center and Bear Sanctuary

With the westward migration the grizzly bear's habitat started shrinking until only one percent remained. Grizzly bear numbers went from approximately 100,000 down to today's figure of less than 900, with eighty-five percent of current death rates attributed to humans.

The Grizzly Discovery Center and the International Grizzly Fund, a nonprofit organization, seek to preserve the grizzly in the wild through education, research, and "ground-level" bear projects.

Teaching tools available to schools around the country and tours of the Discover Center, help kids realize bears aren't monsters that kill every human they come across. Nor are they cuddly pets to toss tidbits to (or worse such as a case where some incredibly ignorant tourists smeared jelly on their hand trying to get bears to lick them!)

In addition, researchers investigate ways to enhance the grizzlies' lives and habitat and study bear genetics and behavior. As a result, the International Grizzly Fund purchases bear-proof dumpsters and food containers and provides them to campgrounds in bear areas in an effort to circumvent conflicts between bears and humans over careless storage of food and trash.

The Grizzly Bear Center and bear sanctuary is located at the west entrance of Yellowstone in West Yellowstone, Montana, where visitors can see grizzlies in a natural setting while learning about bear preservation. It's open year round. Contact it and the International Grizzly Fund at P.O. Box 856, West Yellowstone, MT 59758, 1-800-257-2570.

Colter Bay Indian Arts Museum

Located at the Colter Bay Visitor Center in Grand Teton National Park, the Colter Bay Indian Arts Museum displays an impressive, if small, collection of Native American relics that offer insights into the daily lives of many Indian cultures. Laurance S. Rockefeller and the Jackson Hole Preserve, Inc. assembled the collection and donated it to the museum. The museum also houses the David T. Vernon Collection of moccasins, baskets, shields, and pipes.

Artistically arranged and displayed, the artifacts date back to early contact between Plains Indians and whites. Wood walls have been silk-screened with enlarged historic

Indian portrait photos called "photomurals." The wood and plexiglass panels were coated with photo chemicals and handled like huge sheets of photo paper and developed by temporarily tacking strips along the edges of each sheet to act as a "pan" for the developing solutions.

Although a bit lean on interpretive information, it's a good idea to take a ranger-led museum tour to get the most out of the museum. Exhibits include many items not commonly seen in museums, making it well worth your time.

Check out the beaver and muskrat pelts (with the heads and fur still on) sewn into bags. They mingle with Bandolier shoulder bags. A feathered dance bustle from 1875 makes you want to start keeping step with the Native American flute music playing in the background. The moccasin display includes a pair with beaded soles and sandals designed by natives of Seneca, New York.

Shields with deer and antelope dew claw decorations, an Apache headdress from 1885, a Hopi boomerang for rabbit hunting, an 1880 Chippewa war club, an antler-handle knife with beaded sheath depict the hunter/warrior's life as well as a hunt and dance scene painted on an elk hide in 1915 by Charles Washakie, son of the famous Shoshone peace chief.

The downstairs section also contains a craft demonstration area where you can learn more about beading and basketry.

Located half a mile from the Colter Bay Junction on Highway 89, 191, and 287, the Colter Bay Museum is free and open daily from mid-May through October 1 (unless the weather has other ideas). For exact hours, contact the Grand Teton National Park, Moose, WY 83012, 307-739-3594.

Jackson Hole Museum

From age seven when W.C. "Slim" Lawrence discovered a trade token at the old abandoned Fort Sanders near his home in Laramie City, Wyoming, he started collecting artifacts and relics of the Old West. Later, this love of history led

Lawrence to co-found the Jackson Hole Museum in 1958 with Homer Richards, a Jackson businessman who donated the building.

Reorganized as a private nonprofit foundation in 1981, the museum today houses and displays items dating back to prehistoric times with a collection of hunter-gatherer stone tools and utensils. The Native American room also contains rare Sheepeater artifacts; Plains Indian ceremonial dresses; trade beads, including "Pony Beads" made of Venetian glass found at trading posts between the eighteenth and nineteenth centuries; cookware; tools and Indian saddles which show Spanish influence in the design of the high horn front and rear.

A "Touch Me" Mountain Man display, featuring hides, a very heavy hunting rifle (how would you like to tote that around the mountains?), animal horns, and an incredibly soft beaver pelt, encourages discovery of the trappings of the fur-trading era of the 1800s. Fur Trade artifacts date from 1810 to 1840 and include firearms, knives, traps, and tools.

A re-created room of the Moosehead Ranch, with its assortment of lodgepole furniture from the Fred and Eva Topping Collection, suggests life on a Wyoming ranch. Cowboy saddles, woolly chaps, hobbles, bits, spurs, and Boone and Crookett record-holding game heads help tell the West's story.

Open from the end of May until the end of September, the Jackson Hole Museum seeks to preserve and interpret the area's rich history. It is located on the corner of Glenwood and Deloney, P.O. Box 1005, Jackson, WY 83001, 307-733-2414.

Murie Memorial Museum

Currently part of the Teton Science School, the Murie Museum contains the extensive natural history collection that belonged to the world renowned naturalists and field biologists Adolph, Olaus J., and Mardy Murie. (More on the

Muries in Section Nine.) Believing as Adolph did that "life is richest where the greatest diversity exists in a natural order," the Muries devoted their lives to the study of North American mammals and birds.

Cited for its historical and biological value, the Murie Collection embodies the kind of field work the Muries did. Over 1,000 mammal study skulls and skins and 600 birds, a number of them rare specimens, allow today's researchers the chance to probe our natural world. Also in the collection are the samples of the bird and mammal scat and tracks Olaus used in compiling *A Field Guide to Animal Tracks*, first published in 1954.

The Murie Museum is free to the public, but you need to call ahead to arrange an appointment to tour the facility. It's situated eighteen miles north of Jackson, off Highway 26, 89, and 187 at the Teton Science School, P.O. Box 68, Kelly, WY 83001, 307-733-4765 phone, 307-739-9388 fax.

National Wildlife Art Museum

The National Museum of Wildlife Art provides year-round multidisciplinary education opportunities for adults and children, promoting education through art. Focusing on first-rate-quality wildlife-related art, the museum also develops and maintains high-quality educational interpretive programs and exhibits through the presentation of its own collections, the use of visiting scholars or artists, and by presenting appropriate temporary exhibits acquired from other sources.

Over a thirty-year period, museum founders Mr. and Mrs. William G. Kerr developed a collection of wildlife art unsurpassed in the U.S., which formed the beginning of the museum in 1987 with 250 works of art. The collection consisted predominantly of images of large mammals native to the American West. By the end of 1992 the museum had outgrown its gallery (where the Gun Barrel Restaurant is now). In 1994 a new facility opened in the current location across from the National Elk Refuge. It contains twelve exhibition galleries, an interactive gallery for children, two full-sized classrooms, a 200-seat auditorium, gift shop, cafe, member's lounge, curatorial/conservation laboratory, library/archives, painting and sculpture storage and exhibit holdings, development and administrative spaces.

Four major groups of artists are represented in the collection—explorer artists, romanticists, illustrators, and modernists. The permanent collection contains a well-balanced mixture of nineteenth- and twentieth-century masters. Media include oil, bronze, acrylic, watercolor, gouache, pastel, lithography, and charcoal.

The museum currently displays 1,327 pieces in its permanent collection, dating from 1819 to the present. More than 100 artists depict western wildlife, including: Titian Ramsey Peale, George Catline, Karl Bodmer, Albert Bierstadt, Antoine-Louise Barye, John J. Audubon, Richard Friese, John Clymer, Charles Russell, Carl Rungius, Bob Kuhn, and Alfred Jacob Miller.

The JKM Collection in the JKM Gallery forms the core of the museum's holding and includes all major North American large mammal species. Robert Bateman's acrylic "The Challenge Bull Moose" offers a perfect depiction of how a moose poses prior to charging with his ears laid back and his massive head down. (If you're in the wilds and come across a moose and it presents this behavior, BEWARE!)

The Rungius Gallery features the second largest public collection of Carl Rungius's work in the world. It also includes his only two known triptychs, the only two bronzes completed during his career, and one of the few complete sets of his drypoints in existence. Rungius (1869-1959) became the first artist of note to focus on wildlife, creating the preeminent record of big game in the first half of the twentieth century. His "The Days of Bison Millions" hung in Jackson Lake Lodge and was commissioned by the New York Zoological Society.

The John Clymer Studio, donated in 1991 by Doris Clymer and the Clymer family, shows a representation of the artist's studio complete with reference books, notebooks of pen and ink "doodles," studio props such as Indian clothing and western saddles, a buffalo hide covered chair, a bear hide rug with head attached, and approximately 200 artifacts collected over his lifetime.

The American Bison Gallery, originally assembled as a traveling exhibit for the 1990 Wyoming Centennial and viewed by over 100,000 people, now contains a permanent installation of over 100 images which chronicle the dramatic cultural changes that occurred from the sixteenth through the nineteenth centuries. The paintings in this collection pull you through the rise, the fall, and the rebirth of the American bison and shouldn't be missed. In William Jacob Hays's "Prairie Fire and Buffalo Stampede" you can almost smell the smoke.

The Dellenback Collection includes fifty aquatints and etchings by Swiss artist Karl Bodmer, 284 books, limited edition monographs, periodicals and catalogs pertaining to the history and art of the American West, all donated to the archives.

The Children's Gallery houses a self-guided discovery center where kids can learn about animals through exhibits where they can touch large game animal hides, see plaster casts of hoof print, wonder at scat encased in clear plastic, and feel animals' survival tools—skulls, horns, antlers, and teeth.

Innovative educational and scholarly programs provided by the museum emphasize art appreciation, art history, natural science, creative writing, and American history.

In addition, the museum hosts two school programs. One is "There's Art to Education" which serves Teton County schools. Its twenty lessons are designed for a specific grade level and usually include a pre-visit by the Curator of Education to the classroom, a museum visit by the class, and post-visit activity. "Pathways—Increasing Environmental

Literacy Through Art," written in cooperation with Teton Science School, is a ten-unit program providing teachers with new ways to integrate science and the arts.

In December 1994 the museum began a unique relationship with the National Elk Refuge, providing space for their interpretive center during winter months when up to 10,000 elk reside on the refuge. This collaboration with the refuge helps serve the educational missions of both organizations.

The National Museum of Wildlife Art is located at 2820 Rungius Road, P.O. Box 6825, Jackson, WY 83002, 307-733-5771 phone, 307-733-5787 fax.

Teton County Historical Center

Open year round on weekdays, the Teton County Historical Center offers rare insight into Jackson Hole's past. The archives includes a 2,200-volume Historical Research library, recordings of local oral history, microfilm of Jackson Hole newspapers (including early issues of the area's first paper, the *Jackson's Hole Courier*) and over 6,000 historic photographs taken from as early as the 1870s.

Historical collections include the John E. Weida Trade Bead, Plains Indians, and early settlement artifacts.

The Teton County Historical Center is located in a historic log cabin on the corner of Glenwood and Mercill. For research assistance or general information about the center, write P.O. Box 1005, Jackson, WY 83001, 307-733-9605.

Wax Museum of Old Wyoming

Since its opening in 1968, the Wax Museum of Old Wyoming has offered sixty life-size realistic figures set in twenty-seven scenes that depict major events and personalities in Wyoming's history. They were five years in the making, and sculptor Kenneth R. Bunn spent eighteen months researching the people and additional months on authentic clothing. (Check out Bunn's life-size bronze cougar titled "Silent Pursuit" at the National Museum of Wildlife Art.)

Even the settings required months of work, locating and collecting the props and household items that lend the realism to each display. The circa 1880s operating table used in the "Big Nose George Parrot" scene, a favorite of kids, turned out to be one of the harder pieces to acquire.

The murals that offset the outdoor settings took renowned western landscape artists five years to complete. They bring scenes like the "Buffalo Hunt" and Fred Hudson's backdrop of the "Green River Rendezvous" to vivid life.

The scenes portray an eerie likeness to reality, but even with the addition of the audio tape that's available at the front desk to further explain the scenes, the information isn't as complete as it could be.

The Wax Museum of Old Wyoming is open year round and is located at 55 S. Cache Street, Jackson, WY 83001, 307-733-3112.

5

School's Outdoors

School time in Jackson Hole around the turn of the century meant walking or riding a horse to a community-built log cabin big enough to serve multiple purposes. The Wolff Schoolhouse (so named because the nearest family was the Wolffs), constructed in 1909, was roomy enough for dancing or other gatherings of the community.

The "playground" consisted of a cleared patch of dirt beside the building. Popular games included hopscotch, marbles, pop-the-whip, and races. Boys chased girls, scaring them with water snakes they captured down by the river.

No school cooked and served lunches in those days. Kids made their own, carrying home-baked breads, cookies, cakes, and homemade cheese to class. Some of the children brought bottles or jars of fresh milk. An unusual favorite was pancakes spread with lard and pepper sprinkled on top. (And we used to complain about peanut butter and jelly!)

As summer approaches in modern Jackson Hole, nature throws open the classroom windows and lets the fresh air in, and the Hole world becomes the classrooms—as diverse as the landscape itself. In every discipline imaginable, historians, ecologists, naturalists, wranglers, authors, and artists teach everything from one-day workshops and hikes to weeks in the field to year-round residency programs. In addition to the incredible scenery and intriguing subject matter, many courses offer the extra bonus of honest-to-goodness college credit!

Following in the traditions (and some literally in the very footsteps) of the Hole's early explorers, the area offers a variety of schools that use the mountains, rivers, and valleys as the classroom. Students from the very young to the life-long learners can experience the vastness of meadows, aspen groves, mountains, and wilderness of the great outdoors.

Snake River Institute

Started in 1988, the Snake River Institute provides "learning adventures," as they call them, which delve into the cultures and communities unique to the American West—present and past. Based out of the historic Hardeman Ranch at the foot of Teton Pass (seven miles west of Jackson, off Highway 22), the "classrooms" consist of a large wall tent and red barns at the edge of hay meadows. Between early May and the end of September, the institute presents over fifty one-day seminars and evening programs geared toward all age groups, eighteen three- to five-day courses for adults and fifteen for kids ranging in age from six to fifteen. Classes are kept small, usually no more than fifteen, with an average of about six to eight.

Executive director Libby Crews states, "We choose our instructors from a national pool not only for their academic qualifications, but for their passion for the subjects they teach, and for their ability to infuse their classes with their enthusiasm. Many of them have grown up and worked in the West; all of them have a special affinity for it."

Amid this splendor, students learn how to read the Jackson Hole valley by wandering through fur trappers' journals, British lords and ladies' travelogues, and Easterners' Western adventure books, as well as visiting the actual historical locations which inspired these writings.

Naturalists and nature writers help workshop attenders discover the Hole's distinctive environment. Shoshone Indians demonstrate the ancient art of conversational Indian sign language and Native American dance styles, as well as Shoshone and Arapaho music, attire, techniques, and spiritual significance. Geologists expose the stories compressed in Wyoming's rocks. Wander back in time on one of Jackson's historic dude ranches with a guide or explore the irony of Indian cowboys.

The Snake River Institute also challenges kids between the ages of six and fifteen with "activity driven" courses. Ranging from two- to five-day programs, the institute encourages children to develop and integrate a variety of new skills and techniques through group participation, self-expression, investigation, and inquiry in classes with a maximum of fifteen students each. Imagine learning how to pan for gold or ride the range in a covered wagon, designing leathercrafts or churning ice cream for a "social" all as part of a course named Frontier Fun.

They also teach fly fishing, field sketching, outdoor cooking, mountain biking, horse sense, painting with plants, old-fashioned log home building, drama, and Native American folktales and dance.

Other courses available throughout the Rocky Mountain region let students retrace the history of the Upper Missouri River and the fur trade that connects it to Jackson's Hole, see the development of Cody, Wyoming's distinctive western furniture, ride Wyoming rails, and experience Shoshone and Arapaho tribal life on the Wind River Reservation.

Scholarships, college and recertification credit, and work-study opportunities all abound at the institute.

Snake River Institute, P.O. Box 128, Wilson, WY 83014, 307-733-2214 phone, 307-739-1710 fax.

Teton Science School

Located eighteen miles north of Jackson on Highway 26, 89, and 187 in Grand Teton National Park, the Teton Science School has functioned since 1967 as an independent, nonprofit center. With a maximum of twelve students per class, the school remains devoted to teaching people of all ages the joys of experiential natural science in the Greater Yellowstone Ecosystem—one of the largest intact natural resource areas left in the lower forty-eight states.

Providing an outdoor education to over 4,000 individuals each year, this year-round school focuses on both residential and nonresidential programs for adults, as well as scheduling short "Explorer Seminars" which get people out into the field for one- to three-day trips between June and September. They also offer week-long "Nature of Jackson Hole" seminars with the option to drop in for a single day of the course. Private nature tours can also be arranged, guided by seasoned instructors specializing in photography, astronomy, bird-watching, and natural history.

Once a dude ranch, the campus sits on the edge of open grasslands where wildlife, including the largest bull elks you'll ever encounter in your entire life, wander, seeking forage. In the field, the students use the hands-on approach to learning. Classes emphasize concepts of ecology and perspectives particular to the Greater Yellowstone region.

An interesting learning opportunity arose after a lightning strike ignited a grass fire not far from the school in the autumn of 1994. Since then, students have experienced

Nature's regeneration process in the wake of the four-day fire that scorched 3,403 acres of sage, forest, and grasslands adjacent to the school, and destroyed the historic homestead site of one of Jackson Hole's early settlers, Joe Pfeifer.

Walks on the wild side include seminars on Yellowstone's bears or wolves, wildflowers, Jackson Hole birds, animal tracks, Hole geology, a constellation show in the night sky, the science of fly fishing, and habits and habitats of mammals such as the famous fur-bearing beaver.

The Teton Science School's nonresidential courses for kids fill fast, and they give students an introduction to science and natural history programs tailored to their interests and learning levels. Nonresidential courses for grades two through six involve kids in the investigative nature of science, turning it into an adventure. Residential programs for students in grades five through twelve enter the field for two-and-one-half- to five-day sessions. Summer courses for junior high, senior high, and college students last from two to six weeks.

The Teton Science School also offers a one-year professional residency graduate level practicum in environmental education and natural sciences.

Teton Science School, P.O. Box 68, Kelly, WY 83001, 307-733-4765 phone, 307-739-9388 fax.

Great Plains Wildlife Institute

Ever wonder what it would be like to participate in an honest-to-goodness, "nonconsumptive" safari, a wildlife field research project, or an animal population survey? Well, at the Great Plains Wildlife Institute (GPWI) you get your chance to experience firsthand one of Jackson Hole's most stunning sights—free-ranging wildlife. And you get to learn how to spot game when you're out in the field either on your own or with family and friends. (Pretty impressive!)

GPWI subscribes to a "learning by doing" philosophy. Wildlife biologists and naturalists who make their home in the area, teach the principles of ecology and ethical wildlife observation techniques through actual field experience. The latter is crucial in locales where long winters place enough stress on the animals, without careless onlookers adding to the struggle to survive.

All of the institute's programs endeavor to keep any negative impact on wildlife to a minimum. Therefore, classes remain small, a maximum of eight. The open-roofed safari vehicles stay out of roadless areas, and personnel utilize only previously existing facilities in the field. Surveys and viewing take place with the assistance of twenty-two strength spotting scopes and binoculars provided by the institute, so as not to disturb the animals.

Depending upon the time of year, clients assist in a variety of on-going wildlife stewardship projects the institute collects data for. Take censuses of trumpeter swans, sage grouse, elk, wild horses, or the nests of birds of prey such as osprey, bald and golden eagles. Document the lambing of bighorn sheep in the Teton Range. Search for river otters along the Snake. Monitor the reintroduction of the black-footed ferret. Listen in on the radio-tracking of elk, mule deer, pronghorn or bighorn sheep. Snowshoe into Yellowstone National Park to follow the movements of porcupines in order to better comprehend how forest fires affect the ecosystem.

Established in 1986, GPWI offers three types of wilderness experiences: four hours, full day, or six day.

Summer sunrise and sunset expeditions offer a four-hour overview of wildlife in the Greater Yellowstone Ecosystem from mid-May through early October. Snacks and refreshments come as part of the deal, but you must be an early riser and prepared for a cold morning for the sunrise safaris which begin promptly at 6:30 a.m. Sunset trips offer a bit more flexibility, starting in the neighborhood of 5:30 to 7:30 p.m., depending on the actual time of sunset. Winter sunrise adventures begin at 8:00 a.m. from early December to early April. All of these are well worth the effort and the thrill to see an unparalleled variety of wildlife (and if you're lucky enough to travel to Jackson Hole in September, you can also hear the bugling elk).

If a few hours don't sound long enough to you, try one of the full-day excursions, summer or winter. Starting at 7:00 a.m. in summer and 8:00 a.m. in winter, spend the whole day with a biologist, learning ways to locate and study the relationship between species, their behavior and habitats, breaking only for the fantastic lunch and snacks which the institute provides.

Or, for a truly in-depth experience, the institute holds six-day safaris. Trek through Grand Teton and Yellowstone National Parks, the Gros Ventre Range, the Bighorn Basin, the Wind River Range, the Beartooth Plateau, and the Great Plains. Travel by means of four-wheel-drive vehicles and rafts (non-whitewater floats down the Snake) in summer and snowshoes, snowcoach, and snowmobiles in winter. Lodging and some meals are included.

Dress casually, but come prepared. Even in summer, the thin high country air can be downright chilly. Wear long pants, sturdy shoes with socks, and bring a jacket. For winter trips, dress as you would for a day of skiing—heavy boots, layered clothing, coat, gloves, and a hat.

Most people come to Jackson Hole to experience nature. A wildlife safari with the Great Plains Wildlife Institute will give you that adventure, plus an unmatched education and understanding of how the ecosystem works and how all of us fit into it.

Reservations are required on all trips. Children ages three to twelve must be accompanied by an adult.

Great Plains Wildlife Institute, P.O. Box 7580, Jackson, WY 83002, 307-733-2623.

Wilderness Guides & Packers School

Looking for a different experience? Try a school that has trained people from all over the globe to become wilderness horsepacking guides, farriers, and managers in the horse industry.

Around since 1973, Bud Nelson's institute has been called the "Grandfather" of wilderness guiding and horse-packing schools. In 1983 the U.S. Armed Services Special Forces unit sent personnel and instructors to learn special-ized packing techniques.

Students master how to pick a good pack horse (and a not-so-bright pack horse), animal husbandry, the secrets to correctly packing panniers (saddle bags for animals), how to lead a pack string, the tricks to shoeing, backcountry safety, in addition to camp cooking techniques and guiding skills such as tracking, campsite selection, and game and fish laws. For good measure, wilderness survival and emergency first aid training rounds out the course of study. Classes are held in the Teton Wilderness Area.

The school offers a basic thirty-day curriculum; four-teen-day horsemanship and packing courses; an advanced two-week leadership, guiding, packing, and management class; as well as three- or six-week horseshoeing and farrier science courses.

As the school only accepts a limited number of students each year, with a class size of ten, you should apply early.

Wilderness Guides & Packers School, Bud Nelson, Direc-tor, P.O. Box 409, Jackson, WY 83001, 307-733-2843.

Yellowstone Institute

The Yellowstone Institute resides in the heart of the Lamar Valley, where trapper Russell Osborne met up with the Sheepeater Indians. The valley earned a nickname of the "Serengetti of North America," as few tourists wander into this remote area in the northeast corner of the park, leaving it a relatively undisturbed haven for an abundance of wildlife.

Historically, the valley played an early role in wildlife management and conservation. In 1907 Lamar Valley became the home base of a federally operated experimental program. As a means of halting the demise of the American bison, the government created the "Buffalo Ranch." Run as close to a cattle ranch operation as was possible when dealing with such a huge, undomesticated animal, Yellowstone started the long process of repopulating the park. In 1924 twenty-two cast members and an incredible array of "extras" arrived at the Buffalo Ranch to begin shooting a silent picture of Zane Grey's *The Thundering Herd*. (See the movies in the next chapter.)

The bison ranch remained in operation until 1952.

So what does all this have to do with the Yellowstone Institute? An old bunkhouse building, surviving from the original ranch, became the school's first real home.

Feeling the need to boost the park's educational role, a nonprofit organization called the Yellowstone Association formed the year of the country's 200th birthday, 1976, as a membership organization in cooperation with the National Park Service. The association sponsored the school, guiding thirty-two students that first year through a new awareness of wilderness education. For three years the school was run out of available park lodging and camps. Then, in 1979, the National Park Service granted a special use permit which allowed the institute to house its students, 125 that year, in the Buffalo Ranch bunkhouse—not only a fitting location for the courses, but in keeping with the school's mission.

Director Don Nelson defines the institute's goals as seeking to educate visitors about Yellowstone's natural and cultural history through a diversity of in-depth, year-round courses. "As the public becomes informed about many facets of Yellowstone, through specific and focused courses," Nelson states, "a caring constituency is created and built upon."

From their handful of students and courses, the institute has developed and implements eighty diverse courses which last between one and five days. Over fifty instructors teach over 800 students everything from grizzly bear and wolf ecology, geology, wildflower identification, and Native American and mountain man history to nature photography and writing and fly fishing, as well as the art of lake canoeing.

"Most of our students are in the thirty-five to fifty-five age grouping," Nelson states. "But an increasing number of students in the twenty to thirty age range are taking courses, probably due to the college credit available."

Imagine getting academic credit for such classes as a Wildflowers Llama Trek or Autumn Canoeing in Yellowstone or Yellowstone Streams through the Eyes of Trout or Wild Edible Plants and Medicinal Herbs or Bears: Folklore and Biology! But these are serious courses with exams, submitting field notes, and completing an approved project. About a third of the classes carry college credit. As an interesting footnote, Nelson says that about forty to forty-five percent of the institute's students come from education— teachers and administrators.

People must love Yellowstone courses as half the students in any given course have completed at least one previous class offered at the institute. Some have graduated from as many as twenty courses!

The institute also creates classes specifically designed for families and children. Courses limited to ten to fifteen ensure personal and individualized instruction. Approximately fifty percent of the courses take place at the Buffalo Ranch home base. Students prepare their own meals, sharing camaraderie as well as recipes. Bunkhouse back porch meals hold special meaning as students look out over the Lamar Valley.

The institute works closely with the natural history interpretation division of Yellowstone National Park, utilizing many Park Service staff members as instructors.

Yellowstone Institute, P.O. Box 117, Yellowstone National Park, WY 82190, 307-344-2293.

6

Hollywood in the Hole

Katharine Newlin married Maxwell Struthers Burt in 1903 and moved to Jackson Hole. They started the Bar BC Ranch in 1908. So what does that have to do with Hollywood in Jackson Hole? In 1919 Katharine wrote a book titled *The Branding Iron*. A year later Samuel Goldwyn (MGM) purchased the movie rights and invited Katharine to write the screenplay, making her the first full-time Jackson Hole resident author to receive Hollywood screenplay credits. And that was just the beginning.

"That's a Wrap!"

As early as 1917 the film medium utilized the natural wonders found in the northwest corner of Wyoming. The Pathe Film Company arrived to shoot a series of shorts, each around 100 feet of film, for news services. Later they spliced sections together to create the film *Yellowstone National Park*.

Ford Motor Company obtained the right to film in Yellowstone in 1921. (Today they still use the area for commercials as you'll see below.)

In 1922 Yellowstone again became the location for another type of movie—an episode serial called *Nan of the North* (not to be confused with *Nanook of the North* filmed in Jackson Hole the previous year). Among the backdrops shot in the park, the hero finds herself stranded on Yellowstone Lake in an episode titled "Adrift." (Do you suppose she heard the "music of the Lake?")

The 1922 filming season proved a busy one for all of the Jackson Hole area. The Famous Players-Lasky Corporation chose the town, Hoback Canyon, and Glacier Canyon near Jenny Lake in current-day Grand Teton National Park to produce *The Cowboy and the Lady*. Director Charles Maigne probably selected the sites because of the accounts his father had told him. The elder Maigne traveled through the Hole and Yellowstone with General Sheridan in 1884.

Two years later, the Famous Players-Lasky Corporation again visited the area, filming segments of *The Thundering Herd* at the Buffalo Ranch in Yellowstone National Park, where the Yellowstone Institute currently runs classes. Oddly enough, this silent picture dealt with the wholesale slaughter of the buffalo, the reactions and retaliations of the Native Americans (using real Native American actors from the Wind River Reservation in central Wyoming), and a white man who forsakes the life of a buffalo hunter. (Pretty innovative stuff, considering it was 1924.)

The Mobile Mountains

The Tetons started earning their reputation as the "most geographically active mountain range in the country" as early as 1925. They provided the background for a movie released as *The Yankee Senor*, originally titled *Don Juan of San Antonio*. As the first title suggests, the story line takes place just north and south of the border (the Mexican border, not Wyoming's).

Also in 1925, the Fox Film Company dropped approximately $100,000 into the Wyoming economy with the John Ford production of *Three Bad Men*. The advance crew rounded up 200 head of cattle, 30 oxen, 500 horses, and 255 wagons to outfit the movie town they constructed.

After *Three Bad Men* came the 1930 Oregon Trail epic titled *The Big Trail* (John Wayne's film debut and he didn't get good reviews. Thank goodness he and the movie companies paid no attention to them!). *Wyoming*, the first in the Jackson Hole area for actor Wallace Beery, who owned a vacation cabin on Jackson Lake, came out a decade later. *Bad Bascomb* (another Beery movie) showed up on the screen during 1946, then filming started for the 1952 RKO release of *The Big Sky*.

Studio craftsmen constructed a sixty-three-foot replica of a keelboat, a flatbottom boat with square ends used throughout the 1800s to transport goods and livestock, and floated it on the Snake River (playing the role of the treacherous Missouri River of the 1830s). Kirk Douglas, Dewey Martin, and the rest of the cast of Howard Hawks' production of *The Big Sky* reportedly learned to take in stride frequent dunkings, intended and accidental, in the Snake's swift and, at times, deadly current. The keelboat remained on display in the park at the base of Snow King Mountain for several years.

Downriver a few miles from *The Big Sky* "set," another crew was shooting what would be the 1953 Paramount release of *Shane*, the movie that rocked a few Hollywood notions about the romantic West. George Stevens, the producer, and A.B. Guthrie, who adapted the Jack Schaefer novel of the same name for the silver screen, wanted to portray the real feel of life in the West of the early 1880s. Stevens researched the photos of William Henry Jackson (see Section Eight, Chapter 3) and paintings of Charles Russell, using the details found in them for creating a realistic set and costumes for the movie.

Stevens located the "town" near the Snake River in the shadow of the Tetons, constructing the series of false-front buildings that represented the rangeland town and homesteader's cabins. The Rockefeller family, visiting the site during the filming, expressed an interest in acquiring the set once Stevens completed the movie. The family wished to relocate the "town" to the Menor's Ferry/Chapel of the Transfiguration location in Grand Teton National Park. The *Shane* set could have rounded out an exhibit of what the development of the West was really like. What a pity this idea never became a reality.

An interesting side note, however: In a 1995 survey, members of Western Writers of America (WWA), an association of professional writers dedicated to preserving and celebrating the heritage of the American West, past and present, voted *The Big Sky* by A.B. Guthrie the Best Western Novel ever written, with Jack Schaefer's *Shane* a close second.

The Big Sky won out over such novels as *Lonesome Dove* by Larry McMurtry, *The Time it Never Rained* by Elmer Kelton, *Riders of the Purple Sage* by Zane Grey, *Hondo* by Louis L'Amour, and *The Virginian* by Owen Wister.

The movie *Shane* (Guthrie's screenplay of Schaefer's novel) took Best Western Film of all time against such competition as *High Noon, Butch Cassidy and the Sundance Kid, Unforgiven, Dances With Wolves, Little Big Man, The Outlaw Josey Wales, The Searchers, The Wild Bunch,* and *The Shootist.*

Survey results were published in the December 1995 issue of *Roundup Magazine,* published by WWA. *Roundup* editor Candy Moulton points to a similar survey conducted a decade ago where the movie *Shane* also won the best film category. "*Shane* endures as one of the great western movies and books because it dispelled myths of the glamorous West, portraying the often harsh, dark reality instead."

After *Shane* came the 1955 movie of the Lewis and Clark Expedition, *The Far Horizons,* starring Charlton Heston, Fred MacMurray, and Donna Reed. Jackson Lake and up-river from Deadman's Bar on the Snake provided the expansive, untamed landscape necessary to the story.

Shooting *Jubal,* a 1956 Columbia production, at the Triangle X Ranch in Grand Teton National Park, so endeared Jackson Hole to director Delmar Daves that he returned to film the 1963 *Spencer's Mountain.*

The local community not only got behind this Warner Brothers production, they played in the film as well. Two hundred residents made a 7:00 a.m. call one morning, and that was for one short segment. In addition, Snow King Mountain became "Spencer's Mountain," home of Henry Fonda's screen family; T.A. Moulton's barn on Mormon Row in Grand Teton National Park played a spectacular backdrop for some outdoor segments. And according to Clark and Veda Moulton, the family got a good laugh when Fonda tried to milk a cow in front of the camera. Several church scenes were shot at the St. John's Episcopal Church, with the Ladies Auxiliary cast as themselves. Members of the LDS Ladies Church Choir backed up actor Maureen O'Hara in the hymns she sang on-screen.

But involvement didn't end with the actual filming. Prior to the movie's world debut at Radio City Music Hall in New York, Warner Brothers held a press premiere at Jackson Hole's Teton Theater just off Town Square, attended by around 250 media representatives, including radio and TV personalities Arthur Godfrey and Art Linkletter.

Yet the biggest geographical leap for the Tetons came in the 1970 United Artists release of *The Unexpected Mrs. Pollifax*. The Tetons transformed into the Albanian Alps, at the time the only location in the "free world" with scenery that resembled Albania. Star Rosalind Russell arrived at the Jackson Hole Airport (also in character by flying the Albanian flag) in Frank Sinatra's Lear Jet—all part of the plot that pitted an American tourist against cold war intrigue, with the C.I.A. thrown in for good measure.

The Aerial Tram at Teton Village got a workout hauling equipment and actors up and down Rendezvous Peak where most of the filming took place. During that time, it was closed to the public.

Other Jackson Hole movies include the 1971 Walt Disney production of *The Wild Country*, which utilized the Moulton homestead cabin from Mormon Row for authenticity; *The Homecoming* that same year, as well as some scenes shot in Town Square for the Jackson Hole ski instructor romance called *Winter Love*; the 1979 Columbia Pictures Wind River rendezvous saga *The Mountain Men*, which captured scenes from Togwotee Pass all the way over to Wilson at the base of Teton Pass; Clint Eastwood's famed fight scene in the Town Square in the 1980 *Any Which Way You Can*; the plunging raft scene as it goes over Fall Creek falls in *The Pursuit of D.B. Cooper* that same year; Sylvester

Stalone's mountain training and conditioning in *Rocky IV*; the 1985 TV mini-series *Dreams West*; *The Wrong Guys* in 1987; *Ghosts Can't Do It* in 1989; video release scenes of *Dances With Wolves* also that year; the 1992 made-for-TV movie *Christmas in Connecticut*; and, of course, the incredible Snake River scenes in *A River Runs Through It* in 1994.

More Recently

A German film crew came to Jackson during the summer of 1995 and shot hours of film which they compressed into a thirty- and sixty-minute documentary on Jackson Hole. One of the highlights of their trip was a stagecoach ride around Jackson's Town Square. The stagecoach ride proved to be not only their first such experience, but the first time to see one of the West's best known symbols.

Other western images found around Jackson Hole provide the background for the 1996 PBS documentary *The West*. The Insignia Films project, five years in the making, includes segments on the mountain man and fur trade era and the effect of white men entering the "Far West."

On the Cutting Room Floor

Jackson Hole also has a history of films which didn't make it—ideas that never became realized on the screen. Of them, the failure of the plans to shoot *The Virginian* in Jackson Hole ranks at the top of the list. During 1921 Douglas Fairbanks intended to film the rustler scenes in the actual locations where Wister came across the people who would end up as characters in the novel, but Wyoming's famous weather (in the form of early snows) forced cancellation of the project.

In a different sort of incident, Hollywood failed to see the potential of another Jackson Hole story, oddly enough once again connected with Wister. Ed Trafton, believed to be the person Wister patterned his villain Trampas after, urged Hollywood executives to film his true story that same year

Fairbanks scrubbed the Wyoming shoot of *The Virginian*. The following letter Trafton typed to a friend on the other side of Teton Pass, dated February 3, 1921, is printed with the permission of the Teton County Historical Society:

DEAR BILL,

YOUR nice letter came last night we were sure glad to here from you, and i know JUST how good you felt when you was pulling into idaho falls HOME. i dont believe i ever will be satisfied any where else, NOW about myself we had to stop work on the NUT LOCK mean while i have written 3 different SCENEARIOS, for the SCREEN.

I have taken the matter up with the secret service man, who convicted me of the YELLOWSTONE PARK stage robbery in 1914, the picture people wanted him to help them film it then, but he was so situated he could not do it at that time, now he is foot loose, and i have taken the matter up with him and i enclose his second letter which is self explanatory, NOW MELROSE is just as anxious to get my SCENEARIO filmed as i am, i have offered to split 50-50 with the men who furnish the money to film the picture, and pay them the cost of filming back, out of the earnings, then i will split 50-50 with him, and i will do the same thing with you, if you can get some of the idaho boys interested, it is the biggest money makeing proposition on the market to day. I have interviewed several of the best SCENEARIO writers and moveing picture men in the business, and they tell me the same thing, that the picture if well filmed should earn $1,000.000 the first year 750.000 the second and 3 to 500.000 the thrid. BUT the way to handle the proposition is to form an independent company and film our own SCENEARIOS, that is the way they are doing and they wont consider any other proposition, that way they get all the money, SAVY? HERE is the proposition,

I have got the goods to produce, I can write the SCENEARIOS, and direct them, all we need is the CAMERA, and money to finance the markeing of the film we aught to film it in 4 weeks, right in los angles or JACKSON HOLE. ONCE we get one film on the market, we will have enough money to produce our own pictures and I can write a doz SCENEARIOS of the JACKSON HOLE and HOLE IN THE WALL COUNTRY. that will make the BILL HART and TOM MIX stories look like 30 cents NOW this i sent BULL, i know what i am talking about. MELROSE, says the same thing, we both send love to you Ed & MOLLY

How ironic when Hollywood of that era wanted larger-than-life adventures for the silver screen.

Selling Hollywood on the concept, however, wasn't the problem in 1965. Warner Brothers was all set to begin filming a movie titled *Jackson Hole* in this very location. Unfortunately "casting difficulties" forced the cancellation for that year. When plans fell through for shooting it the following year, the company scrubbed the entire project.

Other Hollywood dreams were never realized, not from technical problems, but because they never received air time. The 1991 TV pilot called *Lakota Moon* serves as a perfect example. Although completed, it was never released.

TV Commercials and Other Advertising

Television commercials require an incredible amount of support personnel and services. Even seemingly simple (low-tech), thirty-second commercials range from a bottom end cost well in excess of a quarter of a million dollars to produce. No detail is too small, such as spraying "dulling" on the chrome surfaces of a new vehicle because it glares from the sun too much, or coating an actor's clothing with "canned dirt" to create the illusion of hard work.

Then there's the setting.

Since 1921 Ford Motor Company has favored Jackson Hole for promotional purposes. The area's mountain back-drops and generally reliable early snows afford an ideal location for winter ads which are shot in November or early December and sent out to Ford Dealer Association members prior to the season.

Of course, things don't always go according to plan. One year the support staff had to resort to shoveling snow onto Jackson streets for the cars to kick through and send up fine plumbs of powder. A police officer redirecting traffic around the location reportedly commented, "Well, that's a first for Jackson, and I thought I'd never live to see the day!"

Then there was the time one of the "showroom quality" trucks on loan from the local dealer for the shoot scraped through scrub brush, badly scratching the finish.

After every drive-through scene, the crew clears off the snow accumulation and wipes the car down so it looks fresh for another take. Shooting lasts five to seven days with lots of film shot on a variety of scenarios—same scene, same make of vehicle, but different colors. Or same car, shot from a different angle. Or same vehicle, different scene. Or. . . You get the idea.

Drivers, who have all attended a special driving school, dress in black and wear dark glasses so they won't be noticed behind the wheel. After all, the idea is to draw attention to the vehicle, not who's driving.

Music Videos

Even music video producers rely on the Tetons' charm to sell their artists. *The Great Adventure*, a religious music video by Steven Curtis Chapman, debuted in 1992. The 1993 Neal McCoy video *No Doubt About It* features a stylized dream home in the earliest construction phase residing in the protection of the grandiose Tetons.

7

Music in the Tetons

The waterfalls on the Yellowstone, the rapids of the Snake, the crunch of ice-glazed snow in a high mountain meadow, and bugling elk orchestrate a unique music throughout the Jackson Hole area. But that doesn't preclude more traditional forms (and a few not so customary types).

Grand Teton Music Festival

During the summer, the Grand Teton Music Festival offers the best in classical music. Thirty-five symphony orchestra and chamber music concerts a year are held in Teton Village at the Walk Festival Hall.

Write to Grand Teton Music Festival, P.O. Box 490, Teton Village, WY 83025, 307-733-1128 phone, 307-739-9043 fax.

Other Music

In addition, the Jackson Hole Chorale puts on an annual Spring Concert, locals play at Dornan's Hootenanny, and the town hosts the "Rockin' in the Tetons" Festival and Bluegrass Festival. Then there's the Jackson Hole Community Jazz Ensemble. For more details, contact the Jackson Hole Chamber of Commerce, P.O. Box E, Jackson, WY 83001, 307-733-3316 phone, 307-733-5585 fax.

Hole Events

1
Spring

Would you believe Jackson Hole and Hawaii have something in common? Besides tourists, that is. Well, they do. Spring.

Sounds pretty far-fetched, doesn't it? Yet, in both locales, spring is a state of mind rather than a tangible season where flowers blossom, grass grows, and leaves bud on trees, signaling the end of winter.

As you'll notice, skiing shows up as part of spring events, and only on very rare years has the Hole run out of the stuff before early summer. On occasion, it lays around all year! (Now you see why you can't necessarily dress by the season but rather for the weather.)

Pole, Pedal, Paddle Relay Race

This homegrown, early April event began in 1974 as a sporty way to celebrate the end of the long Wyoming winter. The contest, with ten different classes ranging from "anything goes all in the name of fun" to serious competitors, includes four relay rounds in the form of alpine skiing, nordic skiing, bicycling, and boating.

209

Racing begins with a giant slalom race, followed by a ten-kilometer cross-country course. And yes, the contestants do stop long enough to swap skis between these two sections.

Next, racers jump on bikes and pedal nearly twenty miles to a designated point on the Snake River where they board rafts, canoes, or kayaks (whichever they prefer) and paddle nine miles down the Snake.

This seriously fun event attracts Olympic-caliber racers and is sponsored by the Jackson Hole Ski Club. For facts and forms, contact them at 307-733-6433.

For other ski events, check out Section Five, Chapter One.

Jackson Hole Guide Kite Festival

Although the art of kite making and flying first appeared in China over two thousand years ago (and was used for military purposes of judging distance between troops and a besieged palace), mid-May of 1995 saw the valley's first annual kite festival. Local kite-building experts conduct workshops and instruct flying know-how. Prizes go to the highest-flying kite (with all contestants' strings measured to 75 feet) and to the best-looking kite that doesn't look like a kite. (Now that's something to aim high for!)

Sponsored by the Jackson/Teton County Parks and Recreation Dept. and Jackson Hole Guide. For particulars, give them a call at 307-733-2430 or 307-439-9025.

Miles for Money

Early May kicks off the Miles for Money fund-raiser for the Learning Center. It features a twenty-two-mile bike-, walk-, roller blade-, and horse-a-thon starting at the Kelly School. Every mile traveled carries a pledge from participants' sponsors. The Learning Center has all the details at 307-733-3791.

Old West Days

What do cowboy hats and boots, black powder guns, and Indian trade beads all have in common? Why, Old West Days, of course! Each Memorial Day Weekend visitors and locals mingle in the spirit of the real Wild West days of the 1800s. Performances by famous singers, cowboy poets, authors, and musicians kick things off on Friday.

Saturday events include a parade, Indian dances, rodeo, cutting horse competition, barn dance, and live country music. Sunday continues with more live music and a carriage-driving competition.

Rodeo 1903 style. It hasn't changed, has it?
Charlie Johnson thrown from a wild steer.
Taken by R.R. Doubleday.

Photo Credit: Teton County Historical Society

As part of the celebrations a Mountain Man Rendezvous at the Fairgrounds runs throughout the weekend. Visitors can meet the modern-day equivalents of John Colter, Jim Bridger, and Davey Jackson as they gather to recreate the famous rendezvous begun during the heyday of the trapping era. The rendezvous strives to make everything as historically authentic as possible, from the tipis to the clothing to campfire cooked fry bread. Tomahawk throws and mountain man historians and poets head up the festivities.

The Jackson Hole Visitors Council has all the details on Old West Days. Call them at 307-733-3316.

2

Summer

Turn-of-the-century western humorist Bill Nye offered a prefect picture of Jackson Hole's short summer season when he wrote, "The climate is erratic, eccentric and peculiar... the early frosts make close connections with the late spring blizzards so that there is only time for a hurried lunch between."

Jackson Hole Wine Auction

The Jackson Hole Wine Auction rounds out three days of wine-related culinary experiences, tastings, and seminars in late June. More than 100 lots of fine wines donated by a variety of California vintners and local wine masters, in addition to some unique travel, adventuring, and culinary packages, take to the auction block. Bidding begins at around fifty dollars per lot. Wine collectors from around the country attend in hopes of obtaining some rare or favored vintage at a great price. Proceeds benefit the Grand Teton Music Festival, 307-739-9043. (For information on what the festival is all about, see Section Six, Chapter 7.)

Collector Car Auction

For two days at the start of July folks get the chance to bid on their dream car. Between 100 and 150 vintage cars and trucks pass over the auctioneer's block. Even if you don't come in with the winning bid, it's fun to cruise through the rows of Bentleys, Mustangs, Corvettes, Model A Pickups, Porsches, Barracudas, and, of course, the classic '57 Chevys.

Contact Silver Auto Auctions at 800-255-4485 for particulars.

Harvest Festival

In mid-July, Teton Village hosts a huge western arts and crafts show. In conjunction with the exhibition and sale, there's a wine tasting party and a children's festival with music, games, and fun art. Call 208-345-0755 for more information.

Teton County Fair

Besides the rides, don't miss the demolition derby, chain saw carving, 4-H exhibits, horse and dog shows (not to be confused with a dog and pony show, which you may also find), fiddle contest, diaper derby, special rodeo, marksmanship matches, live nightly entertainment, and, of course, the cotton candy!

The 4-Hers also host a livestock auction where the animals (steers, lambs, swine, and rabbits) the kids have fed, sheltered, groomed, shown, and loved for the past six months bring in big bucks on the auction block, all to benefit the community.

Activities, action, and fun are held annually at the end of July at the county Fairgrounds. Call 307-733-0658 for a current listing of dates and events.

Teton Tri-Altitude Triathlon

The mid-August Teton Tri-Altitude Triathlon challenges participants to survive some grueling changes in elevation and temperatures. The first leg shakes out with a chilly quarter-mile swim in Slide Lake. But the goosebumps soon disappear during a twelve-kilometer mountain bike ride, in the mountains, of course. It's also a good leg warmer for the home stretch, a five-kilometer run. Contact the Jackson Hole Chamber of Commerce for current sponsors, 307-733-3316.

Jackson Hole Horse Trials

For three days in late August, the Teton Equestrian Club and the Spring Creek Equestrian Center sponsor the Jackson Hole Horse Trials. Horse and rider test their endurance in a variety of events—dressage, stadium jumping, and a cross-country gallop course. Back in the early 1900s, this type of horse-riding competition was designed to test cavalry officers' abilities to handle their mounts in these three disciplines. In each section, the riders score by penalty points on their performances, with the lowest tally, after all three events, deciding the winner.

The Jackson Hole competition attracts riders from the Rocky Mountain region, Southwest, and California, as well as riders who are on the circuit. Many say they find stadium jumping the toughest of the three courses. The number and tightness of turns, the delicate rails so susceptible to being knocked down, producing penalty points, require skill and more.

For competition events and schedules, call the Spring Creek Equestrian Center at 307-739-1460.

3

Fall

Shortly after, if not before, the quaking aspen leaves turn brilliant gold, snow falls (the Wyoming reason for this season's name), hailing the return of autumn. In addition to the change of colors and the crisp edge that seeps into the air, the valley transforms. Kids return to school so family vacations end. Visitation slows. The tempo relaxes. Wild animals drift down from the high country, and the elk return to the valley.

Romancing the Elk: A Twilight Wildlife Encounter

September's crisp mountain air fills with the majestic calls of one of North America's truly magnificent animals, the wapiti. The bulls bugle during this time of the mating season to warn off rivals. If that fails, antlers will clash in an incredible courting battle. One of the best ways to learn more about the meaning behind these dazzling displays is to experience them with a wildlife biologist.

Call the Great Plains Wildlife Institute at 307-733-2633 for reservations for an evening of "Romance of the Elk." (For more details about the institute, see Section Six, Chapter 5.)

Moose Chase Marathon

Started in 1994, the Moose Chase Marathon takes place in early September. Over 150 team and individual runners participate annually in this twenty-six-plus-mile run. The course, which begins at Fall Creek Road, is scenic and grueling, with runners traveling by Pritchards Pass, the Snake River, Teton Pass, and winding up in Teton Village. A starting elevation of 5,850 feet gains until it finally climaxes at 6,300 feet at the finish.

Sponsored by a wide range of Jackson area businesses. Contact the Teton County Parks and Recreation Dept. for particulars at 307-733-2430.

Rendezvous Mountain Bike Hillclimb

During mid-September, mountain bike enthusiasts line up to tackle the "Big One," Rendezvous Mountain, in the annual 7.2-mile mountain bike hillclimb. Over fifty racers participate in the seven categories which range from beginner to expert/elite. All find a challenge in the climb's 4,139-vertical-feet course to the top of Rendezvous Peak (the mountain people enjoy skiing down in winter).

Registration and course information comes from the Teton Village Sports Shop at 307-739-2740.

Fall Arts Festival

This "cultural oasis" takes place during the latter half of September as a celebration of the Arts. Activities include a Gallery Walk (see Section Six, Chapter 1 for more on this tour), the Jackson Hole Quick Draw, the Arts for the Park competition, and the Western Vision Miniature Show and Sale (more on these below).

Contact the Jackson Hole Chamber of Commerce for all the details and current sponsors, 307-733-3316.

Jackson Hole Quick Draw

During mid-September 1995, Jackson Hole held its first annual Quick Draw contest at the corrals and barnyard of the Spring Creek Resort. Many of the artists who participate in the Quick Draw live in the area and show their work in Jackson galleries.

"The Quick Draw is a way to elevate participation in the Fall Arts Festival," explains Sara Flitner of the Jackson Hole Chamber of Commerce, one of the contest's sponsors.

"It's filled with lots of energy, although it can be nerve-racking for artists."

At the Quick Draw, these high-caliber artists work under pressure and sometimes less-than-ideal conditions. In one hour they produce a piece of artwork which is then auctioned off.

"The concept behind the Quick Draw," expounds Flitner, "is to provide a way to get viewers to participate in art activities. By getting involved, viewers reach a better understanding of art. On the other hand, artists don't want to leave the impression they can turn out masterpieces in an hour."

In an atmosphere of fun, artists create paintings out of oils, ink, and pastels, all the while chatting with watchers. Models include members of the audience, Spring Creek's horses, and the mountain vistas. Artists hurriedly add last-minute touches as time is called, then hand the "finished piece" to the auctioneer (sort of like kids turning in test papers. A lot of the artists have that kind of harassed/relieved look on their faces). Proceeds go toward future Fall Arts Festival events.

Moynihan Gallery has all the details about the nationally and regionally recognized artists participating in the Quick Draw. Call them at 307-733-0870.

Arts for the Parks Awards

The annual Arts for the Parks competition and exhibition celebrates this country's 370 national parks, monuments, and historic sites. Out of the thousands of entries submitted which depict well- and little-known parks and monument sites, the National Park Academy of the Arts announces the jurors' selections for the top 100 paintings, which are displayed at Jackson Lake Lodge in Grand Teton National Park during mid-September, kicking off a nationwide tour. The Academy hopes the tour will enhance public awareness and support of the National Park System, while giving the artists national exposure.

Winners are chosen on the basis of artistic merit, content, and portrayal of a special relationship with the national park they painted. A portion of revenues generated from the art competition is contributed to the National Park Foundation, a cosponsor since the competition began in 1986, to provide for maintenance and preservation of the National Park System. The grand prize winning image becomes part of the National Park Foundation's permanent collection.

Jackson Lake Lodge also hosts a special banquet where artists receive cash awards in several categories, including the grand prize winner's $50,000. The second 100 finalists' works are also shown at various locations around Jackson Hole.

Call 800-553-2787 for details on the Arts for the Parks program and exhibition. Reservations are required for the awards banquet. It's a great chance to not only view exceptionally high quality art, but meet the artists as well.

Western Vision Miniature Show and Sale

As part of the mid-September arts festival, the National Wildlife Art Museum sponsors their annual Miniature Show and Sale. Nationally known artists display and sell over 100 paintings and sculptures, all measuring no more than nine-and-a-half by twelve inches.

Funds benefit the National Wildlife Art Museum. (More on the museum in Section Six, Chapter 4.) Contact them for all the details at 307-733-5771.

Jackson Hole Wildlife Film Festival

Over 350 wildlife filmmakers enter the biennial Jackson Hole Wildlife Film Festival held at Jackson Lake Lodge in Grand Teton National Park. An international panel of judges select winners in twelve categories. In conjunction with the festival, filmmakers participate in conferences, screening, and lectures.

Tickets are available for public screenings of the finalists' films. Call 307-733-7016 for times and details.

Quilting in the Tetons

Early October is time to bring out the quilts (for exhibit as well as home use), and Jackson Hole does it with a quilting display, how-to classes, sewing workshops, lectures, and a quilt work fashion show.

Workshops and exhibits are sponsored by the Teton County Extension Office. Call them at 307-733-3087 for details of all the events scheduled.

4

Winter

By the time autumn "officially" ends, Jackson Hole looks like a winter wonderland scene found on a Christmas card. Having caught its breath during the fall, the valley gears up for snow, skis, snowboards, snowmobiles, and a unique mix of winter events that blend traditions with typical western experiences.

Cowboy Ski Challenge

In late February skiers shine up their boots and stampede to Jackson Hole Ski Resort for the Cowboy Ski Challenge. Activities begin on Saturday with a free ski clinic for cowgirls and boys. After lunch, gunfire signals the start of the Duel Races down Eagle's Rest where contestants must concentrate on NOT skiing into the moose that have been known to wander onto the slopes during the race. Cowpoke skiers maneuver gates carrying lariats (occasionally between their teeth!) to reach a plastic bull's head on a bale of hay. Once the "bull" is successfully lassoed, contestants saddle a horse and lead it over the finish line.

In the team division, teamsters must pack two mantees loaded with such items as bales of straw and fence posts.

"Many of these cowboys and cowgirls have never skied before," says Lori Kyle, Chamber of Commerce special events director. "They're out of their element, but the fear factor is nonexistent. They're having a lot of laughs."

On Sunday, the "snow arena" at Teton Village becomes the site of the Dutch Oven Cook-off, filling the town with the aroma of down-home campfire victual. Then the Winter Rodeo commences with a snow-covered obstacle course, novelty rodeo events like nothing you've ever seen. "Cowboys come in off the nearby ranches and from towns all over Wyoming and surrounding states to participate in the weekend's events," explains Kyle. "And it's a heckuva lot of fun for everyone to watch."

The Chamber, in conjunction with the Jackson Hole Visitors Council and numerous local businesses, sponsors the weekend's roundup of entertainment, competitions, and "foot-stompin' fun." Call 307-733-3316 for information and times.

Wild Game Dinner

The Wild Game Dinner began in 1972 as a simple spaghetti dinner. Today, a lavish feast of donated foods, as well as prizes, games, raffles, and an auction all provide a festive night out on the town the Jackson Hole way. Everything from airline tickets to elk antler chandeliers go on the auction block.

Proceeds from the mid-November dinner benefit the children with disabilities or developmental delays from birth to five years old. Approximately fifty area kids attend the Learning Center preschool each year. The center sponsors the Wild Game Dinner. As only a limited number of dinner tickets are available, make reservations by calling the center at 307-733-3791.

Horse-Drawn Cutter Races

On President's Day weekend, the horses, rigs, and racers line up for the annual Jackson Hole Shrine Club Cutter Races—the western version of chariot racing. (And you don't have to be Ben Hur to participate!)

Saturday and Sunday each see twenty-one races run on the quarter-mile track at the Melody Ranch.

For over a quarter century, two-horse teams with a driver have sped over a snow-covered track, seeking the fastest performance. Only one year did Mother Nature force organizers to call the race due to warm weather.

Cutter Race.

Photo Credit: Wyoming Travel Commission

The Jackson Hole Shrine Club sponsors the cutter races with proceeds benefiting the Shriners Hospital for Crippled Children in Salt Lake City, Utah. For information or tickets call 307-733-6257.

Christmas in Jackson Hole

A wide variety of events take place throughout the month of December—something to suit everybody on your list.

The Festival of Light, sponsored by the St. John's Hospital Auxiliary oversees a special tree lighting ceremony, with music by the Jackson Hole Chorale and the Jackson Hole Community Band. Skiers participate in Torchlight Parades at each of the ski resorts, adding spectacular color to the night.

Very Jackson-style happenings include sleigh rides at the National Elk Refuge, a Christmas Race Camp for skiing, a Christmas Tree Festival, and a Children's Art Extravaganza.

Christmas themes come to life in performances by the Jackson Hole Theatre Company and the Jackson Hole Chorale Christmas Concert. Regional arts and crafts abound at the Christmas Bazaar. And, of course, don't miss Santa in the Town Square. Contact the Jackson Hole Chamber of Commerce at 307-733-3316 for sponsoring groups' phone numbers.

Grand Teton Music Festival's "Music on Exhibit"

Starting each January and continuing into March, the Grand Teton Music Festival performs an evening of chamber music at the National Wildlife Art Museum auditorium. For details, schedules, and tickets, contact them at 307-733-1128.

Check out the chapters in Sections Four and Five for other unusual and sporty events in the Hole.

If you would like a current, complete listing of Jackson Hole's calendar of events, contact the Jackson Hole Visitors Council at P.O. Box 982, Dept. 41, Jackson, WY 83001, 800-782-0011.

Watching Wildlife: A Hole New Meaning

1

National Elk Refuge*

No North American wild animal carries a more majestic presence than the elk, or *wapiti*, the Shawnee name which means "white rump." Seeing them starve by the thousands brought about a conservation movement decades ahead of its time in the form of the National Elk Refuge. Bordering the northern edge of Jackson, it serves today as the home of the world's biggest free-ranging elk herd.

In the Beginning

The development of the refuge began and remains inseparable from that of Jackson Hole. Homesteaders and ranchers who settled in the valley from the early 1880s through the start of the twentieth century appropriated

---

*   Sections of this chapter were excerpted from *The Living West*. See the bibliography for details.

huge portions of the elk's habitual winter range, leaving insufficient forage for the wapitis to survive on. Add several severe winters between 1890 and 1911, and the results were a heavy death toll. (As an example, a 1897 report estimated up to 10,000 of the 15,000 to 25,000 elk that wintered in the valley starved that year. Old-timers also claimed a person "could walk miles on strewn bodies of dead elk" the winter of 1908-09.) Topping it off, tusk hunters in search of elk canine ivory, which fetched as much as a hundred dollars a pair, killed countless more. (Hunt the tuskers in Section Four, Chapter 1.)

Visionary Stephen Nelson Leek

The tragic starvation and slaughter of Jackson Hole's elk herd led to one man's fight for the wapiti.

Born in 1858 in the Canadian Province of Ontario, the son of a Welsh emigrant farmer, Stephen Nelson Leek came to the U.S. with his family while still a child. Like countless others who arrived in the Jackson Hole valley in the late 1880s, Leek took up the life of a hunter-trapper at the age of thirty. A family member later commented that Leek "knew this was to be his home and took to his heart the beauty of the scenery and the wonder of the abundant wildlife."

Leek established a ranch at the lower end of Jackson Hole. But as with modern times, a single source for income makes life iffy at times. So Leek started a guide business, which led to an interest in wildlife and their environment.

Leek concentrated on guiding only indoctrinated sportsmen. They hunted only the most worthy trophies of the chase. He stood for controls designed to protect the status quo, the wild animals and their environment. The difficulty of this position was that already environmental pressures were running ahead of the remaining wildlife as there were more wildlife around than the remaining winter ranges could support. Thus, he found himself, or thrust himself, in a leadership position of the 1890s and 1900s conservation movement.

The chief difficulty was that new settlers with their fields and their fences had cut off the wildlife's established migration routes to winter ranges. Furthermore, their cattle and horses grazed the summertime meadows that had traditionally produced winter forage which sustained the wild animals. A tragedy was in the making.

Leek prevailed on other settlers to provide a portion of their hay harvest, and he began to write about the plight of the starving elk. (One year the body count numbered approximately 2,000 wapitis dead, all within a one-mile radius of Leek's home.) Even more effectively he trained the camera George Eastman gave him while in Jackson Hole on a trip on the elk themselves. Later labeled "the Father of the Elk," Leek's self-taught ability with a camera and connections acquired through the hunting lodge became the spearhead behind his push to save the elk.

Stephen Leek's famous photo of the starving elk.

Photo Credit: Teton County Historical Society

Elected to the Wyoming House of Representatives in 1909, Leek pushed a bill through that made it a felony to kill an elk for its teeth. (Follow the elimination of the tuskers in Section Four, Chapter 1.)

At the same time Theodore Roosevelt and Gifford Pinchot were pushing the acts through a reluctant Congress, forming what would become the National Forest, Leek and others sought the establishment of the nation's first great major wildlife refuge—the National Elk Refuge in Jackson Hole.

In 1912 Congress appropriated $45,000 for the purchase and maintaining of lands for a winter elk refuge. A series of presidential executive orders between 1914 and 1916 set aside 1,760 acres of purchased land and 1,000 acres from the public domain.

The Refuge Today

Currently the refuge encompasses 24,700 acres, approximately twenty-five percent of the elk's historic winter range. It provides adequate natural and supplemental feed for 7,500 elk during the six-month period they spend in the low country.

Preserving and managing a winter range for wapitis is the main mission of the National Elk Refuge. As part of this, the refuge works to enhance the natural ecosystem, thus reducing the need for supplemental food, currently in the form of alfalfa hay pellets.

Another goal involves providing habitat for endangered and threatened species of plants and animals. The refuge also seeks to develop and manage wetlands for the perpetuation of migratory birds. In 1938 four endangered trumpeter swan cygnets were introduced to the refuge, the first successful transplant of this kind in the United States. Other species that currently inhabit the area include peregrine falcons, whooping cranes, sandhill cranes, bald eagles, and Canadian geese. A stop at the wildlife viewing area from

Highway 191, 89, and 26 can fill in a Jackson Hole bird checklist in no time!

One of three National Wildlife Refuges within the Greater Yellowstone Area, the elk refuge also furnishes some unique research opportunities for a variety of animal and plant species and their relationship within the ecosystem. Approximately twenty-five percent of the herd that winters on the refuge comes from Yellowstone. Another quarter wanders in from the Bridger-Teton National Forest, while half enter from Grand Teton National Park. Many migrate up to sixty-five miles to reach the refuge.

"Elk are therefore very representative of the ecosystem approach to wildlife management," states James M. Griffin, an assistant refuge manager attached to education and visitor services. "Elk migration and management are integral to a Greater Yellowstone Area educational and interpretive message now and in the future."

For more information about the National Elk Refuge, contact them at P.O. Box C, Jackson, WY 83001, 307-733-9212.

2

Grand Teton National Park*

Gazing at the Teton Range with only a necklace of clouds veiling the highest peaks, you wonder why people put up such a fight when it came to protecting such unmatched beauty. Or why the debate continues.

---

* Sections of this chapter were excerpted from *The Living West* and *Trails & Tales: Day Hikes and Historic Sites on the Way to Yellowstone*. See the Bibliography for details.

Before Grand Teton National Park

Before the controversy which preceded the creation of Grand Teton National Park, the *Caspar Tribune-Herald* called the forty-mile stretch of highway on the way to Jackson—the one that currently affords that indescribably scenic vista of the Teton Range on Highway 26, 89, and 191—"a long lane of unsightly structures that would mar the primitive beauty of the area."

Commercialism, driven by the tourist industry and the popularity of Yellowstone in post-World War I, brought a flood of entrepreneurs to exploit Jackson Hole. By the 1920s an endless stream of billboards, telephone wires, fast food joints, cheaply constructed overnight cabins, junk cars, and gas stations obstructed the now world famous view of the Tetons.

Locals grew concerned but didn't fancy Yellowstone National Park superintendent Horace Albright's desire to include the Tetons and Jackson Hole in with Yellowstone. Forest Service employees feared the loss of jobs should the Tetons be removed from their jurisdiction and placed in the hands of the Park Service. Ranchers feared the loss of grazing rights, granted to them by the Forest Service. Dude ranchers, including Struthers Burt of the Bar BC, feared the influx of tourists in their automobiles in search of plush accommodations would ruin the wilderness experience for vacationing guests. As cheap exploitation occurred, Burt and other ranchers switched sides in order to protect their cherished valley. But by then concern over the lost tax revenue by removing a huge chunk of land from the tax base added fuel to the fire against government control of the valley and the mountains, keeping the anti-park flames burning brightly.

Yet some of Jackson Hole's earliest settlers recognized the value the valley had for nurturing the spirit rather than the pocketbook. Pierce Cunningham circulated a petition during 1925 calling for the government to preserve the land south of Yellowstone "for the education and enjoyment of the Nation as a whole." (Follow Cunningham's early struggles in Section One, Chapter 4.)

Enter John D. Rockefeller Jr. and the Snake River Land Company

John D. Rockefeller Jr. and his family journeyed to Yellowstone for a vacation in 1926. Albright took the family into Jackson Hole via Jackson Lake, where the sun highlighted the Tetons and wildlife went about their lives undistrubed. The next day, the shrewd Albright drove the group back to the park through the tourist trap described by the *Caspar Tribune-Herald*. Then Albright outlined his dream to the philanthropist.

Wanting to preserve the pristine condition of the "grandest and most spectacular mountains" he had ever seen, Rockefeller orchestrated the Snake River Land Company, a dummy corporation that began purchasing ranches and tourist properties along the Tetons and in the river valley as they came onto the market—all in secret so landowners wouldn't jack up the price as soon as they learned who funded the company.

Robert Miller, Unknowing Front Man for His Enemies

Robert Miller first came to Jackson's Hole at age nineteen. Within three years, he and his bride Grace settled permanently on their homestead and sank roots that would forever change the face of Jackson. By age thirty-seven, Robert Miller owned the Jackson State Bank, controlled a major cattle operation, made money developing real estate, and was a Forest Service supervisor.

Miller, like a lot of Jackson residents, opposed expanding Yellowstone National Park to include the Tetons. He agreed, however, to work with the Snake River Land Company in purchasing lands that were coming on the market, but the secrecy surrounding the company's backer and its purpose probably extended to Miller as well.

On December 31, 1929, the year Congress passed a bill setting aside six small lakes at the foot of the Tetons and the surrounding National Forest Service lands as Grand Teton National Park, Miller resigned from the company under a cloud of suspicion that ranged from learning how Albright and Rockefeller had used him, to Miller abusing his position at the bank to force sales by threatening foreclosure. Whichever the case, when Rockefeller's involvement become public knowledge (after Miller quit), the Snake River Land Company's subterfuge eventually exploded in a furor that pitted neighbor against neighbor, friend against friend, as the issue divided the Jackson Hole community.

In 1933 Wyoming's senators demanded a Senate investigation into the dealings (or perceived misdealings) of the Snake River Land Company, which at the time had acquired 35,000 acres from 320 different landowners for a cost of over a million dollars. Eastern reporters flocked to Jackson, expecting to witness the hottest scandal in the nation. But no wrongdoing could be found. Rockefeller neither coerced, threatened, nor cheated landowners out of their property. The acreage went for or above market value. End of scandal, but not of the controversy, for as National Park Service director Arno B. Cammera said in 1935, "Because civilization has moved into the choicest areas faster than they could be established as national parks, some parks must now be carved out of developed areas." And the issue of what to do with all that Snake River Land Company land, and even Jackson Hole itself, still loomed unresolved on the horizon.

The Jackson Hole National Monument

Until 1942 the Wyoming delegation successfully impeded all Congressional attempts to add the Snake River Company's purchases to the National Park Service system. So Rockefeller found another route. With the help of Secretary of the Interior Harold Ickes, he convinced President Franklin D. Roosevelt to issue an executive order in 1943 that created the Jackson Hole National Monument. The proclamation preserved close to 200,000 acres of Teton National Forest, other federal lands, and Rockefeller's Snake River Land Company holdings.

At this point the outrage hit national proportions with comparisons drawn to everything from demonic bureaucrats to a sneak attack the likes of the all-too-recent Pearl Harbor.

Bills made it through both houses of Congress to abolish the monument, only to be vetoed by the President, inciting further anger. In hopes of ending the fight, Roosevelt then asked Congress to pass legislation that would reaffirm the ranchers' grazing privileges, reimburse Teton County for the lost tax revenues on the land, and guarantee no privately owned land in the valley would be confiscated or citizens forced off their property. This appeased all but the most radical factions.

The Long Road to Today's Grand Teton National Park

It took thirty years and many compromises to settle the whole mess and turn public, National Forest, and Rockefeller's privately held land into the current Grand Teton National Park. And what residents once considered a threat to their livelihood now stands as a major benefit to the whole country, not just the locals.

In addition to the now famous uncluttered view, Grand Teton National Park offers 485 square miles (310,521 acres) of hiking, camping, packing, mountaineering, biking, floating, boating, fishing, skiing, snowshoeing, homesteading history, and wildlife watching opportunities to over three and a half million visitors annually.

This visitation, nearly the same as what Yellowstone receives but a sixth the size, creates challenges for GTNP. In the past, the park closed down during winter, giving the land and the wildlife a chance to recover from the summer hordes. Not so any more. Winter recreational use increases each year, and in addition to concerns over where the funds will come from to maintain staff and facilities for winter use, park officials worry about the impact on wildlife at a time when animals can least handle the stress of encounters with humans.

Another borderline crisis facing the park stems from airport expansion. The Jackson Hole airport is the only one in the country located within the boundaries of a national park. Town growth has spurred the need to increase the size of the airport, while at the same time limiting its impact.

Then there's the buffalo. The Jackson Hole Wildlife Park in Grand Teton National Park reintroduced sixteen free-ranging bison to the Jackson Hole area in 1969. By 1994 the herd had increased to approximately 215. GTNP, the National Elk Refuge, Wyoming Game and Fish, the National Wildlife Health Center, and the Bridger-Teton National Forest have developed a bison management plan they hope will maintain a viable herd of 150-200, while at the same time, minimizing bison-human conflicts within recreational use areas and private and park property damage caused by the buffalo. All this clashes at Mormon Row.

The herd grazes on the grasses that used to be the hay fields along Mormon Row, increasing bison numbers. The much photographed Moulton barns, belonging to the park, reside on the Row, as does Clark and Veda Moulton's home, the one acre of private property left on the Row. Visitors interested in Jackson Hole history, as well as hikers and bikers who enjoy the level scenic route through the valley, all travel down Mormon Row and come face to face with the bison herd and potential problems. It's a juggling act that's struggling for a balance that even officials within the park itself can't agree on. How do you maintain a "natural" park without endangering human lives or valuable cultural features?

*Bison grazing near Mormon Row in
Grand Teton National Park*

Photo Credit: Sierra Adare

For information about Grand Teton National Park, contact the headquarters at Drawer 170, Moose, WY 83012, 307-739-3300.

3

Yellowstone National Park*

Thanks to the farsightedness of a few adventurers, an artist, and a photographer, the face of Yellowstone National Park has changed very little since the last glacier receded around 10,000 years ago, leaving the park a mecca for travelers seeking the plethora of natural wonders that are easily accessible today.

But it wasn't always this way.

Early Exploration

Archaeologists estimate Native Americans hunted and fished the Yellowstone Plateau for at least 11,000 years. When the Lewis and Clark Expedition of 1803-1805 made the first recorded contact with the descendants of these prehistoric peoples, they told of strange spectacles and warned against tarrying in a country filled with restless spirits. Obviously it worked, for the expedition did not venture into Yellowstone.

John Colter, one of the expedition's members, however, did become the first white man to traverse the valleys of the "stinking water" and trembling earth that rumbled like thunder. He did this on his own in 1807. Of course, no one believed his "tall tales" any more than they believed famed mountain man Jim Bridger years later.

Sixty-five years passed before the maps Colter drew of his journey were finally authenticated by the first "official" government-sponsored survey of the Yellowstone Plateau.

---

*   Sections of this chapter were excerpted from *The Living West* and *Trails & Tales: Day Hikes and Historic Sites on the Way to Yellowstone*. See the bibliography for details.

Ferdinand V. Hayden

In 1871 the director of U.S. Geological Survey, Dr. Ferdinand V. Hayden, lead a group of thirty-four men and seven supply wagons north from Ogden, Utah. Among the party were the two men most responsible for pulling American's heartstrings taut enough to rally them into creating the country's first national park—landscape artist Thomas Moran and photographer William Henry Jackson. Inspired by Moran's painting of the "Grand Canyon of the Yellowstone," Congress paid $10,000 for the privilege of hanging it in the nation's capitol. Jackson's photos of the Yellowstone's geysers, waterfalls, hot springs, and wildlife became the hit of the nation's Centennial Fourth of July Celebration in 1876.

The road into Yellowstone—the early years.

Photo Credit: Park County Historical Society

William Henry Jackson

At age fifteen, William Henry Jackson gained his first exposure to photography when he took a job as a photo retoucher. After a conscripted stint in the Union army and later a broken engagement, Jackson headed West. He dabbled at life for a while—punching cows, wrangling horses, and wandering—before starting a photography business with his brother in Omaha, Nebraska. In 1869 they won a profitable contract from the new transcontinental railroad. The following year, Ferdinand Hayden asked twenty-eight-year-old Henry to sign on as photographer for the U.S. Geological Survey of the western territories. Jackson's equipment weighed in at over 300 pounds, and he had to have a specially designed portable darkroom tent made for the trip. A mule called "Hypo" packed the camera gear through the uncharted territory for Jackson—except for places where Hypo refused to go. Then Jackson became pack mule as well as photographer.

Reflecting on his life, Jackson said, "If any work that I have done should have value beyond my own lifetime, I believe it will be the happy labors of the decade 1869-1878."

Jackson's photos, captioned and bound in volumes and handed to every member of Congress, were instrumental in convincing the government to set aside Yellowstone. Yet, what could have been a disaster with terrible ramifications for the creation of Yellowstone National Park struck while the Heyden expedition spent five days in Chaco Canyon before proceeding north to current-day Wyoming. Jackson chose that portion of the survey to experiment with a new type of film. Of the hundreds of negatives he shot of the phenomenal Chacoan ruins, not a single one could be developed. Fortunately, he used standard film and the tedious wet-plate processing for Yellowstone's natural wonders.

Late in his life, Jackson compiled the journals and notes taken on the Heyden survey and wrote an autobiography which he called *Time Exposure*. In it he told of yet another potential disaster for the fate of Yellowstone.

Jackson wasn't the only man photographing Yellowstone during 1871. A Chicago man named T.J. Hine joined the Barlow-Hemp expedition and actually arrived back in "civilization" sooner than Jackson. Hine's series of Yellowstone pictures stood to upstage any Jackson would later produce. But fate again stepped in. Hine's return to Chicago coincided with an event synomous with the town itself—the Great Chicago Fire. Hine lost every negative in the fire. Jackson snidely remarked that he owed a "debt of thanks to Mrs. O'Leary's cow."

Jackson died at age ninety-nine, having done things that photographers then and since have only dreamed of.

Yellowstone National Park

On March 1, 1872, Congress set aside over 2.2 million acres (3,472 square miles) of some of the most unique terrain found in the world, "set apart as a public park or

Feeding the bears in Yellowstone circa 1900.

Photo Credit: Park County Historical Society

pleasuring ground for the benefit and enjoyment of the people" as attested to by President Ulysses S. Grant, his vice president, Schuyler Colfax, and Speaker of the House James G. Blaine.

Yellowstone's Natural Wonders

A thousand Yellowstone wonders are calling.

John Muir, 1898

As near as geologists can tell, volcanic eruptions started occurring in the park 2.5 millions years ago, forging the Yellowstone Plateau. These eruptions continued until about 70,000 years ago, forming a series of volcanic craters called calderas. The West Thumb of Yellowstone Lake is an example of a small caldera that has been filled in from centuries of snow-melt streams. Overall, the Yellowstone caldera spans more than thirty-five miles across. Water, seeping into the ground and reaching the hot magma deep in the earth, heats the springs and geysers. Combinations of superheated water and steam rise to the surface, venting in the form of fumaroles (primarily just steam), mudpots, hot springs, and what Yellowstone is most famous for—geysers.

Scientific explanation removes some of the magic of geyser eruptions, until you actually experience one! People have attempted to describe the marvel for a hundred and fifty years. Possibly, naturalist John Muir best conveyed an understandable comparison in his 1898 *Atlantic Monthly* article titled "The Yellowstone National Park." He wrote:

> Some of these ponderous geysers columns are as large as sequoias—five to sixty feet in diameter, one hundred and fifty to three hundred feet high—and are sustained at this great height with tremendous energy for a few minutes, or perhaps nearly an hour, standing ridged and erect, hissing, throbbing, booming, as if thunderstorms were raging beneath their roots, their sides roughened or fluted like the fur-

rowed boles of trees, their tops dissolving in feathery branches, while the irised spray, like misty bloom is at times blown aside, revealing the massive shafts shinning against a background of pine-covered hills.

The exact number of geysers in Yellowstone remains a mystery. At least seventy (approximately a fourth of the world's geysers) exist in the Upper Geyser Basin, the home of Old Faithful. Recent earthquakes in the region have disrupted its eruption schedule from an average of every sixty-five minutes to about every seventy-five minutes.

Often ignored for Old Faithful, Norris Geyser Basin contains lesser known gushers, but their thermal features know no parallel, being the hottest and most active in the park. From a vantage point directly above Echinus Geyser, observers witness the entire sequence of how a geyser erupts. Water at least 527 (with some estimates reaching as high as 706) degrees slowly pools on the surface. To relieve the pressure it boils, then explodes in a characteristic column of water, mist, and steam. Then it drains back into a tube-like fissure at the base of the pool. Every thirty to ninety minutes, the process repeats itself. (Be careful to keep the spray off your glasses and camera lens as the siliceous sinter in the water will permanently spot them.) Another of Norris's geysers that spouts at irregular intervals ranging from days to years apart, Steamboat is the world's tallest geyser, reaching 380 feet.

Water creates other spectacles in Yellowstone. One hundred and fifty waterfalls have been cataloged in the park. The best known and one of the most spectacular cuts through the Grand Canyon of Yellowstone, which runs twenty-four miles long—at its widest 4,000 feet and 1,200 feet at its deepest. The Yellowstone River whittled the canyon out of the geyser basin's volcanic rock, weakened by hot water and acidic gases. The canyon's striking colors come from oxides and minerals leaching out of the decaying rocks. Two falls rush through the canyon—Upper Falls (109 feet) and Lower Falls (308 feet).

The Lower Falls, Crand Canyon of Yellowstone.

Photo Credit: Sierra Adare

Lava Creek Canyon also supports twin falls. The upper Undine Falls drops sixty feet, while the lower one cascades fifty feet. Eighty-four-foot-high Gibbons Falls plunges over the edge of a volcanic crater created 600,000 years ago.

Mammoth Hot Springs stands as a different sort of thermal phenomenon. Seven hundred gallons of water flow daily over its colorful and much photographed travertine terraces stairstepped into the side of the mountain, adding approximately two tons of new deposits every twenty-four hours. Early tourists reached the springs by climbing aboard a six-horse stagecoach departing from Gardiner, Montana. The U.S. Army stationed in the park between 1886 and 1916 kept visitors from taking away chunks of the formation as souvenirs.

Mammoth Hot Springs.

Photo Credit: Wyoming Travel Commission

Unfortunately, the army didn't arrive in time to save the majority of another of Yellowstone's lesser known wonders—a petrified redwood forest dating back millions of years. "Human erosion" plundered all but one fossilized tree stump, now protected by a tall iron fence.

Yellowstone houses a variety of additional geologic treasures. The 260-foot-tall pinnacle of breccia is called simply "the Needle." Indians pilgrimaged to quarry stone for tools and arrowheads from Obsidian Cliff. A strange columnar basalt from an ancient flow of lava remains a permanent forty-five-foot awning over the highway at Overhanging Cliff.

Then there's Yellowstone's much-taken-for-granted natural wonder which Muir expounded on, writing, "The air is electric and full of ozone, healing, reviving, exhilarating, kept pure by frost and fire, while the scenery is wild enough to awaken the dead."

Yellowstone National Park Stats:
- Lowest elevation 5,314 ft. at north entrance
- Highest elevation 11,358 ft. at the summit of Eagle Peak
- Summer temperatures ranging from a high of 98 degrees to low of 9
- Winter temperatures ranging between mid-30 above to 66 below zero
- 80% forested land
- 10% open meadows
- 10% covered with water
- 97% of park wilderness
- 3% of park taken up with roads and building
- 1,210 miles of well-marked hiking trails
- 12 species of trees
- over 80 types of wildflower species
- 60 kinds of mammals
- 225 bird species, with 70 species wintering in the park

For more information about Yellowstone National Park, contact their headquarters at Mammoth, WY 82190, 907-344-7381.

4

Bridger-Teton National Forest*

The Bridger-Teton National Forest began as one of four divisions of the Yellowstone Timberland Reserve, created in 1891, the nation's first such forest reserve, as part of Congress's forest conservation policy. (The name changed to the National Forest in 1907.) The reserve encircled Yellowstone National Park, taking up approximately 9,500 square miles (almost double the land mass of Connecticut), which encompassed chunks of Idaho and Montana, as well as Wyoming.

A.A. Anderson, the Reserve's First Superintendent

According to a 1927 article A.A. Anderson wrote for the *Annals of Wyoming,* up until the creation of the Yellowstone Timberland Reserve, sheepman used to set fire to the dense pine trees in order to make it easier to trail their sheep and to increase the pasturage. Anderson witnessed so many fires burning in the forest, he believed they threatened not only the trees, but every living thing in the forest.

In an effort to curtail this potential for disaster, Anderson appealed to President Theodore Roosevelt's well-know interest in natural resources preservation. Anderson wrote that he proposed the reserve and sent along a map that outlined possible boundaries (although the reserve had been supposedly set aside a decade before). According to Anderson, Roosevelt issued a proclamation and sent it to the Secretary of the Interior establishing the reserve. Effective

---

*   Sections of this chapter were excerpted from *Trails & Tales: Day Hikes and Historic Sites on the Way to Yellowstone.* See the bibliography for details.

July 1, 1902, Roosevelt appointed A.A. Anderson to the position of Special Forest Superintendent.

This gave Anderson authority over all sheep and cattle grazing permits within the reserve, and this made for some very mad sheepherders. They gathered above the saloon in Meeteetse, Wyoming. Anderson, who also attended the meeting, could feel the hostility which threatened to turn into a lynch mob. He managed to calm the group, but nothing was resolved.

In fact, while on a trip back East the following year, Anderson received a letter from the famous showman Buffalo Bill Cody which read in part: "I personally advise you not to return to Wyoming this spring, because, if you do, the sheepmen will kill you." Cody's postscript acknowledged "but there's no use sending you this letter, you will come anyway." Anderson did, and at least two attempts were made on his life, both by fire. A sudden change in a sixty-mile-per-hour wind stopped the first from consuming Anderson's ranch. He barely escaped the second, which struck not long afterward when Anderson awoke as the house burned around him.

The following years proved rocky, with sheepmen defying the permit system, tuskers killing elk, illegal poaching, and disputes over Native American hunting privileges.

In his article Anderson recognized that civilization would pressure the nation's remotest areas. He wrote, "Soon every patch of wilderness that remains will be a true oasis."

The Bridger-Teton National Forest Division

Actual establishment of the Bridger-Teton National Forest division came in two phases. The Teton section started in 1908 with 1,694,574 acres. The Bridger division, named for mountain man Jim Bridger, took in 1,744,702 during 1911 by a presidential executive order. The two merged in

1973, a combining total of 3.4 million acres, making it the second largest national forest outside Alaska.

The Bridger-Teton National Forest Today

The forest faces a similar delicate balancing act as Grand Teton National Park. Forest proximity to GTNP and Yellowstone places it within the sphere of controversy. Competition for resources remains fierce. As part of the "overthrust belt," the oil and gas industry show considerable interest in BTNF. The natural diversity of timbered areas attracts the commercial timber industry. Livestock grazing adds yet another dimension.

On the other hand, increased recreational use (up to almost two million visitors annually) greatly impacts forest land. Excessive human use is causing overcrowding and loss of wilderness characteristics in certain areas of the Teton, Bridger, and Gros Ventre Wildernesses.

Of the 2,500 miles of roads that exist in BTNF, about 1,300 miles have been created by motorists in four-wheel-drive or other off-road vehicles and represent a threat to the soil, water, and wildlife. In an effort to minimize the damage and danger, forest service personnel are attempting to close off or limit use on some of these unofficial roads, particularly those that have the potential to disrupt sensitive wildlife areas.

BTNF is home to three federally classified endangered bird species—the bald eagle, the American peregrine falcon, and the whooping crane. Among other endangered, threatened, or regionally sensitive species are the Kendall Warm Springs dace, and the Bonneville and Colorado River cutthroat trouts. Over 1,000 species of plants add to the complexity of the forest's environment.

Currently BTNF has set up a research partnership with the Teton Science School to compile data that will help formulate site management objectives and plans. This project, a collaboration between education and research, utilizes the school's students to conduct targeted field projects and resource assessments in the 40,000-acre Ditch Creek Management Area.

For more information on the Bridger-Teton National Forest, contact the Forest Supervisor's Office, 340 N. Cache Street, P.O. Box 1888, Jackson, WY 83001, 907-739-5500.

Section Nine

Sites on the National Historic Registry *

Menor's Ferry

Around the start of the twentieth century, a shrewd businessman named William D. "Bill" Menor saw an opportunity. No reliable means of transportation existed across the very unreliable Snake River which divided the Jackson Hole valley. Most of the residents lived on the east bank, while the best access to timber, hunting, and huckleberry picking was on the opposite side.

About 1894 Menor established the first ferry on the Snake, and it stayed busy during times of high water. During the summer lull, people could generally cross on horseback or pulling a wagon without much trouble.

Menor used a cable system to pilot his ferry. When he turned the pilot wheel, the cable tightened and aimed the pontoons toward the distant bank. Water current pushing against the pontoons shoved the ferry across the river.

The ferry's design of two sharp-prowed pontoons across which a flat platform sat at right angles (something along

---

*   Sections of this chapter were excerpted from *The Living West* and *Trails & Tales: Day Hikes and Historic Sites on the Way to Yellowstone*. See the bibliography for details.

the lines of a catamaran without a sail) allowed Menor to carry a four-horse team and a wagon fully loaded with logs (and later a motorized coach full of dudes headed to one of the early dude ranches in the area).

A wagon and team cost its owner fifty cents per ride, while a horse and rider shelled out twenty-five cents. Pedestrians could cross for free—provided Menor happened to be ferrying over a wagon at the same time.

By 1918 Menor grew tired of the business and sold his squatted-on homestead (no claim ever showed up under Menor's name) to Maud Noble and her partner Frederick Sandell, who operated the ferry until 1927 when the Bureau of Public Roads built a steel truss bridge just below the ferry crossing, effectively putting it out of business.

Today, the Menor's Ferry site, located just north of the Moose entrance to Grand Teton National Park, offers visitors a peek into Jackson Hole's early transportation woes.

Miller Cabin

Robert Miller came to Jackson's Hole in 1885 as one of the throng of bachelors. While trapping for a year or so, he searched out the perfect spot to homestead. The place he picked had a good flowing spring and even a cabin. Rumor claims it belonged to the outlaw Teton Jackson. How ironic that a hideout cabin would become the initial headquarters for the National Elk Refuge!

But first it became the first home that Robert brought his bride, Grace, to in 1893—although some soul in need of a prospecting flume made off with the floorboards while Miller was off in Illinois marrying Grace.

The history of the Miller Cabin, currently located in the National Elk Refuge, would rate as just another episode in the settlement of Jackson's Hole had destiny not stepped in, putting each of the Millers, and even the cabin site, in the spotlight of controversy.

Robert and Grace Miller beside their home in what would become the National Elk Refuge.

Photo Credit: Teton County Historical Society

Both Robert and Grace led illustrious lives, helped shape modern-day Jackson Hole, and skated on the edge of a new and developing philosophy of politics and conservation.

Leek's Lodge

In 1924-25 Stephen N. Leek established a semipermanent camp on the east shore of Jackson Lake in current-day Grand Teton National Park. He designed the camp to cater to the needs, comforts, and pleasure of an eastern recreation-oriented clientele—hunters, fishermen, and "dude" horsepackers. Enthusiasts flocked to the camp in such numbers, Leek decided in 1926 to build a permanent lodge. Within a year the completed structure, made of pine and fir cut in the vicinity, included lounge, dining room, office, and kitchen.

As soon as guests entered the front door a predominant impression of space—both horizontal and vertical—immediately overwhelmed them. A massive fireplace made of native stone took away the chill during spring and fall. Since outdoor winter sports would not become commercially profitable for another three decades, Leek closed the uninsulated lodge over winter.

But the most significant thing about the lodge remains the man who built it.

St. John's Episcopal Church and Rectory

Congregational members completed this one-story log structure in 1916. Located at 117 North Glenwood in Jackson proper, the church portrays a characteristic turn-of-the-century style building and detailing. In fact, the church, with its log gable ends and steep-pitched, trussed roof typifies the rural West so well, it became the setting for the church scenes in the movie *Spencer's Mountain*.

Services are held every Sunday; one in the summer of 1995 was attended by President Bill Clinton.

Rosencrans Cabin Historic District

Rudolph "Rosie" Rosencrans came to America from Austria. He spent some time in Jackson Hole prior to 1900, working for the LP&O Ranch as a hired hand. In 1903 he started a long career as a forest ranger in the Teton Division of the Yellowstone Forest Reserve.

With the help of his friend John Alsop, Rosencrans built the first ranger station. It stands today as part of the Buffalo District of the Bridger-Teton National Forest.

After a sometime wild but rewarding career, Ranger Rosencrans retired in 1928 due to failing eyesight.

On September 22, 1970, he died at the age of ninety-four. He is buried south of his cabin. In tribute, the Forest Service named a prominent ridge just east of his gravesite in the Buffalo Fort Valley after him.

Old Faithful Historic District

The Old Faithful Historic District lies along a low rise south of the Firehole River on the Grand Loop Road between Madison Junction and the West Thumb area. Volcanic cliffs and lodgepole pines shape much of the terrain to the northeast and east, while sparse vegetation surrounds the Old Faithful Geyser. Wet meadowlands cover the western side of the district. It consists of twenty buildings, including the famed inn, constructed between 1894 and 1940. Historically, the area played a significant role in the development of concessions needed to accommodate the thousands of people who came to view the park's best-known symbol—the Old Faithful Geyser.

The Old Faithful Inn, designed by Robert Reamer and built in 1903-04, stands as one of America's grand old hotels. Reamer's strategy incorporated the idea of enhancing rather than detracting from the spirit of the wilderness when erecting the rustic log inn. This concept of architectural sensitivity to the environment set the standard for construction by the National Park Service for succeeding decades.

Old Faithful Inn in Yellowstone National Park.

Photo Credit: Sierra Adare

4 Lazy F Ranch

Dude ranches began springing up in the valley around the turn of the century. The 4 Lazy F Ranch, built in Moose, Wyoming in 1927, started out as a summer home for its owners, the William Frew family of Pittsburgh, Pennsylvania. The "dudes" consisted of invited guests of the family.

Throughout the late 1920s and early 1930s, as the Frews expanded the facilities and expanded their guest list, the ranch developed into a small but classic western property of long, horizontal structures that suggest the wide open spaces—exactly what city slickers expect to find at a dude ranch.

Chapel of the Transfiguration

The Chapel of the Transfiguration sits in the valley between the Teton Range and the Snake River. Built with native lodgepole pine logs, the church follows in the tradition of the Western Craftsman style of architecture. The Western Craftsman Movement originated as a reaction to the machine-made confections of Victorianism around the turn of the century, first in England, then later in the United States.

In the 1901 charter issue of *The Craftsman*, an American Arts and Crafts publication, Gustav Stickley, an early practitioner of the style, characterized it this way. "Present tendencies are toward a simplicity unknown in the past. The form of any object is made to express the structural idea directly, frankly, often almost with baldness."

The Western Craftsman style shows up throughout the Rocky Mountain region, associated mainly with dude ranches. The chapel's construction style can be seen in many rural Western lodges, post offices, railroad depots, and, oddly enough, gas stations built in the early 1900s.

In 1925 Maud Noble (of Menor's Ferry fame) donated the land for the chapel. Local craftsmen from surrounding ranches built and furnished the church, patterning the design after "Our Father's House" on the Wind River Indian Reservation in Ethete, Wyoming. The chapel originally served the employees and guests of the outlying dude ranches, the Hole's main industry, dating back to as early as 1890.

The chapel's fixed-sash window over the alter forms its most striking feature. The window frames a spellbinding view of the Grand Teton massif.

Sunday services are still held in this chapel during the summer, giving tourists to Grand Teton National Park a taste of faith in the wilderness.

AMK Ranch

The AMK Ranch exemplifies a twentieth-century rural vacation home. The lodge, ranch house, as well as a series of cabins, dot the eastern shore of Jackson Lake, positioned to maximize the view of the lake and the Teton Range to the west, currently part of Grand Teton National Park.

The ranch developed in two phases: The first was during the 1920s, by owner William Louis Johnson, and the later, more extensive construction of 1936-37 came through the ranch's next owner, Alfred Berol (aka Berolzheimer), an officer and later the CEO of the family-owned Eagle Pencil Co. As a result visitors see two interpretations of Rustic architecture, that while visibly different, coexist well.

The district includes one lodge, one summer home with nearby garage and covered walkway between them, small cabins for smokehouses, storage buildings, boathouse, and caretaker quarters. Even the outhouse's design stayed consistent with the style of the main or Berol Lodge. Massive log columns frame the front door. Furthermore, the architect utilized naturally curved log pieces for eaves trim, in keeping with the earlier Johnson House.

Old Administrative Area Historic District

Old Administrative Area Historic District represents a concise statement of the National Park Service Rustic style of the 1930s. Part of Grant Teton National Park, the Public Works Administration in conjunction with the Civilian Conservation Corps built the district between 1934-39.

Park Service architect Keith Matson designed the overall site, following prescribed depression-era architecture— labor-intensive building techniques and lots of hand-crafted workmanship. As an example, note the rough cut "mill-waste" type trim and minimal exterior decoration.

As with the Old Faithful District, the administrative area harmonizes with its environment, a textbook example of the Rustic style outlined in 1918 by National Park Service director Stephen Mather—eleven years before Congress established the park. The house's front porch opens to a spectacular view of the Grand Teton.

During the thirty years the district served as Grand Teton National Park's headquarters and main offices and sometimes as a command post for local forces intent on increasing the park, crucial changes took place that led to the expansion of the park to its present size.

Bar BC Dude Ranch

A historic district which encompasses thirty-seven structures, the Bar BC Dude Ranch lies on the west bank of the Snake River near Moose, Wyoming, in Grand Teton National Park. The log buildings, with rough-hewn timbers and naturally stained exteriors, capture the essence of pioneer living.

At first glance, visitors see a haphazard collection of cabins scattered about. On closer inspection, however, a subtle pattern emerges, depicting the centers of activity, the main lodge, dining hall, and horse corrals and sheds, within easy access of the central path between the cabins.

Built in 1910 as a dude ranch by its owners, Struthers and Katharine Burt and Horace Carncross, the Bar BC helped define and set the standards for the industry in Jackson Hole. It remained in operation until after World War II.

The Brinkerhoff

Constructed in 1946 at the end of World War II, the Brinkerhoff represents the final chapter of private development on U.S. Forest Service leases within Grand Teton National Park. At one time, 111 such leases existed within the present park boundaries. The National Park Service acquired the Brinkerhoff property late in the 1950s. They converted the lodge into VIP retreat housing, which dignitaries such as Richard M. Nixon and John F. Kennedy used while they held public office. The politicians' presence, like the recent vacationing President Clinton, brought in a lot of press favorable to the park which resulted in stimulating the tourist industry and park visitations. This, in turn, led to the park's image as a retreat of the presidents during the 1960s.

The Brinkerhoff's design is classified as "exaggerated rustic." It overlooks Jackson Lake and Mount Moran, with a commanding deck that runs the length of the house dominating the front. Log columns frame the side entry, lending support to the gable roof. Wood shutters on the first- and second-story windows add the lodge's only decorative touches.

Andy Chambers Homestead

The Andy Chambers Ranch Historic District stands as the only remaining, nearly intact example of the homestead ranches on the once densely settled Mormon Row within the boundaries of modern-day Grand Teton National Park. Between 1900 and 1920, Mormons comprised the bulk of homesteaders to Jackson Hole, making a significant contribution to the development of local agriculture.

In 1908 Teton National Forest officials returned some lands north of the Gros Ventre River to the public domain. Mormons, led by T.A. and John Moulton, filed on lands east of Backtail Butte. Others soon followed. Within a few years a discernible community had materialized, and, although it never developed into a town due to its proximity to Kelly and Jackson, valley residents dubbed the area "Mormon Row" because of the religious preference of many of its settlers.

Eventually the homesteaders built a church on the Row, officially turning their crude places into permanent homes. By the 1920s the frontier had pretty much disappeared, and Mormon Row became more and more a typical rural western ranching site.

Residents of Mormon Row patterned it after the Mormon line village in Grouse Creek, Utah. In both cases, homesteaders attempted to maintain an orderly community as dictated by the church, while utilizing the local topography to best advantage.

The Row's central feature, the church, no longer stands. Nevertheless, its locale remains apparent in a tree-lined parcel of land on the road. Chambers built his home near what turned out to be the center of the settlement, about a quarter of a mile from the site of the former church.

Kimmel Kabins

Kimmel Kabins typifies the popular motor courts of the 1930s. Eleven cabin in all, along with the lodge/dining hall and a quaint foot bridge, the complex straddles Cottonwood Creek south of Jenny Lake in today's Grand Teton National Park. Motor courts attempted to blend the rough and ready pioneer log cabin atmosphere with separate, individual facilities convenient to motorists. Noticeably absent are any animal tending areas such as barns and corrals, thus reinforcing that Kimmel Kabins catered to the new generation of tourists rather than emerging from humble dude ranch beginnings.

J.D. and Lura Kimmel built the compound in 1937. They operated it during the 1937 and 1938 seasons.

During the interval between World War I and World War II, as many as a dozen tourist motor courts dotted the landscape of present-day Grand Teton National Park. Kimmel Kabins alone survives, an example of the forerunner to the modern motel.

Murie Ranch

The STS Ranch near Moose, Wyoming, started out as a guest camp. Built during the 1920s, with the house added during the 1930s, it currently consists of the main house and a studio. Olaus and Margaret Murie, an accomplished pair of naturalists, artists, and authors, purchased the defunct ranch in 1945.

That same year, as World War II drew to a close, Olaus, having recently retired from the U.S. Bureau of Biological Survey (now the Fish and Wildlife Service), took over the executive director position for the Wilderness Society, a growing organization leading the fight to preserve the land in its natural state.

For a hundred years, voices had stressed the need to conserve the nation's wild treasures, succeeding in the creation of the National Park and the National Forest services. But too many areas were falling through governmental cracks, hence the American Wilderness Society.

For eighteen years, the Muries' house in Moose became the setting for many debates and decisions that shaped Wilderness Society's policies and plans.

During the late 1940s and early 1950s, Murie and the Society lobbied Congress on behalf of several pressing issues. They succeeded in the effort to expand Grand Teton National Park (1950) and helped stop the Bureau of Reclamation's plans to build a dam in the heart of Dinosaur National Monument (1950-53). Murie also nudged Congress into creating designated wilderness areas within the national forests and played a major role in the establishment of the Arctic National Wildlife Range in 1960. Unfortunately, he didn't live to see the fulfillment of the crown jewel of his wilderness watchdogging. Congress passed the Wilderness Act in 1964 a year after Olaus's death.

White Grass Dude Ranch

During the early 1900s, a couple of partners named Hammond and Bispham built up a cattle ranch in the White Grass Valley (currently in Moose). Nestled between the forest and the Teton Range rising thousands of feet above the valley floor, the ranch overlooked the southern portion of Jackson's Hole.

Although they ran cattle until after World War I, by 1919 the owners decided to convert the property to a dude ranch, a reflection of the growing popularity and profitablilty of the industry. After the transformation, the reins passed into the hands of Hammond's son-in-law, Frank Galley, who continued the operation until his death in 1985, making it the longest-lived active dude ranch in Jackson Hole.

Gap Puche Cabin

Like many of the early 1900s residents, John Peter Nelson first experienced Jackson Hole through a hunting expedition. He fell in love with the place. When it came time to return home to Michigan, Nelson only stayed long enough to pack up his family and return to settle permanently in the valley.

Nelson worked for the Redmond family on the Red Rocks Ranch for a while, then later operated Menor's Ferry for a couple of years.

Nelson's son, Actor, married Vivian Smith, whose family came to the Hole via Missouri. Actor and Vivian's brother, Charlie, built the Gap Punche Cabin at the confluence of Crystal Creek and the Gros Ventre River about 1929 as a base of operations for their mining claim along the Gros Ventre River. This area saw many a mining claim filed during the late 1920s and early 1930s.

Neslon and Smtih constructed sluice boxes beside the river and panned for gold. And they found what they searched for. All excited, they took their precious metal to Salt Lake City to be assayed. It rated high, but alas, it proved too fine to collect in profitable amounts.

Since mining hadn't panned out (where this expression actually comes from), John Wort and his partner Steve Callahan converted the cabin into a base for outfitted trips around 1930.

John Wort, born in Jackson in 1900, learned the business from his dad, Charlie, a pioneer settler of the valley in

1893. Over the insuing years, the Worts would become one of the town's most socially and economically prominent families, with business enterprises including a livery stable, real estate, boat concessions on Jenny and Jackson Lakes, and the Wort Hotel, in addition to outfitting.

At the time they took over the cabin, John and Steve hired themselves out as guides to half a dozen hunters at a time, conducting approximately twenty to thirty parties during the course of the hunting season.

They charged $35 per day with a one-week minimum— not much by today's standards, but very steep for the Depression era, suggesting their clientele ranked among the very well to do.

Most hunters arrived in the Hole on the Union Pacific Railroad, which deposited them in Idaho. From there, the hunters boarded the "mail" stage to Jackson until it stropped running at the end of 1930s. By then, many clients drove their own automobiles.

Wort and Callahan guided elk hunts primarily. If clients bagged an elk right away, most stayed to hunt deer or bighorn sheep. Similar to modern hunting camps the Gap Puche Cabin served as a base camp kitchen. Hunters slept in tents set up around the cabin.

If various drainages along the Gros Ventre River turned up no game, Wort and Callahan established "spike camps" in the back country where they camped out rather than return to base. Between hunting seasons, they stored gear in the cabin.

In about 1935 Billy Stilson bought Callahan's interest in the outfitting company. Around 1938 or 1939 the Stilson family obtained full control of the business, including Gap Puche Cabin.

At the insistence of the Forest Service, Stilson and his fifteen-year-old son Vern moved it to its present location in 1942 or 1943. Stockmen who drove cattle through the area claimed the cabin disrupted the movement of the cattle causing them to stop and mill around. The Stilsons numbered each log before tearing the cabin apart, making it easy to rebuild on a stone foundation at its new location. Other than a couple of rotted logs replaced and a board and tar paper roof substituted for the sod one, the cabin remains exactly as it did when first built.

Stilson's family continued to operate the outfitting business in virtually the same manner as had John Wort and Steve Callahan until Billy died in 1956, at which time the business passed into the hands of his son Keith.

In 1976 Keith Stilson sold the outfitting business, cabin and all, to Gap and Peg Puche, owners of Crystal Creek Outfitters, continuing the cabins' long tradition as a base camp for guided hunting trips.

The cabin resides today within the Birdger-Teton National Forest, eleven miles from Kelly, Wyoming on the Gros Ventre River Road.

Cunningham's Cabin

J. Pierce and Margaret Cunningham, some of the early homesteaders in Jackson's Hole, established the 160-acre Bar Flying U Ranch in 1890. (Eventually they managed to increase their holdings to 560 acres.)

For the first five years they lived in the two-room "dogtrot" style log cabin, much like the one John Holland and John Carnes built across their mutual property line. The Cunningham's later converted the primitive cabin into a barn and smithy. Today, it still stands on the original homesite.

An architectural form native to the Appalachian mountains of the eastern United States, the "dogtrot" cabin consists of two small, usually single-room square cabins connected and covered by one gable roof, in this case a sod roof. The open veranda between the rooms (where dogs like to lounge, hence the name) offered cool ventilation in summer and could be closed off during Jackson's long, cold winter, making a handy storage space for a plentiful supply of dry firewood.

Cunningham Cabin in Grand Teton National Park.

Photo Credit: Sierra Adare

Cunningham's assembly technique required no nails or pegs. He cut each log with a "saddle-V" notching system, called a "saddle and rider" corner, so the timbers fit together as tightly as today's prefabricated Lincoln log houses.

In the early days, the Cunninghams raised cattle and hay. Then in 1928 they sold the ranch and moved to Idaho. The cabin might have fallen into obscurity had it not been for one sensational event that occurred on April 15, 1892. The Cunninghams, who spent the winter on another ranch on Flat Creek, let a couple of horse wranglers named George Spencer and Mike Burnett use the sod-roofed cabin while they pastured a fine-looking herd at the north end of the valley.

Come spring, five men snowshoed over Teton Pass, passing themselves off as "deputy sheriffs" and spreading rumors that Spencer and Burnett had stolen the horses up in Montana. Enlisting the aid of a few locals, the posse headed for the Bar Flying U Ranch. The "deputies," who held no legal jurisdiction in Wyoming, lay in wait in the barn until just after daybreak when Spencer appeared to tend to the horses. They ordered the wrangler to surrender. But Spencer, an excellent marksman, pulled out his six-shooter. The "posse," however, shot him full of holes before he could do any damage.

Burnett then emerged from the cabin, holding both a rifle and a pistol. He fared no better. The posse then buried the wranglers in one unmarked grave in a draw southwest of the Cunningham cabin.

Currently part of Grand Teton National Park, the cabin stands as a reminder of Jackson Hole's best and worst historical traditions.

Bibliography

Adare, Sierra. *Backcountry Cooking: Feasts for Hikers, Hoofers and Floaters.* Boise, ID: Tamarack Books, 1996.
_____. *Trails and Tales: Day Hikes and Historic Sites on the Way to Yellowstone.* Boise, ID: Tamarack Books, 1998.

Barry, J. Neilson. "John Colter's Map of 1814." *Annals of Wyoming* 10.3 (1938): 106-10.

Bauer, Clyde Max. *Yellowstone—Its Underworld: Geology and Historical Anecdotes of Our Oldest National Park.* Albuquerque, NM: University of New Mexioc Press, 1948.

Betts, Robert B. *Along the Ramparts of the Tetons: The Saga of Jackson Hole Wyoming.* Niwot, CO: University Press of Colorado, 1978.

Bonney, Lorraine G. *Wyoming Mountain Ranges.* Helena, MT: American Geographic Publishing, 1987.

Bonney, Orrin H. and Lorraine G. *Battle Drums and Geysers.* Chicago, IL: The Swallow Press, Inc., 1970.

Burt, Struthers. *The Diary of a Dude-Wangler.* NY: Charles Scribner's Sons, 1924.

Carney, Ellen. *The Oregon Trail: Ruts, Rouges & Reminiscences.* 2nd ed. Wayan, ID: Traildust Publishing Co., 1993.

Crutchfield, James A. "Robert M. Utley." *Roundup Magazine* 2.6 (1995): 40.

Davis, Robert B. Unpublished manuscript, "Sheriff Malcolm Campbell Recalls Romantic Past."

Dominguez, Steve. Unpublished manuscript, "Tukudeka Subsistence: Observations for a Preliminary Model."

Ferrin, Nellie Wilson. Unpublished manuscript, "Life Story of Eligah Nickolas Wilson."

Frison, George C. *Prehistoric Hunters of the High Plains.* 2nd. ed. San Diego, CA: Academic Press, Inc., 1991.

Fritz, William J. *Roadside Geology of the Yellowstone Country*. Missoula, MT: Mountain Press Publishing Co., 1985.

Fryxell, Fritiof. *The Tetons: Interpretations of a Mountain Landscape*. Moose, WY: Grand Teton Natural History Association, 1984

Ghent, W.J. "A Sketch of John Colter." *Annals of Wyoming* 10.3 (1938): 106-10.

Gilbert, Bill. *The Trailblazers*. New York: Time-Life Books, 1973

Harry, Bryan. *Teton Trails: A Guide to the Trails of Grand Teton National Park*. 3rd ed. Moose, WY: Grand Teton Natural History Association, 1987.

Hayden, Elizabeth Wied. "Driving Out the Tusk Hunters." *Teton: The Magazine of Jackson Hole* Winter/Spring 1971: 22+.

_____. *From Trapper to Tourist*. 1957.

Huey, William R. *In Search of Hollywood, Wyoming: The Silent Years 1894-1929*. 1985.

Huidekoper, Virginia. *The Early Days in Jackson Hole*. Moose, WY: Grand Teton Natural History Association, 1978.

Unpublished manuscript. "Judge White Story."

Knowles, Thomas. *The Living West*. New York: Wings Books, 1997.

Larson, T.A. *History of Wyoming*. 2nd ed. Lincoln, NE: University of Nebraska Press, 1982.

Lawrence, Verba. Unpublished manuscript, "If These Cabin Walls Could Talk."

Mattes, Merrill J. *Colter's Hell and Jackson's Hole*. Moose, WY: Yellowstone Library and Museum Association and Grand Teton Natural History Association, 1962.

Moulton, Candy Vyvey. *Legacy of the Tetons: Homesteading in Jackson Hole*. Boise, ID: Tamarack Books, 1994.

_____. *Roadside History of Wyoming*. Missoula, MT: Mountain Press Publishing Co., 1995.

Moulton, Clark. Unpublished manuscript, "Mormon Row History."

Murie, Margaret and Olaus Murie. *Wapiti Wilderness*. New York: Alfred A. Knopf, 1966.

Nelson, Fern K. *This Was Jackson's Hole: Incidents & Profiles from the Settlement of Jackson Hole*. Glendo, WY: High Plains Press, 1994.

Ortenburger, Leigh. *A Climber's Guide to the Teton Range*. San Francisco, CA: Sierra Club, 1965.

Payne, Helen C. Unpublished manuscript, "Make it Wyoming: Biographical Sketch of Rudolph Rosencrans."

Potts, Merlin K, ed. *Campfire Tales of Jackson Hole*. 2nd ed. Moose, WY: Grand Teton Natural History Association, 1990.

Russell, Osborne. *Journals of a Trapper: Or Nine Years in the Rocky Mountains, 1834-1843*. 1921. Ed. Aubrey L. Haines. Boise, ID: Oregon Historical Society, 1955.

Saylor, David J. *Jackson Hole, Wyoming: In the Shadow of the Tetons*. Norman, OK: University of Oklahoma Press, 1970.

Shimkin, D.B. "Wind River Shoshone Enthnogeography." *Anthropological Records* 5.4 (1947): 245-284.

Smith, M.J. "John Colter." Park County Chapter of the Wyoming Historical Society, 1957.

Trenholm, Virginia Cole and Maurine Carley. *The Shoshonis: Sentinels of the Rockies*. Norman, OK: University of Oklahoma Press, 1964.

United States National Park Service. *Exploring the American West 1803-1879*. Washington, DC.

Urbanek, Mae. *Wyoming Place Names*. Boulder, CO: Johnson Publishing Company, 1967.

VanDerveer, Neilie. Unpublished manuscript, "Jackson Hole: Early Settlement."

VanDerveer, Neilie. Unpublished manuscript, "Jackson Hole: The Famous Herd of Cattle."

VanDerveer, Neilie. Unpublished manuscript, "Jackson Hole: The Ghost of Nightcap Bay."

VanDerveer, Neilie. Unpublished manuscript, "Jackson Hole: An Old Time Industry."

VanDerveer, Neilie. Unpublished manuscript, "Jackson Hole: A Rendezvous for Outlaws."

Watson, John. "The Friendly Bandit of Yellowstone Park." *American West* Dec. 1987: 43-47.

Wilson, Elijah Nicholas. *The White Indian Boy*. Ed. Howard R. Driggs. Yonkers-on-Hudson, NY: World Book Company, 1919.

Wister, Fanny Kemble, ed. "Owen Wister's West: The Unpublished Journals." *The Atlantic* June 1955: 52-57.

Wister, Owen. *The Virginian*. New York: The Macmillan Company, 1902.

Personal Oral Interviews:

Albrecht, Scott. 24 April 1995.
Anderson, Peter. 24 April 1995.
Breffeilh, Andy. 15 May 1995.
Bressler, Kathy. 1 May 1995.
Bricher-Wade, Sheila. 28 April 1995.
Cavazos, Jose. 16 September 1995.
Connelly, Karen. 15 September 1995.
Cooke, Anne. 17 September 1995.
Corney, Jeff. 30 August 1995.
Dunkelberger, Kristen. 4 September 1995.
Finck, Scott. 1 May 1995.
Flitner, Sara. 16 September 1995.
Fought, Scott. 14 September 1995.
Frank, Don. 18 May 1995.
Fritts, Evelyn. 15 September 1995.
Gear, W. Michael. 2 April 1995.
Grubb, Bob. 10 October 1991.
Hartman, Marilyn. 10 May 1995.
Hartman, Marilyn. 24 April 1995.
Kruzich, Marty. 15 September 1995.
Lindsay, Jan. 30 October 1995.
Mattheis, Gary. 15 September 1995.
Miles, Richard A. 15 September 1995.
Mitchell, Mary. 15 September 1995.

Moulton, Candy. 30 April 1995.
Murray, Earl. 13 June 1995.
Nickell, Scott. 15 September 1995.
Northup, Kay. 16 September 1995.
O'Mara, Yvonne. 15 September 1995.
Otto, Charles. 14 Spetember 1995.
Overcast, Beth. 15 September 1995.
Parker, Carol A. Mortillaro. 18 May 1995.
Peterson, Evertt. 1 May 1995.
Pierce, John. 25 August 1995.
Price, Stephen. 14 September 1995.
Rawhouser, Ruth. 16 September 1995.
Segerstrom, Tom. 15 September 1995.
Valentine, Kimberly. 5 April 1995.
Whitman, Betty 14 September 1995.
Whitman, Ward. 14 September 1995.
Wild, Tom. 14 September 1995.
Wipfler, Katharine. 16 September 1995.
Wright, Jason. 14 September 1995.
Yverneult, Dominique. 3 September 1995.

Correspondence:

Anderson, Pete. Letter to the author. 5 June 1995.
Bogle, Judy M. Letter to the author. 23 May 1995.
Carson, Andy. Letter to the author. 30 May 1995.
Crews, Libby. Letter to the author. 20 April 1995.
Devin, Kristen. Letter to the author. 25 April 1995.
Fifer, Tracie. Letter to the author. 1 October 1995.
Flitner, Sara. Letter to the author. 27 October 1995.
Getler, Joy. Letter to the author. 18 April 1995.
Griffin, James M. Letter to the author. 1 April 1995.
Kreilkamp, Ann. Letter to the author. 18 July 1995.
Lindsay, Jan. Letter to the author. 31 October 1995.
Martin, Pat. Letter to the author. 14 April 1995.
Nelson, Don. Letter to the author. 14 April 1995.
O'Connell, Carmen. Letter to the author. 25 April 1995.

Parker, Carol A. Mortillaro. Letter to the author.
   21 April 1995.
Perkins, Donald S. Letter to the author. 23 May 1995.
Trafton, Ed. Letter to Mrs. Grace R. Miller. 18 July 1921.
Utley, Robert. Letter to the author. 3 September 1995.
Van Orden, Kelly. Letter to the author. 19 April 1995.
Webb, Melody. Letter to the author. 3 September 1995.
Williams, Jackie. Letter to the author. 31 October 1995.
Wipfler, Kathy. Letter to the author. 19 September 1995.

Newspapers:

Jackson's Hole Courier
Jackson Hole Guide
Jakson Hole News
Oakland Tribune
Salt Lake City Hearld
The New York Times
Casper Tribune-Herald
Casper Star Tribune
Idaho Falls Post Register
Wyoming Eagle
Cheyenne Daily

Index